EX AUDITU

An International Journal of Theological Interpretation of Scripture

Volume 6 1990

Ex Auditu is published annually by Pickwick Publications, 4137 Timberlane Drive, Allison Park, Pennsylvania 15101-2932, U.S.A.

Subscriptions
- Individuals:
  - U.S.A. - $15.00
  - Canada - $12.00 (in U.S. Funds)
  - All other countries - $15.00 (in U.S. Funds)
  - Students - $10.00
- Institutions:
  - U.S.A. - $25.00
  - Canada - $20.00
  - All other countries - $25.00 (in U.S. Funds)

Indexed in *Religion Index One: Periodicals*, published by the American Theological Library Association, Chicago, Illinois, available online in the ATLA Religion Database through BRS Information Technologies (Latham, New York); DIALOGUE Information Services (Palo Alto, California); *Interlationale Zeitschriftenshau für Bibelwissenschaft und Grenzgebeite; Religion and Theological Abstracts.*

Please address all subscription correspondence and change of address information to Pickwick Publications.

ISSN 08883-0053

EX AUDITU

An international journal of theological interpretation of scripture

THE EDITORIAL BOARD MEMBERS AND CONSULTANTS represent various disciplines and denominations. Theological Interpretation of Scripture is a task to be taken seriously by scholars who are committed to the Christian faith and tradition. However, as one editorial consultant stated: "let people gradually get used to the idea that a sane hermeneutics is both oriented in advance toward agreement/consent and is simultaneously exigent, discriminating, critical."

EX AUDITU

Volume 6 1990

CONTENTS

Introduction
Robert A. Guelich

"Chosen by Grace. . . Empowered to Serve Faithfully"
Jack Dean Kingsbury 1

Damnation and Salvation - Prophetic Metahistory and the Rise of Eschatology in the Book of Isaiah
Klaus Koch 5

Some Prophetic Antecedents of Apocalyptic Eschatology and Their Hermeneutical Value
Leslie Allen 15

Inspiration or Illusion, Biblical Theology and the Book of Daniel
John J. Collins 29

The Vision on the Mount: The Eschatological Discourse of Mark 13
George Beasley-Murray 39

The God of Peace Will Shortly Crush Satan Under Your Feet: The Function of Apocalyptic in Paul
David M. Scholer 53

Eschatology in the Book of Revelation
Adela Yarbro Collins 63

From Strangers to Citizens: Eschatology in the Patristic Era
Agnes Cunningham 73

Happily at the Edge of the Abyss:
Popular Premillennialism in America
Timothy Weber 87

Eschatology and Systematics
Gabriel Fackre 101

Ethics and Eschatology
John Howard Yoder 119

The Apocalypse. Hope, Resistance and the Revelation
of Reality
Christopher Rowland 129

INTRODUCTION

The theme of this year's North Park Symposium was fraught with ambiguities. The fundamental term, "eschatology," can refer to a category of systematic theology pertaining to the doctrine of the "last things" involving the consummation of God's work either in history or at the end of history, while as an adjective "eschatological" carries a much broader meaning referring to God's ultimate redemptive activity in history commencing with the work of Christ. Does "eschatology" belong exclusively to the future? Indeed is their a specific future in "eschatology?" Does "eschatology" provide a hope or a mandate or both? What difference does it make for the life of faith?

These and related questions lie behind the topic, "Prophetic and/or Apocalyptic Eschatology?" discussed in consort by representatives of the classical theological disciplines: K. Koch; L. Allen; J. Collins (Old Testament); G. Beasley-Murray; D. Scholer; A. Collins (New Testament); A. Cunningham; T. Weber (Church History); G. Fackre (Systematics); J. H. Yoder (Ethics). Their papers follow as articles in this issue. The article by C. Rowland is an adaptation of chapter from his work *Radical Christianity* (Maryknoll, NY: Orbis Books, 1988) 66-81.

As frequently happens with academic types much energy was expended on even further definitions. The common assumptions—a) that "prophetic eschatology" indeed reflected a future hope but anchored in God's redemptive work in and through history and b) that "apocalyptic eschatology" reflected a future hope based on God's cataclysmic activity to interrupt and eventually end history by ushering in the final day of salvation and judgment—drew much attention. First, the differences proved a caricature, since elements of so-called "apocalyptic eschatology" can be found in the Prophets and so-called "prophetic eschatology" can be found in the Jewish and Christian apocalypses, as well as in contemporary "eschatologies." Second, the debate over the very nature and meaning of "apocalyptic" as a genre and an eschatology frequently preoccupied the discussion among the biblical scholars. Consequently, concern with defining the "what" tended to preempt the discussion of the "so what."

Should one choose, then, between the alternatives of the theme—"Prophetic and/or Apocalyptic Eschatology?"—the option was unanimously "prophetic and apocalyptic eschatology," since this alternative apparently assumes a false dichotomy between the two. The difference, if any, between the two is more one of degree than essence. The Symposium reflected a strong conviction that God was indeed at work "eschatologically" in the world giving hope but especially a mandate for the people of God. At the same time, the Symposium reflected an equally strong conviction that God was going to work "eschatologically" in the world thus re-enforcing the mandate but especially giving hope to the people of God for the future consummation of God's redemptive work personally, socially, and globally. How shall we thus live the life of faith? In the light of this prophetic and apocalyptic conviction and hope. This dual perspective comes through loud and clear in the homily by J. Kingsbury that concluded the Symposium.

The goal of the Symposium and *Ex Auditu* to provide a platform for "theological exegesis" with view especially to the consequence for the life of faith continues to be the ideal toward which we strive. We look forward to the coming Symposium on the critical topic of "Christology and Incarnation."

March, 1991

Robert A. Guelich
The Editor

"CHOSEN BY GRACE . . . EMPOWERED TO SERVE FAITHFULLY"

JACK DEAN KINGSBURY

TEXT: Matt 24: 45-51: *In his eschatological discourse in Matthew, Jesus narrates the parable of the good or wicked slave to his disciples. Hear, then, the parable:* (45) *"Who is the faithful and wise slave, whom his lord has put in charge of the slaves in his household, to give them their food at the proper time?* (46) *Blessed is that slave whom his lord, when he comes, will find so doing.* (47) *Truly, I say to you, he will set him over all his possessions.* (48) *But if that wicked slave says in his heart, 'My Lord is delayed,'* (49) *and begins to beat his fellow slaves and eats and drinks with the drunken,* (50) *the lord of that slave will come on a day when he does not expect him and at an hour he does not know,* (51) *and will cut him in two, and put him with the hypocrites; there people will weep and gnash their teeth."*

Grace, mercy, and peace be unto you all. Amen.

Introduction

Without question, Matthew knew of the "delay of the Parousia." Indeed, the words the slave utters in this parable allude to this: "My lord," the slave says, "is delayed." Despite, or perhaps because of, the delay of the Parousia, Matthew has imbued his Gospel with a lively eschatological hope. He affirms that God is in control of history and all creation. He denies that history is either aimless or eternal. He affirms that now the church is living in the interim between the resurrection and the end but that God, at the appointed time, will bring all things to their consummation. The risen Jesus will appear in splendor as God's regent; he will reign over a renewed creation; and he will call all people everywhere to account. It is against the background of this lively eschatological hope that we are to hear this parable of the good or wicked slave. It is through this parable as Word of God that the risen Jesus draws near to us—draws near to us at the close of this Symposium on this 19th Sunday after Pentecost—and declares to us, "You who are my disciples, remain faithful to me amidst the decisions of life!"

I

Almost daily, we are confronted in our lives with situations in which we must decide whether or not to remain faithful disciples of the risen Jesus. Paradigmatically, the slave in this parable is confronted with just such a situation and just such a decision. The setting is clear. The lord of this slave is away on a journey. Because the lord has particular trust in this slave, he has placed him in charge of his fellow slaves, to see to it that they are taken care of and receive their food at the proper time. Given this responsibility, the slave has a fundamental decision to make: Will he do as his lord has commanded? Or, lured by the belief that his lord will be a long time in coming, will he indulge himself—indulge himself by mistreating his fellow slaves and carousing with his friends? How will the slave decide? Will he decide to remain faithful to his lord? Or will he decide to indulge himself?

In a manner similar to this slave, we are continually confronted in our lives with situations in which we must decide whether or not to remain faithful disciples of the risen Jesus. On the surface of things, most of these decisions we must make seem trivial and not all that momentous. And yet, if we attend to the language of Jesus in this parable, he tells us that precisely the opposite is true. He tells us that these seemingly trivial decisions we must make in the course of our daily lives are, in fact, of ultimate consequence. Jesus tells us this by casting the alternative outcomes of the slave's decision in terms that are starkly--even harshly and offensively—eschatological in nature.

On the one hand, should it happen that the slave remains "faithful" to his lord, "blessed" is he. As this word "blessed" is intoned, all the beatitudes that Jesus has pronounced throughout the whole of Matthew's Gospel suddenly begin to reverberate in our minds, especially those beatitudes that we know so well, those that occur at the beginning of the Sermon on the Mount: "Blessed are the poor in spirit, for theirs is the kingdom of heaven!" (5:3); "Blessed are those who are persecuted for righteousness' sake, for theirs is the kingdom of heaven!" (5:10). And so it is with this slave: "Blessed" is he should he remain faithful to his lord, for his lord will set him over all his possessions! The one outcome of the decision the slave must make alludes to the eternal bliss of God's glorious kingdom.

On the other hand, should it happen the slave acts "wickedly," his lord, says Jesus, will come at a time when the slave does not expect him and he will "cut the slave in two" (dismember him), place his portion with the hypocrites (put him with the evil and the godless), and visit on him the pain of weeping and the gnashing of teeth. This other outcome of the decision the slave must make alludes to condemnation to eternal fire and punishment. In truth, the decisions we must make in our daily lives whether or not to remain faithful disciples of the risen Jesus are not trivial but are laden with ultimate consequences.

II

As we face these decisions we must make, the good news is that the risen Jesus does not simply leave us to our own devices but graciously empowers us to choose to remain his faithful disciples. As the slave in this parable faces the decision he must make, his lord does not simply leave him to his own devices, does not simply cut him adrift, does not simply abandon him to decide however best he can. Notice! His lord first of all invites him to make his decision within the framework of the relationship of trust that they share. In placing this slave in charge of his fellow slaves, the lord of this parable was not acting capriciously or simply on the spur of the moment. On the contrary, the lord "chose" this slave and "elevated" him to a position of special responsibility. The lord has trust in this slave. Accordingly, as the slave makes his decision whether or not to remain faithful to his lord, he makes his decision within the framework of the relationship of trust that they share.

In the second place, the lord invites the slave to make his decision whether or not to remain faithful to him in the knowledge that the lord anticipates that he will choose to remain faithful. In this parable, Jesus does not place the alternative outcomes of the slave's decision on an equal plane. Jesus does not tell the parable in such fashion as that the slave is depicted as standing before two, equally-weighted choices. Jesus' narration of this parable does not proceed something like this: There is this slave whom his lord has placed in charge of his fellow slaves; "if" he is faithful, blessed is he; "if" he is wicked, cursed is he. No, Jesus' parable goes more like this: There is this slave whom his lord has placed in charge of his fellow slaves; "blessed" is this slave when the lord comes and finds that he has been faithful; but "if" he is wicked, cursed is he. What this kind of language shows is that the lord of the parable anticipates that the slave will choose to remain faithful. Plainly, the slave makes his decision whether or not to remain faithful to his lord in the knowledge that his lord anticipates that he will choose to remain faithful.

As we face the decisions we must make whether or not to remain faithful, the risen Jesus does not simply leave us to our own devices. Instead, he graciously empowers us to choose to remain his faithful disciples. The decisions we must make, we make within the framework of Word and sacrament. Remember? In baptism, the risen Jesus came to us, he called us to become his disciples, and we responded to his call the way Peter, Andrew, James, John, Matthew, and all Christians down through the centuries have answered it: by leaving behind the "former" way of life, by giving to him our total allegiance, and by becoming his disciples. And in the Supper the risen Jesus shares with us, he sustains us in our life of discipleship. In this Supper, the risen Jesus urges us to come to his table regardless of how many "wrong decisions" we may have made, he forgives us these decisions and remembers them no more, and he strengthens us to stand firm in all the "situations of decision" we shall confront in this time between resurrection and consummation. As we face the decisions we must make, the risen Jesus does not simply leave us to our own devices, but graciously empowers us to choose to remain his faithful disciples.

III

Accordingly, empowered by the risen Jesus, we do choose to remain his faithful disciples amidst the decisions of life. As Jesus concludes his parable of the good or wicked slave, we recognize that it remains open-ended: Jesus does not go so far as to tell us how the slave finally decided. Although the slave was prompted to do as his lord had commanded and to take care of his fellow slaves, we are not told whether, in fact, he did decide to do this, or decided instead to ignore the responsibilities entrusted to him and to indulge himself at the expense of his fellow slaves. In point of fact, this parable can have no conclusion and must remain open-ended.

The reason this parable must remain open-ended, of course, is that it is we hearers who are the ones who must conclude it. Every time we are confronted in our lives with a situation in which we must decide whether or not to remain faithful disciples of the risen Jesus, we assume the position of the slave in this parable. As we assume this position and make our decision, the alternatives are plain: Will we prove ourselves to be "faithful," or will we prove ourselves to be "wicked"? There to be with us in making the decision is the risen Jesus. Through the powerful Word of his parable, through eschatological promise and warning, he places the decision we must make in sharp perspective: Ultimate consequences attend it, and we make it not apart from him, but in relationship to him. Following the promptings of the risen Jesus, we do make our decision, we do choose to remain faithful to him, and we do "act out" the conclusion to the parable—and then there will be the next time we are confronted with a situation in which we must make a decision.

Conclusion

So then, today—at the close of this Symposium on this 19th Sunday after Pentecost—the risen Jesus draws near to us and declares, "You who are my disciples, remain faithful to me amidst the decisions of life!" We hear this injunction of the risen Jesus. Hearing it, we look to him—we look to Word and sacrament—for the strength to follow it. And we do follow it; we do remain faithful to him amidst the decisions of life.

Amen.

DAMNATION AND SALVATION

Prophetic Metahistory and the Rise of Eschatology in the Book of Isaiah

KLAUS KOCH

The Old Testament prophets describe a world of conflicts. According to the prophetic utterances there is a deep split between right and wrong in their society, and the majority of the nation is on the wrong side. The rich oppress the poor. The desire for luxury dominates their thinking. But the split is not only within the society. There is also a gap between the entire nation and its God. Worship and sacrifice have become an instrument of human hybris. So God has departed from his people or will do so in the near future. Even the relation to nature is disturbed. "Shall not the land tremble on this account?" Amos calls (8:8). "The weeks appointed for the harvest—your iniquities have turned these away," Jeremiah maintains (5:24-25). The disturbance of all their fundamental relations will necessarily lead to decline and catastrophe.

The pessimistic description of Israel and its living conditions in the prophetic scriptures, starting with the eighth century B.C.,[1] contradicts the far more optimistic consciousness of pre-prophetic times. According to 2 Samuel 7, for example, Israel is planted by God, it dwells on its own place and will no more be disturbed, "and violent men shall afflict them no more" (7:10). We find the same consciousness in some Psalms or in early layers of the historical Books. Israel, righteous as it is, has received its *menuha* which means rest as well as freedom. But now, in the middle of the eighth century, the critical prophets like Amos, Hosea, Micah and Isaiah, contradict the common opinion and deny the generally assumed righteousness of the people. Therefore they have to announce doom and catastrophe. But from Amos to Malachi they also look beyond their own times. The present situation is seen in a historical, or better metahistorical framework, because not inner-worldly relations, but divine-human correlations determine the course of history. Looking back to the past the prophets see an epoch of harmony between Yahweh and his people at the end of a long salvation history. Looking forward to the future they announce a renewal of salvation and of an intact relationship between God and God's people following damnation and catastrophe. All the gaps mentioned above will then be closed.

In the course of the prophetic movement this futuristic aspect was stressed more and more. In this connection eschatology, whose definition has been much debated, arises. Building on the proposals of Gerhard von Rad,[2] I shall take it as the doctrine of a future epoch which transcends the present conditions of history, which goes beyond everything that has transpired since creation. According to this definition, eschatology is not the abrupt end of creation and history, but their fulfillment in the annihilation of evil and a subsequent new creation in accordance with God's intention for humankind since time immemorial. Within the development of the Old Testament witness concerning history and eschatology, the prophetic message stands midway between the earlier conception of salvation history and later apocalyptic visions.

In the apocalyptic view the split between good and evil goes back to the first human beings. And it involves not only human society but also the angelic world. Therefore the future salvation will consist of a real new aeon. As the apocalyptic view will be the subject of another paper of our symposium,[3] my concern will be to trace the growth of eschatology by means of one passage in First Isaiah and another passage in Second Isaiah.

I. DAMNATION AND SALVATION ACCORDING TO FIRST ISAIAH

In the first chapter of Isaiah there is a saying about the whoring city of former righteousness, i.e. Jerusalem. It seems to me to be a very characteristic instance of the prophetic description of God's attitude regarding his chosen people in salvation and damnation. In the formerly oral stage of transmission this utterance, Isa 1:21-28, probably was an independent unit. Now at the beginning of the written Book it presents a summary of the prophetic message.[4]

> How the *faithful city* has become a harlot, she that was full of *justice*!
> *Righteousness* lodged in her, but now murderers.
> Your silver has become dross, your wine mixed with water.
> Your princes are rebels and companions of thieves. Everyone
> loves a bribe and runs after gifts.
> They do not defend the fatherless, and the widow's cause does
> not come to them.
> Therefore the Lord says, the Lord of hosts, the Mighty One of Israel:
> Ah, I will vent my wrath on my enemies, and avenge myself on my foes.
> I will turn my hand against you and will smelt away your dross
> as with lye and remove all your alloy.
> And I will restore your judges as at first, and your counsellors
> as at the beginning.
> Afterward you shall be called the *city of righteousness*, the *faithful city*.
> Zion shall be redeemed by *justice*, and those in her who repent
> by *righteousness*.
> But rebels and sinners shall be destroyed together, and those
> who forsake the Lord shall be consumed.

A. The Structure of the Utterance and its Meaning

What Isaiah formulates is a very artfully crafted composition in the Hebrew original. In accordance with a common usage of the genre of prophecy it is divided into two parts. First there is an indication of the present situation and its metaphysical background, then a prediction of future and coming developments. The two parts are both interrupted and connected by a metalinguistic rubric hinting at the divine logic: "Therefore the Lord says, the Lord of hosts, the Mighty One of Israel." This inserted sentence demonstrates that God's speech and action is the decisive link between the present and the future of the people.

Still another point of the structure is meaningful. The righteousness of the faithful city is mentioned at the beginning of the utterance as well as at the end. The term righteousness refers to the past state in the beginning, but it also refers to the goal of the coming events. It embraces the epoch of salvation and the time of damnation and appears as the decisive factor for both of them as well as for the coming new creation. At the beginning and at the end, righteousness seems to be more a divine gift and endowment than a human achievement. Nonetheless righteousness should become human behavior. That was the very purpose of God's action. But the prophet accuses his compatriots for having done the contrary. What is mentioned of human actions in 1:21-23 are strictly actions against righteousness. Let us consider the implications of such unjust behavior in the view of our author.

B. The Evil State of Jerusalem and the Consequences

Although Isaiah does not use the term damnation, the concept of damnation or rather condemnation is implied in our text, as well as in many others. What are the conditions by which God is obliged to condemn the people?

1. The human misdeeds which the Lord recognizes are those of the *ruling* class of Israelite society: "Your princes are rebels." They neglect their responsibility and their solidarity with the weak members among the people, with the orphans and widows, and they are open for every kind of corruption.

2. However, the actual *violation is against God himself,* although there is no direct reproach dealing with religious trespasses. The Mighty One of Israel is oppressed if widows and orphans are oppressed. Where corruption and bribery flourish, there the Lord is ultimately the person affected. God is not only the transcendent guardian of the poor and outcast people on earth, but has some kind of mystic union with everyone of them (cf. Jesus' speech in Matt 25:34-40).

3. So God's reaction in 1:24 is a necessary *divine reflex against affliction.* Hard pressed, God has to defend himself. In the Hebrew original there is no mention of any divine wrath in this connection. The RSV translation is somewhat misleading. The foes in Jerusalem society are called *tsaray,*" those who afflict me." They afflict God himself! God will secure a space for his own living. Therefore, he is obliged to avenge himself. But "avenge," Hebrew *naqam,* does not express a furious outburst of emotion, but the realization of the desire for restitution of the integrity of the community to which one belongs.

4. An *unavoidable doom* will destroy the city. There is no longer a call for repentance either to the princes or to the present generation. In the Hebrew original the beginning of the utterance is *êkâ* which does not only imply the outcry, "How the faithful city has become a harlot," but characterizes a mourning song for a dead person: "How dead has become the harlot, who was formerly a faithful city."

5. A collective disaster is hanging over the city. Although the ruling princes are the specific evildoers, every inhabitant will be included because a human being is always an inseparable member of his community.

So far five points in the text have been noted, explaining the disturbed relations among the members of the Judean community and the disturbed relationship between the people and its God, but also announcing the unavoidable divine reaction and therefore the inevitable disaster. We call these issues in the prophecy "damnation." However, we should be aware that our text does not hint at an isolated sentence of a transcendent judge far away from human affairs, nor at a single intervention of punishment from above. Before the eyes of the prophet an ongoing process of growing alienation and separation between Yahweh and his elected people unfolds, ending in a necessary and total decline of the human partner because of God's withdrawal and even God's hostile attack against them. Isaiah's sermon itself--the word of the Lord uttered by a human speaker--is one stage in this process. According to the superscription of chapter 1, it happens "in the days of Uzziah, Jotham, Ahaz, and Hezekiah, kings of Judah," i.e. in the interval between human misbehavior and divine reaction. It is a necessary preparation for the latter. So the word of the prophet is primarily a word to his generation in its specific historical situation and only secondarily a message for later generations also.

Let me add a remark about fulfillment. In fact the predicted doom of Jerusalem became an outward reality, although not in his own days as Isaiah probably presumed. In 587 Jerusalem was totally destroyed by the Babylonians. Her princes disappeared forever. All the inhabitants had to feel the burden of the hand of the Lord lying upon them. This may be taken as clear evidence that prophetic predictions are not only moral reproaches and threats. They look forward towards a realization in the visible world. It is remarkable that most of the predictions of doom uttered by the pre-exilic prophets were fulfilled in the later history of Israel. Nonetheless they still remain paradigmatic for us by demonstrating the intimate connection between sin and disaster.

C. The Future Salvation of the City

The ultimate goal of our text is not the severe critique of the contemporary society with the consequences of decline and devastation, but the announcement of the creation of a state of salvation. Regarding the positive development expected for the more distant future, there are also some remarkable features in Isaiah's text.

1. Salvation is not only an ideal or a promise for a distant future. It had already been a *reality in former days*. Once there was a time of happiness and salvation for Jerusalem, when she was "full of justice, righteousness lodged in her." We know from other Isaianic passages that in his opinion it was the time of king David which represented a primeval epoch of an undisturbed relationship between Yahweh and Israel and therefore a state of salvation for all inhabitants of his home city (cf. 7:17; 29:1).

2. The circumstances of that beginning will come again, will be renewed. "Afterwards you shall be called the city of righteousness." *The blessed future will correspond to the blessed past,* both being antithetic to the misery of Jerusalem's present.

3. The future righteousness of the renewed Jerusalem will be a *divine endowment,* not a product of human action and achievement. The second part of the prophecy twice uses the Hebrew word *weashîbah* regarding God's condemning as well as his saving action. This verb literally means "to turn back, to return." Thus 1:25 properly reads, "I will return your judges as at the first." Behind both condemnation and salvation the same divine energy stands whose goal clearly relates to the latter state. It is God who creates Jerusalem as a city of righteousness. According to 1:26 the city gains this status before any human action is mentioned in 1:27.

4. The former righteousness of Jerusalem at the beginning was no less God's gift

to his people than will be the latter righteousness. According to the prophetic Books there is *no justice and righteousness* at all on earth except where the Lord has created it. Humans are not righteous by nature. The consciousness and competence for doing right among humankind depends on religious factors. They are strengthened by God's ongoing word and his hidden, but always effective wisdom. And both should be transmitted by Jerusalem, by his elected people as "the salt of the earth" (Matt 5:13).

Again I am obliged to return to the Hebrew language. In it there are two different, but nevertheless related terms for righteousness. Both of them appear in our text. There is no possibility of distinguishing them in modern translations, although the connotations are somewhat different for Hebrew speakers and listeners. Regarding the city and its endowment in the past and in the future, 1:21 and 26 use a masculine noun *tsedeq*. In the first place it is metaphorically described as a person lodging in the city. The *tsedeq*--righteousness is always an integral wholeness and a kind of hypostasis or sphere originating in God's own being.

Alongside this noun stands another one, *tsedaqah*. It is a feminine noun of the same linguistic root and refers either to a single act of righteousness, sometimes even a divine act, or to human righteous behavior. In our text *tsedaqah* appears in 1:27 concerning the conduct of those who repent after the turning point of history, after the Lord has started with a new era in Jerusalem. It is not their repentance which makes Jerusalem into a righteous city. On the contrary, the gift of *tsedeq* from above makes repentance as human *tsedaqah* possible. *Tsedaqah* his always a consequence of foregoing *tsedeq*.. The divine source of human ability for righteous living is also stressed by the metaphorical images of 1:22. The silver once possessed by them was certainly not their own product but a gift of creation. And the wine they diluted had been given to them as a special blessing. Silver and wine are images of the God-given *tsedeq*.

5. We now come to the decisive aspect concerning our issue: Righteousness, either divine or human, always implies salvation. This is a very important factor in the OT view of human existence. If we translate *tsedeq*. and *tsedaqah* with *righteousness*--and there scarcely is another possibility in English, then the translation is rather inadequate. The range of meaning of the two Hebrew nouns is much wider. They not only refer to a moral mind set and moral behavior, but also include the harmony of the person performing it with the surrounding society and nature. Thus *tsedaqah* includes the connotation of health, wealth, reputation, in short every kind of salvation. He who acts righteously will certainly become happy and blessed in the course of time. An evildoer, however, will end in distress and disaster. On both sides there is an invisible as well as inseparable connection between deed and destiny. Whoever performs righteousness will live out of that righteousness, whereas whoever performs iniquity, will die in that iniquity. It belongs to the order of creation that every sinner harms primarily himself and every just person earns happiness. Commonly no divine intervention is necessary for this process. So righteousness and salvation are in the end one and the same thing.[5]

But there are special cases where a whole community or nation is so corrupt that the few righteous persons can no longer gain their happiness within such a society. Just that happened in Jerusalem, and now God is ready to intervene. Damnation takes place. God turns his hand against the guilty party to accelerate the process between deed and destiny, to bring it to a sudden end. But this kind of revenge is never the ultimate goal of the Lord. Damnation is always a preliminary act for salvation, as it is clearly expressed in our text.

Thus I have examined another five points in the message of our text to demonstrate the other, the positive side of the coin. Despite the dangerous catastrophe coming upon Jerusalem, God's will of salvation will remain and will succeed in the end. Both damnation and salvation, however, are not isolated phenomena. They are bound together by a complicated web of divine and human correlation in the history of Israel.

Let us ask the same question as we did above: What about the fulfillment of the positive elements within Isaiah's prediction? Astonishing for us, the religious and political society of Jerusalem raises a much greater problem regarding its historical realization than do the statements of a coming decline. True, Jerusalem was rebuilt after the exile. In 515 B.C. a temple was again dedicated and worship and offerings began anew. In the province of Judah a new leadership arose, governors, high priests and scribes. But as far as we can see, the moral standards became no better than they were in pre-exilic times. No exceptional righteousness grew up and filled the city. As time passed, the people and the apocalyptic writers continued to long for an eschatological renewal and a final salvation as strongly as Isaiah had. And later on New Testament authors saw this kind of prediction fulfilled in Christ and his Church. Perhaps they were correct regarding Christ and his righteousness. Concerning the Church, however, we are still waiting for righteousness and full justice. None of our communities has so far become a real "city of righteousness." Hence, eschatology is still our hope--and our theological task.

D. Metahistory as a Prophetic Concept

What is the general understanding of the divine-human relationship in the interpreted text? What are the connections between the traits of damnation and those of salvation? If God exists—and Isaiah is convinced of that—his compatriots and his city are doomed to death because of their lack of righteousness. But the view of the prophet is not restricted to the precise present. He looks back into the history of his people Israel and remembers a positive starting point created by God's endowment of righteousness. And he looks forward to a better future for his people created and nurtured by divine acts of salvation. To recognize the essence of God and his attitude toward his human creatures it is necessary to look not only at the present situation but also to become aware of the past and the future viewed from religious and moral vantage points. This is what I call metahistory. I have analyzed the different patterns of metahistorical thinking evidenced by the individual prophets in my two-volume work entitled *The Prophets*. The underlying concept, however, is the same. For all the prophets God is not only beyond history, but also within earthly history. Hence, speaking of God's will and intention is not meaningful unless the dimensions of time and history are considered. The essence of history does not consist in outward facts and their empirically observable causalities. There is a hidden background of God's action and reaction and of human righteousness or sin, with both aspects of human behavior producing their corresponding destiny. For this backbone of history Isaiah uses the expression, "the work of the Lord," in 5:12-19.

II. TRANSCENDED DAMNATION AND ESCHATOLOGICAL SALVATION ACCORDING TO SECOND ISAIAH

One hundred and fifty years after Isaiah's preaching in Jerusalem the majority of the leading class of his people was deported to Babylonia and had to live there in prisoner-of-war camps. Among them another prophet arose whom we call Deutero-Isaiah since his utterances have been added to the book of First Isaiah and are now found in chapters 40ff. Under the altered conditions of his time Deutero-Isaiah continued the principal message of Isaiah and other pre-exilic prophets. But that implies that condemnation has come to an end. The turning point in history has been reached. Now salvation in its fulness will commence. Deutero-Isaiah's promises of salvation go far beyond the expectations of his famous predecessor. In his opinion God will do much more for Israel than mere renewal of the time of King David. God will create a state of salvation which had never been before. This is what modern exegetes call "eschatology," i.e. the doctrine of a principal change in the destiny of the world which brings forth structures and circumstances never having obtained since the beginning of creation. Eschatology includes the conviction of a final, everlasting and incorruptible community between God and humankind. Let us look at Isa 51:4-8:

> Listen to me, my people, and give ear to me, my nation;
> for a law will go forth from me,
> and my *justice* for a light to the peoples.
> My *deliverance* draws near speedily, my *salvation* has gone forth,
> and my arms will rule the peoples;
> the coastlands wait for me, and for my arm they hope.
> Lift up your eyes to the heavens,
> and look at the earth beneath;
> for the heavens will vanish like smoke,
> the earth will wear out like a garment,
> and they who dwell in it will die like gnats;
> but my *salvation* will be for ever,
> and my *deliverance* will never be ended.
> Hearken to me, you who know *righteousness*,
> the people in whose heart is my law;
> fear not the reproach of men
> and be not dismayed at their revilings.
> For the moth will eat them up like garment,
> and the worm will eat them like wool;
> but my *deliverance* will be for ever,
> and my *salvation* to all generations.

In this sermon to a distressed people living under hard pressures in a foreign land the stress on salvation is much stronger than in the text of First Isaiah quoted above. The very expression "salvation" appears no less than three times in the five verses. The range of hope has evidently become greater. The future horizon is widened both in space and in time. Coastlands far away are mentioned along with a coming divine justice as a light for all nations. Even the realm of human society is transcended. In the fundamental alteration sky and earth are involved. This tendency to universalism is lacking in the first part of the Book. Nonetheless God's chosen people retains a special position. Its members have the divine law in their hearts, they know God's righteousness more precisely than others, presumably because of Israel's history (51:7). Now they represent the reviled and weak among the nations. Therefore God takes special care of them.

According to Deutero-Isaiah's view Israel will maintain its exemplary position within humankind. But the eschatological salvation will radiate beyond the narrow limits of past history. Like the dimensions of space, those of time are also extended. Now there is a stress on the eternal and immutable status of the future salvation. "My salvation is to all generations." Twice this sentence stands at the end of a passage marking the apex of the promise. What the RSV translates as deliverance in these verses is nothing other than the noun *tsedaqah,* translated as righteousness in the text from chapter 1 quoted above. Again our modern languages are unable to encompass the entire range of connotations of a religious term in Hebrew. What the prophet means is a salvation given by God which endures because the people are given a new capacity for proper behavior. According to the prophetic mind God's delivering actions are a consequence of his righteousness. Because of that connection this deliverance creates human righteousness within the people concerned. By God's act of righteousness they themselves gain the ability to act righteously and justly, and in doing so they will maintain salvation.

So much for this passage from Deutero-Isaiah, which in my opinion is characteristic of his overall message. In its essence his preaching is the same as that of First Isaiah. For both prophets damnation as well as salvation belong to the complicated network of the divine-human relationship, i.e. to a metahistory behind the political and military factors of common sense history. Nevertheless there are new features in the sermon of the second prophet. In the later epoch of prophecy to which Deutero-Isaiah belongs eschatology has developed. God's intentions with humankind appear still more marvelous than imagined in former times. The knowledge of God has become deeper and clearer within the prophetic movement. We saw above that a prophetic utterance always looks for an outward realization in history. Regarding the fulfillment of the Deutero-Isaianic prophecies, however, the problems involved are even greater for our understanding than with First Isaiah. In the following centuries of the history of Israel there is no sign of any realization of this superb eschatological expectation.

III. A CONCLUDING GLANCE AT THE NEW TESTAMENT

In 1 Cor 1:28-30 the Apostle Paul writes:

> God chose what is low and despised in the world, even things that are not, to bring to nothing things that are, so that no human being might boast in the presence of God. He is the source of our life in Christ Jesus, whom God made our wisdom, our righteousness, and sanctification and redemption.

In this passage Paul makes recourse to the Old Testament conviction of God's intimate connection with the weak in the world. He goes farther and maintains that in Christ Jesus the hidden goal of divine providence in history has been reached, because in his person Christ incarnates God's righteousness. This is one side. The other side is Christ's transferral of righteousness to humankind. Through him human beings receive wisdom, righteousness, sanctification, redemption. Although the term salvation is not used, it is clearly circumscribed by these expressions. According to the Christian faith Jesus, in his life, death and resurrection, is primarily the fulfillment of the prophetic expectations.

But it is by no means God's intention that Jesus should be an isolated phenomenon of righteous living and salvation. He is predetermined to endow his followers with righteousness and salvation. Again human responsibility is stressed. Christ waits for good fruits from his believers. Under the continuing and enduring circumstances of the current world this aim becomes only partially realized. We Christians are still far away from the city of righteousness dreamed of by Isaiah and from the world-wide salvation which Deutero-Isaiah emphatically announced. So eschatology is still needed. Metahistory continues, and so it is our task as theologians to look for the signs of the times in the continuing history of church and society.

NOTES

1. K. Koch, *The Prophets,* vol 1: The Assyrian Period (Philadelphia: Fortress Press, 1983).

2. G. von Rad, *Theologie des Alten Testaments,* vol 2 (München: Kaiser Verlag, 1960) 1. G = Old Testament Theology, vol 2 (New York: Harper & Row, 1962).

3. Cf. the contribution of J. J. Collins in this volume.

4. Cf. my *Prophets,* 138-140.

5. K. Koch, "Is there a Doctrine of Retribution in the Old Testament?" in *Theodicy in the Old Testament,* ed. by J. L. Cranshaw (Issues in Religion and Theology 4; Philadelphia: Fortress Press, London: SPCK, 1983) 57-87.

An Announcement

North Park Theological Seminary in Chicago, Illinois is pleased to announce that the second Symposium on Theological Interpretation of Scripture will take place October 18-20, 1991. The Symposium will start at 1:30 p.m. on October 18 in Nyvall Hall and will extend through noon on October 20.

The theme of the symposium will be Christology and Incarnation. The following persons have agreed to make presentations:

Ralph Klein	*Old Testament*
James Luther Mays	*Old Testament*
I. Howard Marshall	*New Testament*
Thomas Wright	*New Testament*
Lawrence Murphey	*Church History*
Fred Norris	*Church History*
Colin Brown	*Systematic Theology*
Priscilla Pope-Levison	*Systematic Theology*
Molly Marshall-Green	*Worship*

Persons interested in attending the sessions should write before September 1, 1991 to:

Dr. Klyne Snodgrass
North Park Theological Seminary
3225 W. Foster Avenue
Chicago, Illinois 60625

Meals may be taken at North Park, and assistance will be provided in finding nearby lodging.

Some Prophetic Antecedents Of Apocalyptic Eschatology And Their Hermeneutical Value

LESLIE C. ALLEN

I. DEFINING OUR TERMS

The last twenty years or so have seen a radical reappraisal of apocalyptic issues, which has made earlier studies look old-fashioned. One may refer to the title of Frank M. Cross's 1969 article, "New Directions in the Study of Apocalyptic," which concentrated on the origins of apocalyptic in late prophecy,[1] and to Klaus Koch's insistence in 1970 that the loose term "apocalyptic" be defined in terms of a literary genre and a historical movement.[2] The challenges of Cross and Koch were taken up in the work of Cross's student Paul D. Hanson. In 1976 he refined Koch's call for precision by specifying three terms: apocalypse as a literary genre, apocalypticism as the ideology of a certain social and religious movement, and apocalyptic eschatology as a religious perspective relating to the future, not confined to apocalypses or apocalyptic movements.[3]

The approach that Koch had taken was also developed in the work of the SBL Forms and Genres Project, initiated in the mid seventies, whose conclusions were published in 1979 in *Semeia* 14. Primacy was given to form in defining an apocalypse as

> a genre of revelatory literature with a narrative framework, in which a revelation is mediated by an otherworldly being to a human recipient, disclosing a transcendent reality, which is both temporal, insofar as it envisages eschatological salvation, and spatial, insofar as it involves another, supernatural world.[4]

This emphasis on form was designed to have an exclusive and inclusive intent: to restrict the application of the term apocalypse to literary works of the Greco-Roman era, composed between 250 BC and 150 AD, and to allow for the enormous variety of content within these works. James Barr has described such apocalyptic literature as

> a kind of conversation, in which over two or three centuries different religious issues are argued out and different points of view are propounded, yet all of them within certain conventions of form and presentation.[5]

This variety has led to a number of proposed modifications of the basic definition of genre, which need not concern us here.

The function of the apocalypse, as well as its form, has been the object of much discussion. One definition that has been offered is to say that it was "intended for a group in crisis with the purpose of exhortation and/or consolation by means of divine authority".[6] Another is that an apocalypse was intended to interpret present, earthly circumstances in light of the supernatural world and of the future, and to influence both the understanding and the behavior of the audience by means of divine authority.[7]

II. HANSON'S RELATING OF PROPHECY AND APOCALYPTIC

We observed earlier that Hanson developed the issue of apocalyptic origins in late prophecy. He has done this notably in his book *The Dawn of Apocalyptic* published in 1975[8] and in a contribution to the *IDB Supplementary Volume* in 1976.[9] He has sought to reestablish along new lines the tenet of critical orthodoxy that apocalyptic literature has essential social and literary roots in the earlier prophetic revelation. However, he has carefully distinguished between the perspectives of prophetic and apocalyptic eschatology. He has defined the former in terms of

> the prophetic announcement to the nation of the divine plans for Israel and the world, which the prophet has witnessed unfolding in the divine council and which he translated into the terms of plain history, real politics and human instrumentality,

while apocalyptic eschatology focuses in

> the disclosure (usually esoteric in nature) to the elect of the cosmic vision of Yahweh's sovereignty—especially as it relates to his acting to deliver his faithful—which disclosure the visionaries have largely ceased to translate into the terms of plain history, real politics and human instrumentality due to a pessimistic view of reality growing out of the bleak postexilic conditions within which those associated with the visionaries found themselves.[10]

Hanson has observed that both made use of "visionary" transcendent imagery that went back to Israel's ancient traditions and beyond to Canaanite mythology, and was preserved in the royal cult of Jerusalem. Such visionary imagery relates to divine warfare, and embraces such motifs as the theophany of the divine warrior, the divine council and heavenly army, and the divine conflict with chaos.[11]

Hanson has seen a movement from prophetic to apocalyptic eschatology along a sliding scale whereby this imagery was increasingly left ungrounded in categories of human history. In *The Dawn of Apocalyptic* he labeled Second Isaiah, which uses such imagery extensively yet anchors it in pragmatic history, as protoapocalyptic in its eschatology. He went on to characterize a number of post-exilic texts as manifesting increasingly apocalyptic eschatology. He called Isaiah 24-27, 34-35, 60-62 and Zechariah 9-10 early apocalyptic; he labeled Zechariah 12-13 middle apocalyptic; and he described Zechariah 14 together with what he regarded as the redactional framework of Third Isaiah, Isaiah 56:1-8 and 66:17-24, fullblown apocalyptic.[12] However, in a much smaller book published in

1987, *Old Testament Apocalyptic*, Hanson no longer calls Second Isaiah proto-apocalyptic. He describes Daniel 7-12 as the only example found in the Old Testament of full-blown apocalyptic, "though Zechariah 12 and 14 come close to that category." The other post-exilic texts cited above, to which are now added Ezekiel 38-39 ("to a certain degree"), Joel 2:28-31, Zechariah 1-6 and Malachi, are described as early apocalyptic.[13] The new categorization represents little fundamental change in Hanson's view of Old Testament apocalyptic texts. However, it does seem to represent a terminological shift, with the purpose of acknowledging more closely the legitimacy of claims made by specialists in the Greco-Roman apocalypses that, whatever transitional elements are revealed in late prophecy, the apocalypse proper is a product of a still later period.

A key element of Hanson's approach to apocalyptic is his sociological emphasis. In this respect he is clearly dependent on Otto Plöger's earlier presentation in *Theocracy and Eschatology*,[14] although Hanson's political reconstructions and chronology associated with texts are different and he explicitly distances himself from Plöger. Hanson envisages a basic struggle within the early post-exilic community between a dominant priestly element and a minority group composed of visionaries and disfranchised Levites. Putting all his apocalyptic eggs into one sociological basket clashes somewhat with an insistence of apocalypse specialists: in terms of social setting the apocalypses are no longer to be categorized as "conventicle" literature, literature essentially associated with membership of a particular underprivileged group within a community.[15] It is not surprising, therefore, that in more recent years Hanson has acknowledged that apocalyptic tendencies may also be discerned in groups possessing roles of leadership and authority who felt powerless against a foreign world power.[16] The implication is that to confine apocalyptic tendencies to minority groups within the community is an oversimplification. Hanson's concession makes room for his eventual inclusion of Zechariah 1-6 as representative of apocalyptic eschatology.[17] Nevertheless, his basic exposition and choice of texts remain essentially tied to his attribution of them to a minority group within post-exilic Judah. Hanson has been accused of uncritically assuming a sociological model derived from quite a different social setting.[18] Moreover, it has been disputed whether some of Hanson's texts can be grounded in class conflict within the community.[19]

It is clear that the last word has not been said on the apocalyptic texts studied in detail in *The Dawn of Apocalyptic*, especially with reference to their political interpretation. However, whatever refinements future scholarship will wish to make, Hanson's assessment of the increasing role of the supernatural over against the historical as the factor that gradually changes prophetic eschatology into an apocalyptic variety will remain an important contribution.[20]

III. EZEKIEL

Let us examine this movement toward apocalyptic in some late prophetic texts, first in the book of Ezekiel. Hanson has given little positive attention to Ezekiel, largely because he could not fit the book into his minority-oriented apocalyptic program. For him the prophet is mainly the father figure of what one might call the other side, the Zadokite hierocracy against whom the dispossessed minority valiantly fought.[21] He treats Ezek 44:4-31 as a post-exilic supplement that sets out the exclusive claims of the Zadokite party.[22] Hanson is here in good company, for Zimmerli among others holds that 44:1-16 is post-exilic.[23] However, one must take into account the judgment of other scholars such as Jon D. Levenson and Ronald M. Hals that there is no warrant to push the passage over into the post-exilic period. My own work in this area envisages literary development in Ezekiel 40-48, within which 44:1-16 stands at the farther end, but sees no grounds for extending the redactional process beyond the end of the exile.[25]

Barr, while rightly denying that the book of Ezekiel is in any part truly apocalyptic in terms of genre,[26] has described it as "the book that more than any other single book must be considered the fountain from which the apocalyptic river flowed."[27] He drew attention to the visions of Ezekiel and to his intricate symbolism. Hanson too has briefly acknowledged such literary apocalyptic features as "the bizarre imagery, the form of the vision and the device of divine interpretation (later developing into the figure of the *angelus interpres*)."[28] What one misses in his comment is an appreciation of traditional imagery of supernatural intervention such as he shows in the case of other texts. Thus the temple stream that enlarges to a river of life in 47:1-12 is an eschatologized version of the cultic river celebrated in a Song of Zion (Ps 46:4). This motif of cultic mythology was probably an extravagant reference to the little Gihon spring, which seems to have had a significant role in the royal cult (cf. 1 Kgs 1:33, 45; Ps 110:7).

The framework of Ezekiel 40-48 is a visionary tour of the new temple, in which the prophet is guided by a supernatural figure. It is a precursor of the guided tours of secret places in the apocalypses. The temple that Ezekiel saw was "a house not made with hands."[29] Significantly in Ezekiel 40-48 there is no call to build the temple, only to observe the regulations for rites and offerings once it is built (43:11; cf. 44:5). The divine initiative of 37:26, "I will put my sanctuary among them," is taken seriously in the vision. The temple was to be Yahweh's creation, built for his people rather than by them. No wonder the post-exilic temple owed little influence to Ezekiel's vision: for the returned exiles to have copied it would have been to fly in the face of heaven. Only God could construct it. Similarly, while the temple envisioned in the Temple Scroll of Qumran is much influenced by the vision, it is acknowledged to be distinct from the eschatological temple that Yahweh would one day "create."[30] In Ezekiel's vision of the new temple as an architectural entity may be found that divorce from pragmatic history and preoccupation with the transcendent which Hanson has found to be the stuff of apocalyptic eschatology.

The invasion of Gog from Magog and his defeat at the hands of Yahweh in Ezekiel 38-39 has been briefly described by Hanson as apocalyptic "to a certain degree."[31] Generally the core of the literary unit is attributed to Ezekiel, and the rest is regarded as a series of redactional amplifications. Some scholars, mainly of an earlier vintage, have denied any input from Ezekiel's hand.[32] Hanson, whose main interest is in the post-exilic period, sides with them. In a footnote in *The Dawn of Apocalyptic* he has described its setting in terms of a post-exilic response from the visionary party as to why "the glorious promises of Ezekiel 36-37 were not fulfilled as expected, once the program outlined in chapters 40-48 had been completed." The answer given in Ezekiel 38-39 is: "Because the evil remaining in the land necessitates further destruction and judgment, after which the restoration will finally occur."[33] For "Israel still stood in the era of divine wrath."[34]

These are surprising statements, hardly grounded in the text. There is no mention at all of "evil remaining in the land." The restored people of God are represented not as sinners but as sinned against by the invader (38: 8, 11-12).[35] It is true that the representation of the invasion owes much to Isaiah 10, which sets forth the divine use of Assyria as the rod of Yahweh's anger to punish a sinful people, before it in turn was to be broken by Yahweh. However, the element of Israel's sin is conspicuously absent from the Gog unit: the motif drawn from Isaiah 10 is used only as an expression of divine determinism worked out through a foreign invader.

The notion of an invasion that shatters the peace of a restored, secure Israel is a strange one, although we have lost a sense of its strangeness because some of the apocalypses wove it into their eschatological timetables. Its roots seem to lie in the fears of the exiles. It is now generally acknowledged that the crises that generate apocalyptic responses can be of many kinds. There may be "situations of conflict or crisis, real or imagined, or . . . the context of fear of such situations."[36] The salvation oracles in Ezekiel seem to reflect a number of such fears and pastoral attempts to assuage them. The prospect of return to the land was not unalloyed joy. Why should not the pre-exilic syndrome of failure overtake the people once more, after the restoration? The ancient saying "The land eats up its inhabitants" (Num 13:32) was recalled with a superstitious shudder. Reassurance comes in 36:13-15: You have no need to worry on that score, for God himself has cancelled out that ancient curse associated with the land. However, there was a new fear: What of the regional neighbors of Israel? Will they not once more be a thorn in our side, when we live in the land? The soothing response is given in 28:24-26: No, God can and will deal with all those aggressive neighbors, and Israel's future is to be a life of security in the land. What's more, it will be Yahweh's means of disclosing his holy sovereignty to the world.

These latter motifs of Israel's security and Yahweh's holiness significantly recur in Ezekiel 38-39. The implicit setting of the unit is once more the exiles' fears concerning the future. What if there is another invasion from outside the land? We suffered so much from far-off foes in pre-exilic times. How do we know it will not happen all over again? Ezekiel often takes the views of the exiles quite seriously and goes along with them before he trounces them. He does so in this case. Re-using the format of an oracle against a foreign nation, he casts their worst fears into an eschatological scenario of invasion—yet it is a scenario directed by Yahweh himself, which he sets up only to destroy it by his own intervention. The text goes on to depict a horrific theophany of judgment. The miraculous intervention serves both to glorify Yahweh as transcendent in his holiness and successfully to put Israel's security to the test. The whole scenario has the function of a fire drill or a smoke alarm, to test the security system and confirm its efficiency.

The human foes in the eschatological drama are entities that reawakened old fears in the Mesopotamian world in which the exiles lived. Meshech and Tubal in east Asia Minor were a threat to the Assyrians toward the end of the eighth century BC. There may be the complementary influence of a much older Babylonian legend of invasion from Asia Minor.[37] The mysterious figure of Gog is best explained as a literary reanimation of King Gyges of Lydia, called Gugu by the Assyrians, a powerful king who reigned in west Asia Minor in the first half of the seventh century. As with the national names, a great figure from the past is evidently used to express a future threat, as we might speak fearfully of a new Stalin or a new Hitler.

These chapters are proto-apocalyptic in their distance from real history. They are set unambiguously in an imaginary future. Moreover, they invoke the sole intervention of the warrior God as the means of resolving the projected crisis that embodies the fears of the exiles. There is not yet, however, a vision of a brand new age inaugurated by the resurrection of the dead.[38] The Gog war is merely a second phase of Yahweh's future dealings with Israel[39] after the first phase of their restoration to the land. Thus P. Grech could refer to Ezekiel 38-39 as "an example of apocalyptic taking off but still touching the runway."[40] H. H. Rowley memorably distinguished between prophecy and apocalyptic with the aphorism "The prophets foretold the future that should arise out of the present, while the apocalyptists foretold the future that should break into the present."[41] Here, while the fully apocalyptic perspective has not yet been reached, there is a straining toward it.

A further feature of the Gog unit that reminds us of the later apocalypses is the re-interpretation of prophecy.[42] The apocalypses are exegetical literature. "All that is past is prologue to what is about to happen; all that has been written and spoken in the sacred tradition was pointing to this [apocalyptic] group and time."[43] We have noted the re-use of Isaiah 10; we may also refer to the way the unit echoes Jeremiah's oracles about the foe from the north, and the cultic tradition of the Songs of Zion concerning the inviolability of Jerusalem, which in these chapters is transferred to the land. These echoes are capped by an explicit reflection about Gog in an editorial amplification: "Thus says the Lord Yahweh: You are the one of whom I was speaking in past history through my servants the prophets of Israel" (38:17). Here the figure of Gog is the "real" focus of earlier prophecy. "The prophetic word was released from the limiting control of the historical situation to which it was addressed."[44] In apocalyptic vein Scripture is claimed as the divine answer to the nightmares that disturbed the hopes of the exiled people of God.

IV. JOEL

A further group of later prophetic oracles that foreshadow later apocalyptic is to be found in the book of Joel. Hanson had nothing to say about Joel in *The Dawn of Apocalyptic*. His silence is explained by an essay he wrote in 1976 in which he distanced himself from Plöger's apocalyptic views of Isaiah 24-27, Zechariah 12-14, and Joel.[45] Plöger regarded these texts as evidence for sharp social dissension within Judah between the theocratic and eschatological parties. Hanson retained from different perspectives the sectarian origin of the first two groups of texts, but his abandonment of Joel suggests that he was not able to find a minority viewpoint expressed there. However, in the *Supplementary Volume* of *IDB* he made a slight concession. In listing texts associated with the post-exilic apocalyptic movement he included Joel with an attached question mark.[46] He developed his thinking further in *Old Testament Apocalyptic,* where he listed Joel 2:28-31 among early apocalyptic texts in which there are visions of the destruction of the old fallen order and the dawn of a new era of blessing.[47] He had much more to say about Joel in his 1986 book *The People Called*. He found in 2:32 "an anti-establishment eschatological spirit," which envisages the downfall of the Zadokite hierocracy and the creation of a new order independent of the cultic apparatus of the Jerusalem temple. In 2:28-29 he discovered an "egalitarian impulse" sounded by a protest group. Moreover, in 1:15 and 2:1-2, 11, 27 the historical crises of the post-exilic period are interpreted as "the final outbreak of evil leading to a fearsome battle in which only the Divine Warrior could prevail."[48] Hanson's view of 2:28-32 is derived from Plöger, to whom he referred. Plöger radically differentiated between the whole community of Judah intended in "all flesh" at 2:28 and "all who call on the name of Yahweh" in verse 32, where he found reference to "a hidden division of Israel," a "conventicle-type limitation."[49] Over against such a judgment may be set H. W. Wolff's explanation of the group in verse 32: "Most likely is meant the same circle of Jerusalemites and Judeans which is addressed throughout the rest of the book."[50] It does seem more natural that verses 28 and 32 should refer to the same group as recipients of God's eschatological blessing and protection.[51]

A sectarian view of Joel has been developed by Paul L. Redditt, who envisages the social situation as one in which

> the prophet attacked the Jerusalem priesthood for allowing the daily sacrifices to cease, with the consequence that the priests relegated the community gathered around Joel and/or his message to the periphery of postexilic Judah's religious life. This peripheral group became sectarian, envisioning a new day when the group would survive any catastrophe associated with the Day of Yahweh, and God would pour out his spirit upon all types of persons, allowing people to turn to God without recourse to a priestly hierarchy.[52]

It must be asked whether Redditt's scenario fits the text. It is difficult to see why Joel would have attacked the priesthood for allowing the daily sacrifices to cease. Since natural supplies were lacking, they had no alternative but to let the sacrifices lapse. To single out the priesthood is to spotlight unfairly one social element among many mentioned by Joel in his survey of reactions to the locust plague in chapter 1. Joel does not seem to be blaming the priests for lack of supplies for the sacrifices (1:13), any more than he blames the farmers (1:11-12) . He acknowledges that the priests were most unhappy about the situation (1:9). Essentially it was a crisis for which there was no human solution. Accordingly Joel calls upon the priests to organize a period of national prayer and lament (2:15-17), and presumably they react affirmatively, because Joel can deliver in God's name a promise that the locust plague will be removed, fertility restored and by implication the cultic clock set ticking once more (2:18-27; cf . 2:14) .

Certainly there is an implication of great evil, as Hanson observed, evil which is left undefined (2:12, 13), yet which is so great that Yahweh could deal with it only by a locust plague that posed a threat to the very survival of the community and was nothing less than a manifestation of the eschatological Day of Yahweh. As in Haggai and Zechariah 1-8, the community as a whole seems to be at fault. It is they who are called to repent via the communal lament issued by the priests themselves (2:12, 16-17) . And when the cultic community led by the priesthood respond affirmatively, it is they who are promised divine blessing. Hanson was right about the attack of the divine warrior in 1:15 and 2:1-27; however, in a prophetic rather than apocalyptic vein it seems to be tied to a pragmatic situation as a providential interpretation of the locust plague.

A sectarian interpretation of the Book of Joel does seem to depend on finding radical discontinuity between 1:2-2:27 and 2:28-3:21. There is indeed a transition from prophetic to apocalyptic eschatology, but nevertheless there is a natural flow of coherence between the two parts of the book. If redaction has taken place, it has been done sensitively and consistently. In form-critical terms the divine message of 2:19b-27, which ends with a recognition formula, "and you will know that I am . . .Yahweh your God," is matched by a further message in 2:28-3:17, which ends likewise. The formulas of knowing God serve to resolve with glorious certainty the cautious question "Who knows?" concerning God in 2:14. The two messages give the literary impression of being divine responses to the lament of 2:17, which are introduced in 2:18-19a. God's saving work is represented in two phases, the fertility and vindication of 2:19b-27, and the blessing and protection of 2:28-3:21, which is introduced by the "afterward" clause in 2:28. We are reminded of the two phases of Yahweh's dealings with his people in Ezekiel 38-39, first restoration to the land and then the quelling of danger to Israel's security in the land. In 2:12-27 there are instances of the prophet's adding or inserting his amplification to reinforce the divine oracle (verses 13-14 after verse 12; verses 21-24 between verses 19b-20 and 25-27), and this phenomenon reappears as the book progresses, in 2:32 after verses 28-31 and in 3:14-16 and 21b.

If a parallel is sought for the twofold nature of the book of Joel, one may compare the Prophecy of Obadiah, of which our book is itself not unaware, as we shall observe later. There the initial problem of resentment against Edom (verses 1-14, 15b) opens out into a deeper problem, the vindication of Israel against a backcloth of suffering at the hands of a host of nations (verses 15a, 16). Moreover, in both Obadiah and Joel there is the same twofold treatment of the Day of Yahweh. In Obadiah it is first inflicted upon Israel in the fall of Jerusalem, and then about to be inflicted upon other nations. For Joel the theme of the Day of Yahweh was a complex of eschatological motifs that threatened not only Israel but also the foreign enemies of Israel, and that furthermore spelled salvation for Israel. A universalistic note is a firm part of the prophetic tradition of the Day of Yahweh.[54] Accordingly, after the initial presentation of the Day of Yahweh as a threat to Israel, there is a natural snowballing process whereby the other aspects are picked up, as indeed occurs in the Book of Obadiah. It is true to the post-exilic period of Judah's history that the pain of exile lingered on as an unhealed wound, so that Judah's deepest need was a final resolution of issues associated with it. The ultimate answer to the taunting question prompted by the locust plague, "Where is their God?" (2:17) is that Yahweh gives proof that he "dwells in Zion" (3:17, 21) through the defeat of the nations. The great machinery of the Day of Yahweh, once set in motion for the judgment of Israel—which Israel survived by means of repentance—rumbles along its programmed course in the rest of the book. For Israel there had seemed to be "no escape" from its path in the first phase of judgment (2:3). However, it veered from that path and was to make the nations its target, so that there was no longer to be any danger for Israel but rather "escape" (2:32; cf. 3:16). They were now safe in the eye of the storm. They were destined to be heirs of eschatological salvation, which was to take the forms of inner renewal (2:28-29) and external prosperity in permanent occupation of the land (3:18, 20).[55] They are characterized in 2:32 as those who "call upon the name of Yahweh" because in response to Joel's appeals they had brought their sincere prayers of cultic lament to Yahweh in invocation of his name (cf. Lam 3: 55-57).

The description of inner renewal in terms of the outpouring of God's spirit at 2:28-29 corresponds to the promises of the law written upon the heart in Jer 31:33 and of the new heart or spirit in Ezek 11:19; 36:26. Here it is expressed in a manner peculiarly appropriate to Joel. It not only eschatologizes Moses' wish in Num 11:29, but also looks back to the situation of Joel 1:2-17, when the community of Joel was out of real touch with Yahweh and only the prophet understood the divine will. No longer would this be true: all would be given prophet-like insight into God's purposes. It is hardly relevant to speak, as Redditt does, of a "democratized view" of prophecy, as if priestly authority were somehow impugned. There was an established, cultically acceptable literary tradition of lay prophets in God's past dealings with Israel. Moreover, priests and prophets had different roles in Israelite religion, as indeed the earlier part of the Book of Joel illustrates.

The Book of Joel fits snugly into late prophecy. Like other manifestations of late prophecy, it looks forward in an apocalyptic direction. In a composition full of echoes of earlier prophecy, the evident citation of Obadiah 17 in 2:32, "On Mount Zion there will be a remnant" or "those who escape," is especially significant. It is reminiscent of the use of past prophecy in Ezekiel 38-39, but in this case both Obadiah and Joel are envisioning the same eschatological event, so that there is no reapplication. As so often in apocalyptic literature, there is a reaction to crisis. There was an immediate crisis, the locust plague, and there was also an earlier crisis which had left the community scarred and deprived, and which still festered deep in their hearts. As for apocalyptic eschatology, in 2:28-3:21 there is an absence of the pragmatic form of divine intervention that was featured in 2:1-11. Yahweh was no longer to work as Divine Warrior through natural means, but now, as in Ezekiel 38-39, to function without earthly intermediaries, intervening with literally cosmic upheavals that are signs of or reactions to theophany[57] and evidently calling upon celestial warriors to execute his judgment in the summonses of 3:13 (cf. Zech 14:5).[58] As in Ezekiel 38-39 and 47, there is in 3:16-18, 21b (cf. 2:1, 32) an eschatologizing use of the Songs of Zion traditions,[59] which used traditional imagery to weave around the temple and Jerusalem a web of divine protection. These are features that an apocalypse would not be ashamed to own. As G. W. Ahlström has observed, "Joel's prophecy is prior to the period of apocalyptic literature, but Joel may be characterized as one of the prophets who served as a source of inspiration for the apocalyptists."[60]

V. HERMENEUTICAL RELEVANCE

Apocalypses and apocalyptically tinged prophecies are a foreign country to us modern, western readers. We are more at home in Romans 13 than in Revelation 13. There is a danger that distaste for what is alien can prevent us from attempting to hear what message such texts have for us and our contemporaries. We must extend to them the courtesy of trying first to understand them on their own terms. One must overhear their message to their original constituencies and try to empathize with their intent. Recent apocalyptic studies have done good work in this area by seeking to overcome earlier academic prejudice. Instead of shrinking from a lust for vengeance such as may be seen in Joel 3, there is a recognition of a "jail-house" perspective that asks for the realization of God's justice and power, which will take the form of vindication of his servants.[61] There is recognition too of the pastoral and psychological alleviation such literature seeks to bring. Apocalyptic literature reinforces the solidarity of the community addressed and teaches how to cope with present distress.[62] It provides a view of the world that will be a source of consolation and/or exhortation, by putting the problems of the present into perspective.[63] Those who are confronted by the seemingly total disaster of the present have meaning and hope attached to it in terms of a cosmic drama, which is the construction of an alternative, symbolic world.[64]

> The projection of the conflict onto a cosmic screen, as it were, is cathartic in the sense that it clarifies and objectifies the conflict. Fearful feelings are vented by the very act of expressing them, especially in this larger than life and exaggerated way. . . . Feelings of fear and resentment are released by. . . presentations of the destruction of the readers' enemies.[65]

The basic problem we have in hearing apocalyptic or proto-apocalyptic texts is that we live in a different season of life. The crisis, real or perceived, that underlies such texts generates disorientation so great that only divine intervention, it is felt, can bring relief. Order has been replaced by chaos that only God's work of new creation can undo. We, however, live for the most part in the season of orientation, in which order tends to prevail, despite ever-changing flies in the ointment. For Theodore W. Jennings writing in 1984 apocalyptic was pertinent to "our era of cataclysmic dread (represented above all by the threat of thermonuclear annihilation)."[66] His emotively intended words fall flat in this post-Cold War era, after the Berlin Wall has come tumbling down like the walls of Jericho.

If I ask myself, as one who has written commentaries on Joel and Ezekiel, how I have treated them hermeneutically, the answer is twofold. First, in my exegesis I have regarded them as expressions of pastoral theology. They provide examples of a perennial deep calling unto deep by echoing desperate cries of need and offering solace in the assurance that God cares and will come to the aid of the needy. Second, I have tended to relate them to systematic theology by tracing the carry-over of their eschatological traditions into the New Testament. The latter expedient involves a distancing of myself from their inherent urgency and immediacy. Systematic theology is intended for the season of orientation. Like the first readers of apocalyptic texts, we also are running a race and making for the finishing post, but in our understanding there are many laps left to run. We function as marathon runners rather than sprinters. To regard such texts as raw material for systematic theology is by no means a purely intellectualizing approach. Systematic theology has a dynamic role in providing a supportive view of the world without which the Christian cannot function.

Interestingly, rabbinic Judaism did something very similar with its apocalyptic tradition. The tradition served to provide language for the end times that would occur when God so willed. Although there was an implicit refusal to recognize that present historical crises were eschatological in character, the task of living out the Torah was given more depth and dimension by attention to the future which is the completion of and integral to the present. To this complex belief system with its subordinate category of eschatology, apocalyptic thought has made a small contribution.[67] No one can investigate the relevance of apocalyptic without reference to Rowley's classic book with that very title. Barr in his wry manner has categorized Rowley as "an expert in apocalyptic, but hardly an apocalyptist at heart."[68] He found it ironic that Rowley, writing in 1942, made no reference to World War II. However, rather like the old rabbis, Rowley was denying any eschatological significance in the war. He explicitly distanced himself from apocalyptic interpretations offered by dispensationalists, for whom Hitler was the Antichrist (and Mussolini was the rider on the black horse of Revelation 6). He also paralleled the rabbis in explicitly confessing his Christian belief in the Second Advent and so its role within orthodox systematic theology.[69] He had no intent to deny eschatology. He acknowledged the debt owed to the apocalyptists concerning hope for the hereafter and the challenge of the Last Judgment.

Rowley gave a revealing title to his fourth chapter, "The enduring message of apocalyptic."[70] It is remarkably similar to the regular formula used in the psalms of orientation, such as "The earth will never be moved" (Ps 104:5), "The king . . . will not be moved" (Ps 21:7), and "I shall not be moved" (Ps 16:8).[71] Rowley was trying to translate the disorientation of apocalyptic into a format meaningful for the season of orientation. He extrapolated from apocalyptic an affirmation that God is in control of history: "The God whose hand we may find in all history will supremely reveal himself in the goal of history."[72] For all the "mistaken hopes" of the apocalyptists, he found a "sound instinct " in their confidence that their little lives were linked to the eternal will and purpose of God. [73]

Carol A. Newsom has claimed biblical warrant for translating the esotericism of apocalyptic into a form compatible with ordinary life. Her warrant is the realized eschatology of parts of the New Testament. Arguing from this premise, she has urged that appropriation of apocalyptic hope consists of experiencing the events of human history as Christians who "participate already in the kingdom of life, where God overcomes the alienation of the world", and who in this way anticipate the final redemption of the world.[74] More specifically, other students of apocalyptic have seen in its message of God-given hope for the oppressed a social challenge for us Christians to open our eyes to oppression in our own times and to express in action God's concern for the ending of oppression wherever we find it in our society.[75] Hanson has seen in apocalyptic not only a call to ultimate trust in God's sovereignty even over death, but also a pastoral challenge to see the situation of the oppressed, such as the blacks of South Africa, through their eyes and to search for the morally mandated response.[76] He has enlarged on this theme in *Old Testament Apocalyptic*. The apocalyptic vision creates the awareness that peacemakers and advocates of justice struggle not by themselves in the fray. It permits them to recognize at their side the God who frees slaves from their bondage and hears the cries of the oppressed and whose loving power draws all reality toward peace and wholeness.[77]

These social applications of apocalyptic eschatology all revert to what approximates to a prophetic type of eschatology. Their premise is that God does not work solo, but uses his church to forward his purposes in human history. Moreover, there is no longer immediate expectation of a new transcendent age inaugurated by God but only of a better tomorrow that will mend the disorders of today. Yet such lesser hopes are essentially grounded in God's ultimate work of salvation, and constitute a series of dress rehearsals for that grand performance. This shift to a prophetic model shows the degree of dynamic equivalence necessary in the translation of apocalyptic if it is to become meaningful not only at the level of systematic theology but also at the grass roots of ethical and pastoral concern. However, if George E. Ladd was correct in categorizing the teaching of Jesus as both eschatologically apocalyptic and ethically prophetic,[78] we have the highest of warrants.

NOTES

1. *Apocalypticism. Journal for Theology and the Church* 6, ed. R. W. Funk (New York: Herder and Herder, 1969) 157-65.

2. *Ratios vor der Apokalyptik* (Gutersloh: Gerd Mohn, 1970), translated as *The Rediscovery of Apocalyptic* SBT 2: 22; Naperville: Allenson, 1972) .

3. "Apocalypticism", *IDBSup*, 29-30.

4 . *Apocalypse: The Morphology of a Genre* . *Semeia* 14 (1979) 9.

5. "Jewish Apocalypticism in Recent Scholarly Study," *BJRL* 58 (1975/76) 35 .

6. D. Hellholm, "Apocalyptic Genre and the Apocalypse of John" in *SBL 1982 Seminar Papers*, ed. K. H. Richards (Chico: Scholars Press, 1982) 168.

7. A. Y. Collins, "Introduction," *Semeia* 36, (1986) 7.

8 . *The Dawn of Apocalyptic: The Historical and Sociological Roots of Jewish Apocalyptic Eschatology* (Philadelphia: Fortress, 1975). In 1979 it was reissued with the addition of an appendix, "An Overview of Early Jewish and Christian Apocalypticism," 427-44 .

9 . *IDBSup*, 29-34 .

10. *Dawn*, 11-12.

11. Cf. P. D. Miller, *The Divine Warrior in Ancient Israel* HSM 5; (Cambridge, MA: Harvard University, 1973) . He has noted a fundamental distinction of the imagery of the divine council in Israelite lore from that of Canaan and Mesopotamia, "between a polytheistic development" in the case of the latter "and a basically monotheistic thrust" (73).

12. *Dawn* 27, 128-29, 368-69, 388-89.

13. *Old Testament Apocalyptic* (Nashville: Abingdon, 1987) 35.

14. (Richmond: John Knox, 1968) from the 2nd German edition of 1962.

15. See, e.g., J. J. Collins, "The Genre Apocalypse in Hellenistic Judaism", in *Apocalypticism in the Mediterranean World and the Near East*, ed. D. Hellhom (Tübingen: J. C. B. Mohr [Paul Siebeck], 1983) 546. Cf. S. J. DeVries' criticism of Hanson on this score in "Time in Wisdom and Apocalyptic," *Israelite Wisdom*, ed. J. G. Gammie (Missoula: Scholars Press, 1978) 275 n.40.

16. "Biblical Apocalypticism: The Theological Dimension," 7 (1985) 3; "Israelite Religion in the Early Postexilic Period," *Ancient Israelite Religion*, ed. P. D. Miller et al. (Philadelphia: Fortress, 1987) 492.

17. *OT Apocalyptic*, 37. Earlier he denied that apocalyptic eschatology featured in Zech. 1-6 on the ground that it was too pragmatic (*Dawn*, 256). M. A. Knibb observed in "Prophecy and the Emergence of the Jewish Apocalypses" in *Israel's Prophetic Tradition*, ed. R. Coggins et al. (Cambridge: CUP, 1982) 175, that in his (earlier) rejection of the apocalyptic nature of Zechariah 1-8 Hanson was unduly influenced by his hypothetical reconstruction of a single post-exilic struggle.

18. R. P. Carroll, "Twilight of Prophecy or Dawn of Apocalyptic?"*JSOT* # 14 (1979) 9-11, 27-28. Hanson drew on Mannheim, Weber and Troeltsch.

19. H. G. M. Williamson, "Isaiah 63, 7-64,11. Exilic Lament or Post-exilic Protest?" *ZAW* 102 (1990) 54, has argued in the case of Third Isaiah that Isa 63:7-64:11 primarily reflects a concern of the whole community rather than a particular party, while D. L. Smith, *The Religion of the Landless* (Bloomington: Meyer-Stone, 1989) 191, has urged that Isa 61:6; 66:21 attest not the exclusive claims of either Zadokites or Levites but the prospect of all Israelites becoming priests to the rest of the world and even of foreigners becoming priests. As for Isaiah 24-27, the assumption of an inner-community struggle in 26:7-19 has been vigorously denied by D. G. Johnson, *From Chaos to Restoration: An Intergrative Reading of Isaiah 24-27,* JSOTS 61; (Sheffield: JSOT Press, 1988) 74-75, 100.

20 . Cf. M. E. Stone's appreciation of this element in "Lists of Revealed Things in the Apocalyptic Literature" in *Magnalia Dei: The Mighty Acts of God*, ed. F. M. Cross et al. (Garden City: Doubleday, 1976) 441.

21. "Behind some of Hanson's analysis is a pejorative view of hierocracy and a positive sympathy for the visionaries" (Carroll, *JSOT* 14 [1979] 26).

22. *Dawn*, 265-67.

23. W. Zimmerli, *Ezekiel* 2 (Philadelphia: Fortress, 1983) 463.

24. Levenson, *Theology of the Program of Restoration of Ezekiel 40-48* (HSM 10; Missoula: Scholars Press, 1976) 153 n.13, cf. 157 n.63; Hals, *Ezekiel*, (FOTL 19; Grand Rapids: Eerdmans, 1989) 320-21.

25. *Ezekiel 20-48* (WBC 29; Dallas: Word, 1990) 254-56.

26. In an earlier generation G. A. Cooke, *The Book of Ezekiel*, (ICC; Edinburgh: T.&T. Clark, 1936) 407, could describe Ezekiel 38-39 as an apocalypse.

27. *BJRL* 58 (1975/76) 19. This judgment goes back to F. Hitzig, *Der Prophet Ezechiel erklart* (KAT; Leipzig: Weidmann, 1847) xiv-v.

28. *Dawn*, 234.

29. J. Skinner, *The Book of Ezekiel* (EB; New York: Armstrong, 1901) 392. Cf. K. Galling in G. Fohrer, *Ezechiel* (HAT; Tübingen: J. C. B. Mohr [Paul Siebeck], 1955) 221; Zimmerli, "Plans for Rebuilding After the Catastrophe of 587" in *I Am Yahweh* (Atlanta: John Knox, 1982) 115-16.

30. Col. 29, lines 9-10. See H. Stegemann, "Die Bedeutung der Qumranfunde fur die Erforschung der Apokalyptik" in *Apocalypticism*, 515; J. Maier, *The Temple Scroll* (JSOTS 34; Sheffield: JSOT Press, 1985) 32.

31. *Old Testament Apocalyptic*, 37.

32. More recently R. Ahroni, "The Gog Prophecy and the Book of Ezekiel," *Hebrew Annual Review* 1 (1977) 1-27, has argued for a post-exilic dating.

33. *Dawn*, 234 n.47.

34. *Ancient Israelite Religion*, 503.

35. Ezek 39:24 is speaking of the exile.

36. T. Olsson, "Social Aspects of Palestinian Jewish Apocalypses,"*Apocalypticism* 31. Cf. G. W. E. Nickelsburg in the same volume: "What counts is not a neutral observer's view of whether

things are good or bad, but the apocalyptist's *perception* and *experience* that the times are critical" ("The Apocalyptic Activity. The Case of Jasmasp Namag," 646).

37. See M. C. Astour. "Ezekiel's Prophecy of Gog and the Cuthean Legend of Naram-Sin," *JBL* 95 (1976) 567-79.

38. According to J. J. Collins, "The Symbolism of Transcendence in Jewish Apocalyptic,"*Biblical Research* 19 (1974) 10, hope for the transcendence of death distinguishes apocalyptic from earlier prophecy.

39. This is what "in the latter years/days" (38: 8, 16, RSV) means here: see Zimmerli, *Ezekiel* 2, 304, 306-7. It is a mistake to relate it to the eschatological formula for a new age, as B. Vawter did in "Apocalyptic: Its Relation to Prophecy," *CBQ* 22 (1960) 41.

40. "Interprophetic Re-interpretation and OT Eschatology," *Augustinianum* (1969) 249 .

41. *The Relevance of Apocalyptic* (New York: Association Press, 1963) 38.

42. Cf. in general L. Hartman, *Prophecy Interpreted* (Lund: Gleerup, 1966) .

43. W. A. Meeks, "Social Functions of Apocalyptic Language in Pauline Christianity,"*Apocalypticism,,* 697.

44. B. Erling, "Ezekiel 38-39 and the Origins of Jewish Apocalyptic," *Ex Orbe Religionum. Studia Geo Widengren . . . oblata,* vol. 1 (Leiden: Brill, 1972) 113; cf. M. Fishbane, *Biblical Interpretation in Ancient Israel* (Oxford: Clarendon, 1985) 477.

45. "Prolegomena to the Study of Jewish Apocalyptic," in *Magnalia Dei,* 400.

46. *IDBSup,* 33.

47. *Old Testament Apocalyptic,* 37.

48. *The People Called: The Growth of Community in the Bible* (San Francisco: Harper and Row, 1986) 313-14.

49. *Theocracy and Eschatology* 103-04; cf. D. L. Petersen, *Late Israelite Prophecy,* (SBLMS 23; Missoula: Scholars Press, 1977) 41.

50. *Joel and Amos* (Philadelphia: Fortress, 1977) 68-69.

51. Accordingly P. L. Redditt harmonized vv. 28-29 with v. 32 by interpreting "all flesh" as "persons of all classes," not every Judean, in "The Book of Joel and Peripheral Prophecy," *CBQ* 48 (1986) 233.

52. *CBQ* 48 (1986) 225.

53. The substantial unity of the book is maintained by Wolff, *Joel and Amos,* 6-8, and W. S. Prinsloo, *The Theology of the Book of Joel,* (BZAW 163; Berlin: de Gruyter, 1985) 122-27.

54. See Zimmerli, *Ezekiel 1* (ET, Philadelphia: Fortress, 1979) 210-12.

55. Structurally 2:30-32 seems to function as a headline for 3:1-17, while 2:28-29 is balanced by 3:18-21.

56. *CBQ* 48 (1986) 233.

57. In 2:2, 10 the cosmic language is applied to the locust plague .

58. For v. 11 see my *The Books of Joel, Obadiah, Jonah and Micah* (NICOT; Grand Rapids: Eerdmans, 1976) 107n7; Wolff, *Joel and Amos,* 73. V. 16 suggests that Israel is not fighting, contra H. P. Muller, "Prophetie und Apokalyptik bei Joel,"*Theologia Viatorum* 10 (1965) 245.

59. Müller, *Ursprünge und Strukturen alttestamentlicher Eschatologie*(BZAW 109; Berlin: Topelmann, 1969) 89, cites Pss. 46:2, 5, 7; 48:2.

60. *Joel and the Temple Cult of Jerusalem,* (VTS 21; Leiden: Brill, 1971) 96.

61. E. S. Fiorenza, *Invitation to the Book of Revelation* (Garden City: Image Books, 1981) 30. Cf. A. Y. Collins, " 'What the Spirit Says to the Churches': Preaching the Apocalypse," *Quarterly Review* 4 (1984) 83: "There are circumstances in which love needs to be subordinated to justice. The challenge in interpreting Revelation is to discern when such is the case."

62. Meeks, *Apocalypticism, ,* 694, 701.

63. Cf. J. J. Collins, *The Apocalyptic Imagination* (New York: Crossroad, 1984) 214, who speaks of a "revolution in the imagination."

64. See A. N. Wilder, "The Rhetoric of Ancient and Modern Apocalyptic," *Interpretation* 25 (1971) 443; L. Thompson, "A Sociological Analysis of Tribulation in the Apocalypse of John," *Semeia* 36 (1986) 164-65.

65. A. Y. Collins, "Apocalyptic and Contemporary Theology," *CTM* 8 (1981) 8-9.

66. *Quarterly Review* 4 (1984) 68.

67. A. J. Saldarini, "The Uses of Apocalyptic in the Mishna and Tosepta,"*CBQ* 39 (1977) 407. Cf. in general J. Bloch, *On the Apocalyptic in Judaism,* (JQRMS 2; Philadelphia: Dropsie College, 1952) .

68. *BJRL* 58 (1975/76) 13.

69. *Relevance,* 163.

70. Cf. the title of an essay by J. Oman: "The Abiding Significance of Apocalyptic" in *In Spirit and in Truth,* ed. G. A. Yates (London: Hodder and Stoughton, 1934) 276-93.

71. See my remarks in *JBL* 105 (1986) 711 and in *Psalms: Word Biblical Themes* (Waco: Word, 1987) 34-36.

72. *Relevance,* 171.

73. *Relevance,* 174 .

74. "The Past as Revelation: History in Apocalyptic Literature," *Quarterly Review* 4 (1984) 51-52.

75. E.g., A. Y. Collins, *Quarterly Review* 4 (1984) 81, 84.

76. *HBT* 7 (1985) 15.

77. *Old TestamentApocalyptic,* 70.

78. "Why Not Prophetic-Apocalyptic?" *JBL* 76 (1957) 192-200. 79. I am grateful to members of the symposium for their stimulating contributions, especially to my respondent, Dr. Jack Levison.

Inspiration Or Illusion: Biblical Theology And The Book Of Daniel

JOHN J. COLLINS

The problem of biblical theology is essentially a problem of genre, in the broad sense, that determines the expectations appropriate to the interpretation of the text.[1] The history of biblical interpretation is marked by the progressive revision of generic expectation.[2] The most obvious conflicts have concerned the historicity of biblical narratives, creation and flood, exodus and conquest, virgin birth and resurrection. While many of these issues are still disputed, the tendency of scholarship has been to place less reliance on historical accuracy and to seek a more positive appreciation of nonliteral modes of communication such as myth and symbol. Nonetheless, the referential value of biblical texts continues to present fundamental problems for biblical theology.

The Book of Daniel has often been a lightning rod in the conflict of generic expectations in biblical interpretation. The tales in chapters 1-6 have a history-like character, but they also present notorious historical problems, such as Nebuchadnezzar's madness and the existence of Darius the Mede. The second half of the book consists of what Sibley Towner has called "a series of failed apocalypses."[3] The consensus of historical critical scholarship is that the Daniel described in the book did not even exist, and that the observation of the ancient anti-Christian polemicist Porphyry, that the book is only accurate down to the time of Antiochus Epiphanes, is a compelling indication of its date. It is not surprising then that the early historical criticism of the book in the 19th century evoked conservative wrath. In the famous words of E. B. Pusey, Daniel was ideally suited to be a battle ground between belief and unbelief: "It admits of no half-measures. It is either Divine or an imposture . . . The writer, were he not Daniel, must have lied on a most frightful scale."[4] Pusey's simple alternatives of truth or falsehood were born of an age of rationalism, but are still compelling not only for many unsophisticated believers, but also for some philosophers of religion of the analytical school.[5] Yet, as John Goldingay remarks in his recent Word Biblical Commentary volume, what was excusable in Pusey is less excusable now that so much more is known about the ancient world in which the Bible was written.[6] I propose to discuss two of the issues that spark perennial controversy in the Book of Daniel: first, the question of pseudonymity and second the failed predictions of the end.

I. PSEUDONYMITY

For mainline biblical scholars (including many who consider themselves evangelical) the pseudonymity of Daniel was established some two centuries ago, and is scarcely an issue worth discussing.[7] A surprising number of quite erudite conservative scholars continue to fight a rearguard action on this issue, but their efforts are misdirected. Many of these efforts are directed towards defending the historicity of the first six chapters of Daniel, but they typically argue that the biblical account is not impossible, rather than establish its probability.[8] So, for example, in his prestigious Schweich Lectures, D. J. Wiseman admits that "There is no reference in the Babylonian Chronicle to any siege of Jerusalem in Nebuchadrezzar's first six years" but nonetheless maintains that the problematic statement in Dan 1:1, that Nebuchadrezzar besieged Jerusalem in the third year of Jehoiakim, "could refer to this time," despite the lack of supporting evidence.[9] Or again, several scholars have suggested that a historical figure (e.g. Cyrus's general Gubaru) underlies the problematic "Darius the Mede," without explaining why he should be named in this way.[10] Such efforts seem to be rather desperate attempts to bring the text into line with the generic expectation of historical accuracy. It would surely be better to forego the attempt to force the evidence, and bend our generic expectations to accommodate the evidence.

A. Canon and Context

Generic expectations are inevitably bound up with the literary context in which a text is read. The rediscovery of the Jewish pseudepigrapha in the late 19th century and more recently of the Dead Sea Scrolls has greatly altered the literary context of the Book of Daniel. In light of this context, pseudonymity should cause no surprise: it is the norm rather than the exception in Jewish apocalypses. This discovery does not in itself explain the phenomenon, but it shows that the practice of pseudonymity in ancient Judaism cannot be denied. No one in modern times has argued for the authenticity of *Enoch*.[11] The pseudonymity of Daniel can not be explained convincingly without taking this non-canonical context into account.

Nonetheless, Brevard Childs has argued at length that biblical books should be interpreted in the context of the scriptural canon. Childs is no literalist, and he does not question the pseudonymity of Daniel, but he proposes to explain it in the following manner: the author "had no new prophetic word directly from God. Rather he understood the sacred writings of the past as the medium through which God continued to make contemporary his divine revelation. His own identity had no theological significance and therefore he concealed it. It is basically to misunderstand the work of the Maccabean author to characterize it as a ruse by which to gain authority for himself, nor was it a conscious literary device. Rather, it arose from a profoundly theological sense of the function of prophecy which was continually illuminated through the continuing reinterpretation of scripture."[12]

This attempt to resolve the problem of pseudepigraphy deserves serious consideration, both on account of Childs' stature in the field and on account of its distinctively theological character. Nonetheless, I find it problematic in several respects. It rests on an exegetical claim that chaps. 7-12 are an amplification of the early visions of Daniel through the study of Scripture. The evidence offered in support of this claim is slight indeed. The strongest case involves the parallelism of chaps. 2 and 7. In Childs' view chapter 7 attests to the truth of the four kingdom schema with reference to the new circumstances of the Maccabean period.[13] This statement is true enough as far as it goes, but it does scant justice to chap. 7, which is presented as a vision in its own right, not as an interpretation. (Contrast Daniel 9 in this respect). The motif of the four kingdoms is overlain with the new imagery of beasts rising from the sea and a heavenly judgment scene. This imagery is not derived from Daniel 2 and can be explained only partially from older Scripture. Childs' inner biblical exegesis leaves unexplained the contrast between the turbulent sea and the man-like figure who comes on the clouds, a contrast best understood against the background of ancient myth.[14] Chap. 2 provides one of the building blocks for chap. 7, but the latter is a new and independent vision. The midrashic element in chaps. 8 and 10-12 is even slighter. Even in chap. 9, where Daniel draws explicitly on older Scripture, the interpretation departs so blatantly from the plain sense of the text (seventy years become seventy weeks of years) that it presents a further set of problems, concerning the nature and validity of such interpretation. Daniel's visions are not adequately described as the reinterpretation of older Scripture. Their primary purpose was to interpret the crisis of the Maccabean period. The interpretation of older Scripture was only one means to that end.

In any case, it is not clear that Childs' interpretation alleviates the scandal of pseudepigraphy, with its implication of deception. While the dream and interpretation in chap. 2 are surely older than chaps. 7-12, their association with Nebuchadnezzar and Daniel is nonetheless fictional (at least according to the critical consensus which Childs appears to accept). In short, the problem of fictional attribution arises already in the oldest stratum of the Daniel tradition. It is not clear why a pseudepigraphic elaboration of an older, legendary, oracle should be less problematic than a new pseudepigraphic vision. It is true enough that the identity of the author had no theological significance and that the author did not seek authority for himself, but for his message. That message, however, was quite novel, and the claim that the author understood it as the interpretation of earlier prophecy is unsubstantiated.

A more helpful approach to the problem of pseudonymity is found by considering Daniel in the context of the extracanonical literature of the period, especially that of other Jewish apocalypses. Pseudonymity was a widespread phenomenon in antiquity. Its motivations were diverse, and differed from genre to genre.[15] Any explanation of pseudonymity in Daniel, however, must at least take account of the highly similar visions that were circulated in the names of Enoch, Ezra and Baruch.

B. Reasons for Pseudepigraphy

In view of the prevalence of pseudepigraphy in the ancient world, the possibility that Daniel uses it as a conscious literary device can not be dismissed out of hand. We must assume at least that the immediate circles of the authors were aware of the manner in which the works were actually produced. On the other hand the attribution of the apocalyptic books was apparently accepted by the general public and there is no evidence that the literary convention was generally recognized in Judaism or early Christianity. Yet these books, whether canonical or not, are all of high moral seriousness, and so it is difficult to dismiss them as mere forgeries or calculated deceptions.

We have a few parallels from antiquity which may throw some light on the mentality of the apocalyptic authors. Plato allowed that "the lie in words is in certain cases useful and not hateful" and gave as an example "the tales of mythology . . . because we do not know the truth about ancient times, we make falsehood as much like truth as we can, and so turn it to account,"[16] and proposed that rulers might find "a considerable dose of falsehood and deceit necessary for the good of their subjects" as "the use of all these things regarded as medicines might be of advantage."[17] No Jewish apocalyptist attains the level of self-conscious reflection we find in Plato, but the philosopher's comments are nonetheless suggestive of ways in which departures from literal truth might be morally justified.

With more specific reference to pseudepigraphy, we know that the Neo-Pythagoreans were accustomed to attribute their treatises to Pythagoras himself as a mark of respect,[18] and even Tertullian, who denounced the author of the *Acts of Paul and Thecla,* held that "what disciples publish should be regarded as their masters' work."[19] Here again there is a limited analogy. The Books of Enoch and Daniel appear to have originated in circles which held these traditional, legendary, figures in high respect. Jewish pseudepigraphic writings were not assigned at random, but were considered appropriate to their supposed authors (e.g. The book of Wisdom was ascribed to Solomon). David Meade's thesis that "in the apocalyptic tradition, attribution is primarily a claim to authoritative tradition, not a statement of literary origins" has much to commend it, if we bear in mind that the line between authoritative tradition and literary origins was not sharply drawn.[20]

A claim to authoritative tradition was, of course, an attempt to enhance the authority of a work. Salvian of Marseilles, who was accused of writing a letter in the name of Timothy in the fifth century, gave an explanation that fits many uses of pseudonyms, ancient and modern: "the author wisely selected a pseudonym for his book for the obvious reason that he did not wish the obscurity of his own person to detract from the influence of his otherwise valuable book."[21] In the context of ancient Judaism, the decline in prestige of prophecy in the post-exilic period made the recourse to pseudonymity all the more desirable, if not necessary. Prophecy did not cease.[22] Josephus mentions several prophets in the Hellenistic period.[23] Yet the Hebrew Bible contains no prophetic book ascribed to a figure who lived later than Malachi, and we have no collections of oracles in the name of a prophet of the later period. Prophets no longer enjoyed the status in Jewish society that they had in the pre-exilic period, and this was surely one reason why the apocalyptic visionaries associated their revelation with ancient authorities. On the other hand, another popular scholarly theory, that apocalyptic writers had recourse to pseudonymity because of fear of persecution, seems to me implausible.[24] We find pseudonymity in works whose authors had no reason to fear retaliation (e.g. the Third Sibylline Oracle) and many apocalypses, including Daniel, glorify martyrdom, and would hardly have hidden the identities of their authors because of fear.[25]

Each of these factors, respect for an ancient figure, the wish to lend authority to the work and the decline in status of prophecy, offers a possible partial explanation for the use of pseudonymity in a morally serious work such as Daniel. All of them, however, are rational explanations, and for that very reason their adequacy is questionable. The work ascribed to Daniel consists of visions and purports to recount ecstatic experiences. We must at least consider the possibility that it describes actual experiences of its author or authors, and that the pseudonymity is to be explained in that context.

It is, of course, difficult to extrapolate religious experience from a literary work, and the issue is further complicated by the pseudonymity. Yet, as Susan Niditch has shown, the apocalyptic writers "certainly know how genuine ecstatics feel, the sort of things they do and see, the sort of role they generally play in communities . . . . "[26] The description of Daniel's vision in Daniel 10, which is partially modelled on Ezekiel's visions, conforms to widespread visionary practice in some of the points that lack scriptural precedent—mourning, fasting and falling into a deep sleep. It is also well known that visionary experience tends to flourish when a society is disrupted and subjected to cultural stress. The persecution of Jews by Antiochus Epiphanes was certainly such a time. Moreover, the early apocalypses of Daniel and *Enoch* did not have clear literary precedents to imitate, as was the case with some later apocalypses. All these considerations add to the likelihood that the visions of Daniel had an experiential basis, and were not simply following literary convention.

Christopher Rowland, building on the work of Johannes Lindblom, has suggested that apocalyptic pseudonymity may be rooted in the visionary experience.[27] He points to "the occurrence, in visionary literature of diverse origins, of the tendency of the visionary to separate his normal experience and his visionary life by speaking of the latter as if it happened to another person." The suggestion is intriguing, but it must be complemented with some explanation of the choice of pseudonyms. The pseudonymous heroes must have been held in exceptionally high regard in the circles that composed the apocalypses. Daniel was a suitable *alter ego* for a visionary because of the way in which Nebuchadnezzar's dream was revealed to him, although the visions in chaps. 7-12 were new revelations, not simply re-creations of the older dream. The visionary of the Maccabean period identified with Daniel and saw history, as it were, through Daniel's eyes. Or again, the Enochic visionaries mentally re-enacted Enoch's ascent to the heavens in search of new revelation, relevant to their own times. Such an explanation is, of course, hypothetical, and I do not know of any way in which it could be verified. It is attractive, nonetheless, because it attempts to deal seriously with the ecstatic, irrational character of the experience that the apocalypse describes.[28] Apocalyptic pseudepigraphy, then, need not be regarded as a calculated deception, but rather as a result of the intense and emotional experience of the visionary.

Yet, however we understand the psychology of the apocalyptic writers, the phenomenon of pseudepigraphy helps underline the fact that their works are fictions, works of imagination, whose truth is of the same order as that of Plato's myths. This point is fundamental for the generic expectations we bring to these works. They are not likely to be repositories of reliable fact, or sources of chronological information about the future. If they have enduring value it is more likely to lie in their affective aspects, the ways in which they shape moods and motivations, than in their propositional content.

II. INACCURATE PREDICTIONS

The fictional, imaginative character of Daniel's visions is indeed forced upon us by the blatant inaccuracy of some of the predictions. Despite the traditional interpretation in terms of the Antichrist,[29] there can be little doubt that Dan 11:40-45 refers to the same historical figure as the preceding passages, Antiochus Epiphanes, and implies that he would meet his death in the land of Israel. This, of course, did not happen. Moreover, Daniel is exceptional among the Jewish apocalypses in attempting to calculate the time of the end, and even gives a number of different calculations. According to Dan 7:25, the holy ones would be given into the power of the little horn "for a time, two times and half a time" or three and a half years. In Daniel 8, the angel Gabriel explains that "the vision is for the end-time" (8:17) or for "the appointed time of the end" (8:19). Within the vision, one holy one asks another how long the desecration of the temple will last. The answer is 1,150 days (2,300 evenings and mornings, 8:14). Again in chapter 12 a "man clothed in linen" asks "How long shall it be until the end of these wonders?" (12:6) and is told "that it would be "for a time, two times and half a time." The duration is further specified in 12:11: "From the time when the continual offering is taken away and the desolating abomination is set up is 1,290 days. This figure is a possible calculation of three and a half years, but it is obviously higher than the 1,150 days of chap. 8. although both calculations start from the disruption of the Temple cult. Yet another figure is given in Dan 12:12: 1,335 days.

The most plausible explanation for the different numbers is that the date was recalculated when the first number expired.[30] Such recalculation of dates in millennarian groups was the subject of a famous study by Leon Festinger, *When Prophecy Fails*.[31] People who make exact predictions do not just give up when the prediction fails to be fulfilled. Instead they find ways to explain the delay. One such way was to make a revised (presumably more precise) calculation. Dan 12:12 uses the same verb "to wait" as is found in Hab 2:3: "if it tarries wait for it, for it will surely come and it will not be late." The Pesher on Habakkuk from Qumran applies this passage to the "men of truth. . . when the last end-time is drawn out for them" (lQpHab 7:9-12). A similar situation is envisaged in Daniel. The "end" which was envisaged after 1,150 days, and then again after 1,290 days, is drawn out, and the faithful must "wait" for the later date. It would seem that there was also some revision of what was expected to happen. The figure in chap. 8 refers to the length of the desecration of the temple. In fact the temple was restored sooner than the visionary expected, after three years. The restoration must already have taken place before the numbers in chap. 12 were added, but it evidently did not constitute the "end."[32] In the final redaction of the Book of Daniel, the "end" involves the resurrection of the dead.

Obviously the final date predicted by Daniel also came and went. If Daniel were evaluated on the basis of its propositional assertions, it would surely have to be judged a failed apocalypse. But it was never so evaluated in antiquity. On the contrary, Josephus, writing more than two centuries later, still praised Daniel because he not only prophesied future things but also fixed the time at which they would come to pass.[33] The failure of the predictions did not prevent the inclusion of the Book of Daniel in the canon.

A clue to the ancient understanding of Daniel's predictions can be found within the Book of Daniel itself, in the reinterpretation of Jeremiah's prophecy in chap. 9. There we are told that the 70 years predicted by the prophet are really 70 weeks of years. Prophecies, and biblical texts are mysteries, like Nebuchadnezzar's dreams, and the literal meaning is not necessarily definitive. Given this kind of latitude in interpretation, a prophecy can hardly ever be finally disproven. Nonetheless, Josephus evidently believed that it still had some referential value, however elusive it might be.

In view of Daniel's allegorical interpretation of Jeremiah, we must question just how literally Daniel's own predictions were meant to be. The context of the persecution would seem to require specificity. Yet the very fact that different numbers are left juxtaposed in chap. 12 would seem to allow for an element of uncertainty. There is then some tension in Daniel between the psychological need of the persecuted Jews to know the duration of their distress and the realisation of the limits of what human beings can know.

A. The Function of Eschatological Predictions

The original function of Daniel can be seen clearly in chap. 11, which outlines the position of the wise teachers or *maskilim*. In the time of persecution, "the people who are loyal to their God shall stand firm and take action . . . . The wise among the people shall give understanding to many; for some days, however, they shall fall by sword and flame and suffer captivity and plunder . . . . Some of the wise shall fall, so that they may be refined, purified and cleansed until the time of the end."[34] It is generally agreed that the "wise" here are to be distinguished from the Maccabees who led the militant resistance. They are more akin to the martyrs in the cave who let themselves be slaughtered rather than profane the sabbath, as reported in 1 Macc 2:29-38. The willingness of the "wise" to let themselves be killed becomes intelligible in light of the conclusion of the passage in chap. 12: "At that time Michael, the great prince, the protector of your people, shall arise. . . . . Many of those who sleep in the land of dust shall awake, some to everlasting life and some to shame and everlasting contempt. Those who are wise shall shine like the brightness of the sky and those who lead many to righteousness like the stars forever and ever." The wise are those who are privy to the apocalyptic mysteries, and believe that they will be elevated to the stars, to join the angelic host, at the time of deliverance. This belief empowers them to lay down their lives rather than compromise their religion in the time of persecution.[35]

The question that arises, of course, is whether they were deluded. Daniel's prediction of the death of Antiochus proved false. The promise of resurrection, by its nature, must await eschatological verification, but it too is part of Daniel's imaginative fiction. The history of apocalypticism is in large part a history of failed hopes and broken promises. Would it not have been better to make some compromises and join the Maccabees?

Perhaps. But the reliability of Daniel's predictions is not the only factor that requires consideration. The moral stance of the *maskilim* and that of the Maccabees would have to be evaluated in their own right. If the wise chose rightly, it was not because the outcome was guaranteed, but because of the intrinsic merit and integrity of their decision.

It is instructive to read Daniel 11 in light of Daniel 3, which also presents a situation of potential martyrdom. The three youths are commanded to bow down before the great statue or be thrown into the fiery furnace. Their response is remarkable: "If our god, whom we worship, is able to save us, he will save us from the furnace of blazing fire and from your hand, O king. But if not, let it be known to you, O king that we do not serve your gods and that we will not worship the statue of gold which you have set up."

It is unlikely that the youths seriously doubted whether their God was able to save them.[36] They had every reason to doubt whether he would in fact save them. The story of the youths in the fiery furnace was atypical of human experience, and of the experience of Jews at any period of their history. The point of the youths' statement, however, is that their refusal to worship the statue is not conditional, and does not depend on any guarantee of deliverance. The hope of deliverance is important, to be sure, as a supporting consideration. Even if hope is disappointed, however, ethical commitment should not be undermined.

The profession of the three youths is suggestive for the hermeneutics of apocalyptic eschatology. The primary value attaches to the ethical stance advocated by the apocalypse. The eschatological expectations are, so to speak, the props. They provide a supportive way of construing reality which is not necessarily reliable in detail, but gives ground for hope, and makes it easier to do what one ought to do anyway.

The ethical values themselves, the convictions about what one ought to do, are derived from elsewhere. In the case of the three young men and of the Maccabean martyrs they are essentially derived from the Jewish Torah, but one might argue that the real issue at stake was freedom of religion, the right of a subject people to follow its own customs. In this respect the values of the visionaries overlapped to a great degree with those of the Maccabees. The main difference is that the visionaries were purists, and were unwilling to compromise some commandments for the sake of the others.

The problem remains whether eschatological expectations can still function as supports when one realizes that they are not necessarily reliable; whether fictions can still inspire when they are recognized as fictions? Fictions, of course, are of different kinds, and fiction and truth are not mutually exclusive. Daniel's prophecies did not fail entirely. The fact that the king died suddenly, in Parthia, may be dismissed as coincidental. That he must die, despite his pretensions to divinity, was inevitable. The kingdom of the Greeks did not prove to be the final world kingdom, but it did prove to be transitory. Perhaps the most fundamental insight of apocalyptic literature is into the fleeting character of human power. In this respect, at least, the truth of the apocalypse is incontrovertible. Such insights are not peculiar to apocalypses, but a book like Daniel expresses them with forceful imagery which lends itself to paradigmatic repetition in new situations.

The positive fictions of the apocalypse, however,—the eternal kingdom of the holy ones, or the resurrection of the dead—defy verification in this world, even in general terms, and must be understood for what they are, projections of human hope. Much of the biblical tradition builds an argument for God's fidelity by rehearsing the history of salvation. Such rehearsals play little part in apocalypses, and virtually none in Daniel. The apocalyptic revelation is addressed to the imagination rather than to the memory. It is a proposal for a way of looking at the world which, in its essentials, cannot be verified factually but only authenticated in value by the kind of action it supports. The relation between ethics and eschatology is reciprocal. The ethical stance of the visionaries, and their commitment to the God of Israel, gives rise to the eschatological vision just as much as it draws support from it.

Brevard Childs has rightly insisted that canonical texts transcend their original historical setting. In the case of Daniel, he points to 4 Ezra 12, Mark 13 and parallels and concludes that "Daniel continued to be read as scripture in the post-Maccabean age, as a true witness to the end of the age, which still lay in the future."[37] That Daniel was read as a witness to the end of the age can not be denied. It continued to be so read down through the Middle Ages and is still so read in some circles. The witness, however, has been an ambiguous one. In so far as it has been taken to promise the imminent end of the age in each generation, it has been misleading. To say that Daniel is a witness to the end of the age may still be bound too closely to the propositional content of the text, and be subject to false generic expectations. Daniel might better be construed in terms of the experience from which the apocalyptic vision arose: as a witness to the transience of human kingdoms, to the integrity of the persecuted and to the ability of the human spirit to view the world in the light of hope in times that invite despair.

NOTES

1. See the comments of John Barton, *Reading the Old Testament* (Philadelphia: Westminster, 1984) 16-19, on "'Genre' in Old Testament Study."

2. The main issues of this history are well described by Robert Morgan and John Barton, *Biblical Interpretation* (Oxford: Oxford University Press, 1988).

3. W. Sibley Towner, "The Preacher in the Lion's Den," *Int* 39 (1985) 157.

4. E. B. Pusey, *Daniel the Prophet* (Oxford: Clarendon, 1865) 75.

5. Views similar to Pusey's, with reference to pseudepigraphy though not specifically to Daniel, were expressed by Michael Dummett and Eleonore Stump at a conference on Philosophical Theology and Biblical Exegesis at the University of Notre Dame, March 15-17, 1990.

6. John E. Goldingay, *Daniel* (WBC 30; Dallas: Word, 1989) xxxix.

7. For a summary of the early historical criticism of Daniel, see J. M. Schmidt, *Die judische Apokalyptik* (Neukirchen-Vluyn: Neukirchener Verlag, 1969) 35-63.

8. See Lester L. Grabbe, "Fundamentalism and Scholarship: The Case of Daniel," in *Scripture: Meaning and Method* (Essays presented to A. T. Hanson; ed. B. P. Thompson; Hull: Hull University Press, 1987) 133-52.

9. D. J. Wiseman, *Nebuchadrezzar and Babylon* (Oxford: Oxford University Press, 1985) 23 .

10. For a review and incisive critique of these proposals see Lester L. Grabbe, "Another Look at the Gestalt of 'Darius the Mede,' "*CBQ* 50 (1988) 198-213.

11. The authenticity of *Enoch* was defended by Tertullian, who argued that the teachings could have been transmitted by Methusaleh to Noah and so to the post-diluvian generations (*On the Apparel of Women* 1.3).

12. Brevard S. Childs, *Introduction to the Old Testament as Scripture* (Philadelphia: Fortress, 1979) 618.

13. A rather similar position is taken by David G. Meade, *Pseudonymity and Canon* (Tübingen: Mohr, 1986/ Grand Rapids: Eerdmans, 1987) 89: "the whole focus of Chapter 7 is to reinterpret Chapter 2 in the light of a new *Sitz-im-Leben*."

14. On the imagery of Daniel 7 see J. J. Collins, *The Apocalyptic Vision of the Book of Daniel* (Missoula: Scholars Press 1977) 95-106; J. Day, *God's Conflict with the Dragon and the Sea* (Cambridge: Cambridge University Press, 1985) 151-167.

15. See B. M. Metzger, "Literary Forgeries and Canonical Pseudepigrapha," *JBL* 91 (1972) 3-24.

16. *Republic*, Book 2, 382C.

17. Ibid., Book 5, 459D; see also Book 3, 414B.

18. So Iamblichus, *De vita Pythagorica* §198.

19. *Against Marcion* 6.5.

20. Meade, *Pseudonymity and Canon*, 102.

21. *Epistola* ix, cited by Metzger, "Literary Forgeries," 8.

22. See F. E. Greenspahn, "Why Prophecy Ceased," *JBL* 108 (1989) 37-49, who points out that the rabbis had their own tendentious reasons for claiming that the spirit had withdrawn from Israel after Haggai, Zechariah and Malachi.

23. *J.W.* 6.5.2 §285-6; *Ant.* 13.11.2 §311-13;20.5.1 §97; 20.8.6 §169.

24. So Paul D. Hanson, *The Dawn of Apocalyptic* (Philadelphia: Fortress, 1975) 252.

25. See further Collins, *The Apocalyptic Vision of the Book of Daniel*, 67-68.

26. Susan Niditch, "The Visionary," in *Ideal Figures in Ancient Judaism* (ed. G. W. E. Nickelsburg and J. J. Collins; Chico: Scholars, 1980) 163. The view that apocalyptic visions have an experiential basis has also been argued by Michael Stone, "Apocalyptic: Vision or Hallucination," *Milla wa-Milla* 14 (1974) 47-56 and in his commentary on *4 Ezra* (Hermeneia; Minneapolis: Fortress, 1990).

27. C. Rowland, *The Open Heaven. A Study of Apocalyptic in Judaism and Early Christianity* (New York: Crossroad, 1982) 243; J. Lindblom, *Prophecy in Ancient Israel* (Oxford: Blackwell, 1967) 43-44.

28. Note also the suggestion of David Aune, "The Apocalypse of John and the Problem of Genre," *Semeia* 36 (1986) 89-90 that the apocalypses were meant to mediate a new actualization of the original revelatory experience through literary devices.

29. See the summary of traditional interpretation by J. A. Montgomery, *The Book of Daniel* (ICC; New York: Scribners, 1927) 468-70.

30.This explanation was proposed by H. Gunkel, *Schöpfung und Chaos in Urzeit und Urzeit* (Göttingen: Vandenhoeck & Ruprecht, 1895) 269.

31. L. Festinger et al., *When Prophecy Fails: A Social and Psychological Study of a Modern Group that Predicted the Destruction of the World* (New York: Harper & Row, 1956). Festinger's theory is applied to OT prophetic texts, but not to Daniel by Robert P. Carroll, *When Prophecy Failed. Cognitive Dissonance in the Prophetic Traditions of the Old Testament* (New York: Seabury, 1979).

32. See my paper "The Meaning of 'The End' in the Book of Daniel," in *Of Scribes and Scrolls. Studies in Honor of John Strugnell* (ed. H. W. Attridge et al.; Lanham, MD: University Press of America, 1990).

33. *Ant* 10.11.7 §267.

34. Dan 11:32-35.

35. See my essay "Apocalyptic Eschatology as the Transcendence of Death," *CBQ* 36 (1974) 21-43, reprinted in Paul D. Hanson, ed., *Visionaries and their Apocalypses* (Philadelphia: Fortress, 1983) 61-84.

36. See the comments of James A Wharton, "Daniel 3:16-18," *Int* 39 (1985) 173.

37. Childs, *Introduction*, 619.

The Vision On The Mount: The Eschatological Discourse Of Mark 13

GEORGE BEASLEY-MURRAY

I. INTRODUCTION

The title suggests a comparison with the more famous "Sermon on the Mount." The Sermon is stated to have been given "on the mountain" (Matt 5:1), the Vision made known "on the Mount of Olives, opposite the temple" (Mark 13:3). Despite their difference in content, they have certain features in common. Both discourses are compilations of largely disparate sayings of Jesus. Both are closely related to the dominant theme of his proclamation, the kingdom of God. The common core of the Sermon in Matthew and Luke begins with beatitudes on the heirs of the kingdom, continues with varied exhortations on love, mercy and judgment, and how to recognize authentic faith, and ends with a parable of judgment. While the Vision on the Mount does not use the expression "kingdom of God" it presupposes it throughout; it begins with a prophecy of the ruin of the temple, warns of tribulations that lie ahead, and ends with a portrayal of the coming of the Son of Man, with appeals to be ready for it. Its outstanding feature is its linking of eschatological instruction and ethical exhortation, for which reason it is often characterized as "eschatological parenesis" or "parenetic eschatology." The Sermon on the Mount is a summary of life under the saving sovereignty of God that has come with Christ and is to come through him; the Vision on the Mount describes a crisis situation for Israel and the Church, yet under the sovereignty of God who fulfills his purpose for humanity through the Son of Man.

Whereas the Church has been confident that in the Great Sermon the authentic voice of Christ can be heard, grave doubts have been voiced as to whether the teaching of Jesus can be discerned in the Vision on the Mount. We must, accordingly, pay some attention to this issue.

II. THE ORIGIN OF THE ESCHATOLOGICAL DISCOURSE

All New Testament scholars know that modern critical discussions of Mark 13 and its parallels take their rise from the work of Timothy Colani. Not all are aware of what motivated his work. Like all other New Testament scholars in Europe in the mid-nineteenth century he was compelled to respond to the writings of David Strauss in Germany and his follower Ernest Renan in France. No works on Jesus produced so great a sensation as those written by Strauss in 1835 and Renan in 1863. When considering the teaching of Jesus on the future Strauss did what all did in that era, he examined the eschatological discourse in Matthew's gospel. He drew attention to the saying in Matt 24:34, "This generation will not pass away till all these things take place"; it follows mention of the ruin of the temple, the troubles of Israel and the Church, and the coming of the Lord at the end of the age. That led Strauss to affirm that history has proved Jesus to be mistaken. He remorselessly exposed the expedients of scholars to evade the charge. For example, to those who held that Jesus was simply impressing on men the necessity of being prepared for the end he replied: " One whose mind is in a healthy state conceives the possible to be possible, the probable as probable, and if he wishes to abide by the truth he so exhibits them to others. The man, on the contrary, by whom the merely possible or probable is conceived as the real is mistaken; and he who, without so regarding it himself, yet for a moral or religious reason so represents it to others, permits himself to use a pious fraud."[1]

On such a view Jesus was either mistaken or a deceiver, and Strauss did not mind which alternative one chose. Renan went further in affirming that this fundamental error in Jesus shows that his system is discredited:

> The world, in continuing to exist, caused it to crumble. One generation of man at the most was the limit of its endurance. The faith of the first Christian generation is intelligible, but the faith of the second generation is no longer so. After the death of John, or of the last survivor, whoever he might be, of the group which had seen the Master, the word of Jesus was convicted of falsehood."[2]

In his later more popular work on Jesus Strauss adopted a more violent attitude. Of the teaching in the Gospels that Jesus is to return as Son of Man he wrote:

> Such a thing as he has here prophesied of himself cannot happen to a man. If he prophesied the like of himself and expected it, then to us he is a fanatic (Schwärmer). If he uttered it of himself without any real conviction then he was a braggart and a deceiver . . . . However sourly it may be received by our Christian ways of thinking, if it becomes established as a historic fact (i.e. that Jesus so spoke), then our Christian ways of thinking must be given up.[3]

It needs little imagination to realize the offence that these allegations caused. One overriding conviction seized the minds of many scholars: eschatology is a stumbling block to faith, and Jesus must be saved from providing it. The most common resort of theologians was to insist on the purely symbolic character of the eschatological utterances of Jesus.

Colani took a bolder line. He affirmed that Jesus rejected root and branch the eschatology of his contemporaries. There is no connection between Jewish messianism and the gospel, neither in relation to the Messiah nor to the kingdom of God. The gospel is the kingdom of God, which gradually extends itself over humanity. Consequently there is no thought of a denouement in Jesus' teaching; for the catastrophes of apocalypses Jesus substituted the concept of an organic development. The whole life of Jesus thus is a contradiction of the notion of a *parousia* of the Son of Man. The fact that the eschatological discourse in the Gospels is similar to Jewish apocalyptic teaching is itself sufficient to show that it could not have been uttered by him. Colani observed that the limit of agreement between the synoptists in their versions of the discourse ended at Mark 13:31, "Heaven and earth will pass away, but my words will not pass away." The answer to the disciples' question in Mark 13:4 as to when the temple will be destroyed accordingly is stated in Mark 13:32: "Of that day and hour no one knows, not even the angels in heaven, nor the Son, but only the Father." The discourse between the question and answer is termed "a little apocalypse"; it is assumed to have originated in the Jewish Christian community.

This hypothesis was received with great relief. Carl Weizsacker, in a work issued later in the year when Colani's book was published, refined it to take account of the presence of authentic sayings of Jesus in the discourse. He suggested that "the little apocalypse" consisted of three short scenes, the birthpangs of the end, 13:7-8; the tribulation of the Jews, 13:14-20; the coming of the Son of Man, 13:24-27.[4] That solution has remained popular to the present day and will be found in the majority of commentaries on the Synoptic gospels.

Experts who have examined the discourse in detail, however, are not so enthusiastic about the theory as the commentators. Of the many scholars who have written on the eschatological discourse in recent years one only, E. Brandenburger, supports it. R. Pesch in his dissertation on the discourse, adhered to it, but abandoned it when he wrote his great commentary on Mark. Among critical writers on the Gospels there is extraordinary divergence of opinion as to the precise content of the supposed apocalypse. In tracing the history of thought relating to the "little apocalypse" I have observed that every statement in the discourse has been claimed for it and every verse has been omitted from it; the extent of the postulated source ranges from three or four sentences to almost the entire discourse. That illustrates the high degree of subjectivity in attempts to define the apocalyptic source. More serious still, the motive which led Colani to eliminate the eschatological discourse from the teaching of Jesus continues to operate. The first scholarly work to be devoted to the discourse of Mark 13 was that of F. Busch, published in 1938. His examination of the literature on the subject led him to the conviction that two supreme motives have actuated the little apocalypse theory, namely a weakened Christology and a low estimate of Jewish apocalyptic. Of the former he said:

> The first presupposition for the grounding of that hypothesIs is the construction of a Christ who in every respect was adapted to the colorless features of a century whose representatives must needs perpetually call the artless, magnificent view of Mark 13 "bizarre." If this presupposition, this prejudice is renounced, then all the reasons for the hypothesis tumble down.[5]

On the latter issue he cited the affirmation of J. Schniewind: "We must free ourselves from the fancy that Jewish eschatology is a collection of absurdities."[6] That "fancy" continues to be met, despite the evidence of the Gospels that Jesus was a Jew through and through, and that the message he proclaimed was God in action to fulfil his promise to establish his saving sovereignty, a message rooted in the heritage of Israel's prophets and their successors.

If the theory of the little apocalypse is questionable, how then did it originate? To that many answers have been given. One to which much attention has been paid recently is the suggestion of Lars Hartman that the discourse is "an exposition on the basis of Daniel, a kind of 'midrash' which is on the way to becoming a 'mishna,' in that its connections with the original text are no longer clear and the traces of exegetical work may have been largely effaced."[7] This "midrash" contains material partly apocalyptic and eschatological and partly parenetic. The apocalyptic and eschatological field has two poles, namely the activity of the Antichrist and the *parousia* of the Son of Man. Hartman considers the possibility that this midrashic core of the discourse goes back to Jesus.

That the discourse contains some very significant connections with Daniel is undisputed, above all its references to the abomination of desolation in 13:14 and its description of Israel's tribulation in 13:19. The portrayal of the *parousia* in 13:24-27 includes associations with many prophetic passages of the Old Testament; its link with other descriptions of the *parousia* in the Gospels prevents it from being viewed as a simple citation from Dan 7:13. Most of the other suggested connections of the discourse with Daniel appear to me to be dubious, while, therefore, the appearance of the abomination and the revelation of the Son of Man may be claimed to form its two poles, they can hardly be said to form the core of the discourse. The thesis of a Danielic midrash as the basis of the discourse may be viewed as a pardonable exaggeration of an important feature of the discourse, namely the significant role within it of Old Testament and apocalyptic concepts, above all, of certain from the book of Daniel.

I myself have set forth the suggestion that the materials of the eschatological discourse, like those of all the other discourses of Jesus in the Gospels, were originally preserved in the primitive Christian catechesis as largely disparate sayings. Signs of rudimentary groupings of these sayings, however, may be discerned, which later became extended. Chief of these are the following:

1) *Sayings on the Distress of Israel,* 13:14 and 19. These were early linked with the prophecy of the doom of the temple in 13: 2. In due time 13:15-16, probably from Q, and 13:17-18 were similarly conjoined, and finally 13: 20.

2) *Sayings on the Distress of the Church,* 13: 9 and 11. That these circulated together is seen in Luke 12:11-12. Mark will have inserted between them 13:10, the saying on the mission to all the world, since it was the witnessing activity of the disciples which was a prime cause of their persecution, and the Church's mission was viewed in an eschatological perspective. Mark 13:12-13a were later conjoined through the same motive, as also 13b.

3) *Sayings on Pseudo-Messiahs and the true Messiah,* 13:21 and 24-26. In these the contrast between the Jewish notion of the secret appearance of the Messiah and the Christian teaching on the *parousia* of the Son of Man is set forth. Precisely the same contrast is set forth without interruption in Luke 17: 23-24. The reference to false messiahs in 13:21 attracted the related sayings of 13: 6 and 22.

4) *Sayings on the Parousia and Watchfulness,* 13:26(-27) and the parable of 13:34-36, without Markan expansions.

The core of groups 2 and 4 (sayings on the Distress of the Church and the *Parousia* and Watchfulness) appear to have been early linked in the catechesis, as appears from their combination in the Epistles (e.g. 1 Thess 4:15-5:11; Rom 13: 11-13; 1 Peter 4:7, 5:8-9). The Caligula episode of A.D. 39-40 could have stimulated the uniting of the sayings in group 1 and linking them with those of group 3 (cf. 2 Thess 2:1-9).

While these elements of Christian catechesis circulated in the early period of the Church, we cannot assume that they existed in the form of a connected discourse. Mark 13 reflects the evangelist's style through its whole length, and moreover it reflects a later period of crisis. It is likely that Mark brought together the varied eschatological traditions that had become associated in this manner and fashioned them into a unity in light of the contemporary situation and the needs of the churches he served. Such would appear, at least, a reasonable working hypothesis.

III. THE *GATTUNG* OF THE ESCHATOLOGICAL DISCOURSE: IS IT AN APOCALYPSE?

Proponents of the little apocalypse theory naturally answer the question affirmatively. E. Brandenburger holds that this is true not simply of the postulated apocalyptic core of the discourse but of the entire composition. "Mark 13 can, indeed, must be called through and through an apocalypse."[8] He defines it as an apocalyptic "school discourse" in answer to a "school question."[9]

Other scholars have denied this, none quite so emphatically as C. C. Torrey, whose acquaintance with apocalyptic literature is illustrated in his work, *The Apocryphal Literature*. He pointed out that "apocalyptic" is a literary term for a particular type of writing, purporting to contain revelations from God through visions and usually by means of an angel, and he affirmed:

> In the thirteenth chapter of Mark there is no indication of any special revelation, no mystery in language (except in v 14), none of the characteristic apparatus of the vision, nothing even to suggest knowledge received from heaven for the purpose in hand. Whatever may be thought of the material of the chapter, or conjectured as to its composition, there is nothing in any part of it that can justify the use of the term "apocalyptic."[10]

Other writers have urged that the discourse is to be viewed as standing in the prophetic rather than the apocalyptic tradition.[11] The discussion is not always clear, since the distinctions between the varied meanings of "apocalyptic," familiar to Torrey, have not always been in mind. Paul Hanson conveniently defined these as: 1) a special kind of literature, developed in the last two centuries B.C. and the first century A.D.; 2) apocalyptic eschatology, concerned especially with the kingdom of God, the judgment and the resurrection of the dead; 3) apocalypticism, i.e. the peculiar world of symbolism drawn from the traditions of centuries and even millennia through which the apocalyptic message is represented.[12] On that basis "apocalyptic" in the sense of apocalyptic eschatology should be the focal point of this discussion. Its uncertainty, however, is compounded by the fact that various prophetic works, such as Ezekiel, Deutero-Isaiah, Zechariah, and Isaiah 24-27 and 65-66, have affinity with the later apocalyptic literature, while the first truly apocalyptic work, the Book of Daniel, has much in common with the prophetic outlook, particularly on the relation of God to history; and scholars still debate whether the Book of Revelation is to be classed as prophecy or apocalyptic! There is much to be said in favor of Morna Hooker's view that Mark 13 is not strictly an apocalypse, but rather is mid-way between prophecy and apocalyptic, having affinities with both.[13]

That position has implications that extend beyond this one discourse. Burton

Mack, in an article in the journal of the Jesus Seminar, maintained that Mark's Gospel not only *contains* an apocalypse, but is an apocalypse, and scholars have failed to take that into account: "By treating the question of the 'little apocalypse' differently than the question of the Gospel itself, the 'eschatological' beginnings of the Gospel have been retained even while dismissing or discounting the apocalyptic endings. But both go together."[14] Ramsey Michaels, in the same journal, accepted the proposition that Mark 13 and Mark's Gospel "go together", but reversed the argument: if Mark's presentation of Jesus and the kingdom is to be taken seriously, then chapter 13 deserves to be taken equally seriously.[15] With that R. E. Clements would fully agree. He pointed out that the little clause in Mark 13:14, "Let the reader understand," is a characteristic expression of the task of the literate teacher in relation to the semi-literate communities of God's people, and he comments: "What is being conveyed by the eschatological discourse of Jesus is not simply a prophecy about forthcoming events, but at the same time a vitally significant evaluation of the import and meaning of those events for all who look to the Hebrew scriptures as the ground and guide of their hope."[16]

The conclusion of his discussion on apocalyptic and canonicity is noteworthy, not alone for Mark 13 but for the theme of our Symposium:

> Apocalyptic patterns of biblical interpretation are to be seen not simply narrowly confined to the Biblical books of Daniel and Revelation, but quite extensively spread throughout the prophetic literature of the Old Testament, widely present in the Biblical interpretations of St. Paul, and, most centrally of all, present in the teaching of Jesus. It may then be hoped that the seeming vagaries and excesses of the Biblical apocalyptists, which have so often in the history of the Christian church been the target of heavy criticism and even outright rejection by theologians, may be seen not to be so repulsive as they at first appear. They belong to a kind of theological necessity to the processes by which the word of God, originally proclaimed orally, came to be preserved and disseminated for the benefit of later generations.[17]

If it be asked why there is such a concentration of concern with apocalyptic expectations in Mark 13 the answer must lie in the critical time in which the discourse was composed, namely the Jewish war with Rome. This consideration holds good whether the author stood at the beginning of the war, or in its midst when the outlook for the Jews was grim, or at its end when Jerusalem lay in ruins and its people were decimated. Eschatological fever was possible at all these points, as the twentieth century with its experiences of wars abundantly illustrates.

It may be noted in passing that the so-called "apocalyptic cipher" of Mark 13:14, "the abomination of desolation," was no cipher to the Jews of our Lord's day. The memory of Antiochus Epiphanes and the deliverance from his blasphemous oppression was kept as fresh in the people's mind through the annual celebration of the Festival of the Dedication as the oppression of the Egyptian Pharaoh and the Exodus through the annual celebration of the Festival of the Passover. To a people under the heel of a power far more terrible than that of Antiochus the possibility of a repetition of that history prior to the ultimate deliverance described in Daniel was evident; how much more so for one who declared that not a stone of the temple would be left on a stone? And how very clear to a generation which had experienced the attempt of a mad emperor to repeat the deeds of Antiochus!

IV. THE PURPOSE OF THE ESCHATOLOGICAL DISCOURSE

A. To inspire faith, endurance and hope in face of the sufferings of the Church and the Jewish nation.

It seems right to place this object first, in view of the frequent habit of stressing the negative objects of the discourse. Warnings of Jesus to his followers concerning the inescapability of suffering are frequent in the Gospels. One such is included in the beatitudes of the Sermon on the Mount: "Blessed are you when men revile you and persecute you and utter all kinds of evil against you, lying as they do so, on my account" (Matt 5:11; cf. "on account of the Son of Man," Luke 6:22). That kind of experience was known from the earliest days of the Church, and certainly was true of the time when Mark was writing. But the concern of Jesus extended also to his people, and Mark included his warnings to them. The point, however, to which the discourse moves is not the abomination of desolation but the *parousia* of the Son of Man. That is the ground of hope, on account of which the Christians can endure all things and abound in the service of their Lord and his kingdom.

B. To warn Christians against false teaching concerning the End.

There is now a consensus among exegetes that the warnings against pseudo-prophets and pseudo-messiahs, which occur in 13:5-6 and 21-22, have been set by Mark at the beginning and the end of the narration of "signs" to draw attention to the danger of listening to such people. The position of these warnings probably indicates that there were prophets both within and without the Christian Church who proclaimed teachings viewed by Mark as highly dangerous.

1. The primary illusion is that the end of the age is immediately at hand, indeed the process has begun already, and Mark counters it at points throughout the discourse. While this is often thought to be a modern interpretation it goes back to the very early years of critical study of the eschatological discourse, e.g. in Pfleiderer's essay, "Über die Composition der eschatologischen Rede Matt 24.4ff,"[18] and, perhaps surprisingly, it was staunchly maintained by Johannes Weiss.[19] F. Hauck averred, "The tendency of Mark 13, despite all tension of thoughts as to the great hope of the End, is directed more to holding back extravagant views as to the near expectation of the End."[20] The motif appears in the warning that opens the discourse: "Watch out . . . . Many will come in my name, saying, 'I am he'" (13:5-6). That is not a Christian utterance, claiming the authority of Jesus for the statement, "I am he." It is the claim of a Jew to be "The Coming One," i.e. the Messiah. In 13: 21 that claim is made on behalf of others in terms of the notion of the "hidden" Messiah, whose presence and identity are kept secret till the time of his appearing; their followers are viewed as saying, "He's arrived! I know where he is! Come and let me show you!" Needless to say, if the Messiah has come, the deliverance is to take place now. Despite the denials of some, the comparison with the teaching in the church at Thessalonica, which Paul had to counter, that the day of the Lord had set in (2 Thess 2:2) is pertinent.

The immediately following statements in 13:7-8 relating to wars, "They must happen, but the end is not yet . . . . These are the beginning of the birth-pangs," rebut the contrary notion that the end has come and that the new age is at the birth. To represent the latter statement, "These are *only* the beginning of the pangs," is, however, an overstatement. J. Gnilka is right in observing, "The two temporal statements of 7b and 8c express both eschatological distance and expectation together."[21]

The paragraph 13:9-13 refers to quite different kinds of sufferings, namely those occasioned through confession of faith in Christ. The statement of 13:10, "And the gospel must first be proclaimed to all the nations," is highly significant for our discussion: first, it is Mark who inserted it between 13:9 and 11 (they occur in Luke 12:11-12 without any break); secondly 13:10 appears to be entirely traditional (from the catechesis?) with the possible exception of the term "first": "the gospel must first be preached to all nations." That is, it must be preached to all before the end comes! That emphasis of Mark not merely corrects apocalyptic excitement; it calls for devotion to the apocalyptic task of taking the good news to all humankind, for such is the divine purpose before the end comes. Matthew spells out the implication plainly: "Then the end shall come!" (24:14). On this Schmithals observed, "13:10 thus is a key to the understanding of the intentions which the Evangelist combines with chapter 13."[22]

2. A corollary of this correction of an extreme near expectation is an implicit denial that the *parousia* will take place in order to deliver the temple from the heathen, or as the immediate consequence of the temple's ruin. Mark's composition of the discourse is set as an exposition of the prophecy of Jesus in 13:2: the temple will be wholly overthrown. The disciples' question as to the premonitory sign that will herald this shocking event is most surely given in 13:14: "When you see the abomination of desolation standing where he ought not . . . then let those who are in Judea escape to the hills." Whatever the precise meaning of these words, it is plain that God has no intention of saving the temple. On the contrary it appears that its destruction is on account of the divine decree of judgment (cf. Mark 11:15-18; 11:12-14, 20-21; Matt 23:34-36, 37-39; Luke 13:1-5; 19:41-44). The abomination of desolation will herald the execution of that judgment. Accordingly the instinctive resort of every Jew to flee for refuge to the temple when disaster threatens is reversed; rather the command is given that all who are outside the city should flee from it, for the day of its judgment has come.

3. This entails a corollary to the corollary: the employment of the Danielic language for the anticipated destruction of the temple, and its kinship with other prophetic proclamations of the judgment of God on Jerusalem, indicate that the end does not fall with that event. "Day of the Lord" it may be, but not every "day" of the Lord signifies the last day. God has something more to accomplish before the final end (e.g. the sending of the gospel to all). That is strangely suggested by the proverbial language of 13:19 concerning the tribulation "such tribulation has not been . . . nor ever shall be!" and the (probably) Markan insertion in 13:24: the cosmic signs of the *parousia* will take place "after that tribulation." It is likely that the description of the *parousia* in13:24b-27 circulated independently without 13:24a, and that the expression "in those days" was added with a strictly eschatological meaning: "those days that end the old age and introduce the new"; but if Mark so found them, the connection with which he now provided them in their new context was highly misleading, hence he added the phrase "after that tribulation." That effectively separated the *parousia* from the ruin of the temple—to the chagrin of the heralds of the immediate end.

V. THE ESCHATOLOGICAL DISCOURSE AND THE PASSION NARRATIVE

That the discourse on the judgments and the deliverance of the Lord should take place at the end of the public ministry of Jesus is entirely in accord with the catechetical tradition. But its position as immediately preceding the passion narrative has long intrigued students of the gospels. R. H. Lightfoot not only believed that Mark designed the discourse as the immediate introduction to the passion narrative, he also saw a great deal of parallelism between the discourse and the passion narrative. This convinced him that Mark viewed the passion narrative as a first fulfillment of the eschatological discourse, "a sign, a seal of assurance, and a sacrament of the ultimate fulfillment" of the *parousia*. On this understanding the passion is an echatological event, participating in the finality of the consummation for which it prepares.[23] K. Grayston reached a similar conclusion. Reviewing the connections between discourse and the passion narrative he wrote, "By these means the crucifixion is seen in its full eschatological significance; and at the same time the eschatological expectations of the Church are controlled by the crucifixion."[24]

To what extent Mark was conscious of the connections pointed out by Lightfoot and Grayston I'm not sure. Of the close link in Mark's mind between the death, resurrection and *parousia* of Christ there can be no doubt. That is demonstrated by the little "discourse" of Mark 8:27-9:1, which is clearly of central importance to the evangelist and his Gospel. The passage describes Peter's confession of Jesus as the Messiah, the first prediction of the passion, a group of sayings on discipleship and the sufferings of Christ, and two sayings on the *parousia* in relation to the disciples. It was the merit of F. Busch to grasp the importance of the connection between Mark 8:27-9:1 and Mark 13. He saw that so surely as Messiahship and suffering belong together, so proclamation of the gospel and suffering of the proclaimers are inseparable, hence "*Mark 13 is an explication of Mark 8:34*."[25] His book is virtually an expansion of that thesis.

D. A. Koch developed this insight in an essay on Christology and eschatology in Mark. He observed that Mark 8:27-9:1 provides a kind of contents list of the second half of Mark's Gospel. The Christology of 8:27-33 and the eschatology of 8:38-9:1 are linked through the use of the title "the Son of Man," so bringing together the passion and resurrection of the Son Man and the *parousia* of the Son of Man, and indicating the identity of the Crucified with the Judge. The discipleship sayings of 8:34-37 are framed between the Christological beginning and the eschatological prospect. Hence the sayings on the present existence of the Church are given a double foundation, through retrospect on the suffering of the Son of Man and prospect of the coming of the Son of Man. Mark 13 is constructed on the same theological basis. The present is a period of afflictions, but the orienting to the Son of Man as the Crucified and as the Judge has the effect of enabling disciples not to withdraw from this situation but to accept it as in accord with the nature and calling of the Church.[26]

This recognition of the relation between Mark 8:27-9:1 and Mark 13 is significant in emphasizing the relation of the discourse to the redemptive action of the Son of Man in his death and resurrection on the one hand and in the *parousia* on the other, and the way of the Church in the time between as a via dolorosa illumined by the Easter resurrection and the *parousia* glory.

VI. SIGNS AND THE INCALCULABILITY OF THE END

This theme is a perennial problem in studies of Mark 13. The discourse depicts a succession of events leading to the *parousia* in answer to questions as to the time when the temple will be destroyed and the sign when it will happen, on the presupposition that temple ruin and *parousia* will occur together. By contrast the Q tradition represents the *parousia* as taking place suddenly and without warning (Luke 17:24, 26-30). Pharisees are told that the kingdom of God comes "without observation" (Luke 17:20-21), and Mark 8:11-12 reports Jesus as emphatically rejecting a demand for a sign "from heaven" to be given by him ("No sign will be given to this generation"). Strangely enough, these two representations of the future appear side by side in Mark 13: the parable of the fig tree (13:28-29) appears to sum up the function of the discourse as indicating signs by which the nearness of the end may be known ("When you see these things happening know that he is near . . . "), yet 13:32 declares in strongest terms the unknowability of the time of the end ("Of that day or hour nobody knows . . ."), and the parabolic sayings that follow emphasize the need for watchfulness in light of that fact. It could be maintained, therefore, that Mark has presented a contradictory picture of the end of the age. Inasmuch, however, as he himself fashioned the elements of the discourse into one that is not very likely. Some preliminary observations may help to dispel some of the fog.

The "evil and adulterous generation" which demanded from Jesus a sign from heaven is rebuked by him for failing to discern signs of the kingdom present in his ministry (Luke 12:54-56), and he warned them of coming wrath for their failure to repent in face of such signs (Matt 11:20-24). His message to John the Baptist conveys the same fundamental idea, although couched in gentler language (Matt 11:5-6). The emphasis in Mark 8:11 is probably on a demand for a sign "from heaven," since the Pharisees suspected that the signs of Jesus on earth were inspired by Satan (Mark 3:22).

Luke 17:20-21 requires to be understood in light of these sayings. The term *parateresis* (observation) is used in secular literature by physicians of the observing of signs and symptoms of the body, and by astronomers and astrologers of the movements of stars and the planets. Jewish priests pursued the latter kind of observation in order to fix the dates of their religious festivals. If, with W. Bauer, we understand *meta paratereos* in Luke 17:20 as "so that its approach can be observed," we need to qualify "observed" with such some term as "accurately." Most apocalyptists believed that God works in history according to a timetable. Consider e.g. 4 Ezra 4:36-37: " . . . He has weighed the age in a balance, and measured the times by measure, and numbered the times by number; and He will not move or arouse them until that measure is fulfilled." With this goes the belief that God has revealed this timetable to certain elect souls (see e.g. 2 *Bar* 54:1-5), and that a comparison of such revelations with events in history will show where one is at any given time in the divine plan. This process is less difficult than it sounds, since it is always assumed by apocalyptists that the close of history is at hand. (For examples of this viewpoint see the Apocalypse of Weeks in 1 *Enoch* 91-93, and the more detailed Apocalypse of the Clouds in 2 *Baruch* 53-74). We know that many rabbis after the Fall of Jerusalem busied themselves with calculations of the time when the kingdom of God should come; according to one system of reckoning it should have arrived in A.D. 70, and those who so believed strove to explain why it failed to come then. It is unlikely that this kind of calculation on the basis of signs did not happen prior to A.D. 70. Jesus in Luke 17:20-21 apparently called on his Pharisaic interlocutors to abandon such futile apocalyptic arithmetic and to recognize that "the kingdom of God is within your grasp," and, by implication, to seize it by receiving the word of the kingdom that he brought.[27]

Anyone who reads the portrayals of the divine revelations of the course of history in such works as 1 *Enoch* 91-93 or 2 *Baruch* 53-74 will readily acknowledge that they are vastly removed from the picture of the future in Mark 13. There is no timetable in Mark's discourse. The warnings given regarding false messiahs and prophets, wars far and near, persecutions for witnessing to the gospel of Christ are not stated in a chronological order, neither are they datable. Rather they characterize the entire period between the resurrection and the *parousia*, which is the eschatological time, the "last times." The one apocalyptic sign in Mark 13 which has reference to a specific event in history is the appearance of the abomination of desolation, and that is stated to answer a question concerning the prophecy of the ruin of the temple in Mark 13:2.

What, then, are we to say of the parable of the fig tree, 13:28-29, with its application, "When you see these things taking place, know that he is near, at the doors?" What things are in mind here? They are happenings future to the time of speaking but prior to the end. In Mark's setting they must include the events described in 13:5-23, but not all in the same manner. It is said of the wars in 13:7, "the end is not yet," and in 13:8 that they are the beginning of birth-pangs; while, therefore, they belong to the "last" times, they are not to be overemphasized as heralding an immediate end. Curiously, the same thing applies to the one clear sign of a historical and geographically locatable event, the appearance of the "abomination of desolation"; while described by means of Danielic language relating to the Day of the Lord which immediately precedes the end, Mark is careful to safeguard against viewing it as integral to the end—the *parousia* comes *after*, not *with* the catastrophe upon Jerusalem. The remaining events in 13:5-23, viewed as premonitory signs of the nearness of the end, are the activities of pseudo-messiahs and pseudo-prophets (5-6, 21-22) and the suffering witness of disciples (13:9-13). The importance of the former is emphasized by Mark's enclosing all other signs between their mention, doubtless because individuals of this sort were creating mischief in his own area by their claims about the immediacy of the end. It is an ironical factor, that a sign of the end can become a means of deception through misleading people to think that the end is nearer than it is! And that was a real concern to Mark! The suffering witness of the disciples is manifestly a sign perpetuated through the whole era of the Church; its nature as a sign of the end is peculiarly in harmony with the fig tree parable, for those suffering in the service of Christ are encouraged to know that the end of their labors is none other than the event that will consummate the kingdom initiated by their Lord, namely his *parousia* in glory.

On no account, however, should the so-called cosmic signs described in 13:24-25 be viewed as premonitory signs of the *parousia*. Brandenburger, following Conzelmann, maintains that Mark looks back on the whole portrayal of signs in 13:5-23, including the catastrophe on Jerusalem and its temple and people, as lying in the past, consequently the only signs referred to in the fig tree parable are the cosmic signs that herald the *parousia*; when they occur, however, it is too late to do anything about it! Brandenburger considers that by this means Mark has released the expectation of the *parousia* from the typical apocalyptic projection of historical-cosmic tribulation of this world time: "It is a fundamentally critical way of thinking, won under actual circumstances, and releases hope from Daniel's pattern of thought."[28] This I view as a questionable interpretation of Mark's intention. The notion of cosmic signs of the coming of God belongs, as Brandenburger himself emphasizes, to the ancient concept of theophany. But the fundamental idea of signs in heaven and on earth is the reaction of creation to the stepping forth of the awesome and terrible Lord of the storm, the Creator himself. The elements of creation go into confusion and fear *because* he appears, not as a sign that he is *about* to do so (see e.g. Jud 5:4-5; Amos 1:2; Hab 3:3-6, 10-11; Pss 77:14-16; 114:1-8). The cosmic signs mentioned in Mark 13:24-26 are, therefore, accompaniments of the appearing of the Lord in his advent, manifestations of his glory rather than heralds of his coming; they serve to characterize the *parousia* as a theophany, the revelation of the divine Son of God.

All this has a significant bearing on the nature of signs in Mark 13. Like the other evangelists, Mark recognizes that the kingdom of God is present in and through Jesus - his ministry, death and resurrection, and that it presses on to his *parousia*. The whole period between the Christ event and the *parousia* is kingdom of God time, for it is characterized by continuing signs of the inbreaking kingdom which comes in its fullness at the *parousia*. All the events described in Mark 13:5-23 have to be viewed as falling under the sovereign rule of God, for the judgments of God are manifestations of the rule of God as well as his acts of salvation. This includes the appearance and works of the abomination of desolation, just as, in the Book of Revelation, the Antichrist is given authority by God to open his mouth in blasphemies and to "act" for forty-two months, the period of the great distress (see Rev 13:5).

There is, accordingly, some justification for F. Hahn to speak of the fig tree parable as the principal item, the "angle-point" of the eschatological discourse. In Hahn's estimate Mark, despite all his apocalyptic points of interpretation, makes this clear through his thoroughgoing relating of the whole discourse to the time between Easter and the *parousia*; thereby he comes closer to the original meaning of the parable and is enabled to bind together Christology and eschatology.[29] This "original meaning" of the parable, I take it, will not have related solely to the presence of the kingdom of God in the ministry of Jesus, but to the complete fulfillment of the kingdom, present and future through the action of Jesus, as the future "when you see these things" of 13:29 indicates. The signs of Mark 13 show God at work in and through the processes of history in the world under the lordship of Christ and through the Spirit in the Church, leading the world and the Church to their destined end in the consummated kingdom of God. Hence the suitability of the conclusion of the discourse in exhortations ever to remain on the alert, ready for the final manifestation of the kingdom in the *parousia* of Christ. This preparedness for the end includes serving the Lord until the end, as the parable of 13:34-36 suggests, and not least in serving Christ in mission and sufferings for the kingdom, as 13:9-11 show. Signs and suddenness are reconcilable when they relate to the Lord of the cross and resurrection and *parousia*.

VII. PERSONAL AND COSMIC-UNIVERSAL ESCHATOLOGY

In an earlier work on the eschatology of Jesus H. D. Wendland drew attention to the double polarity contained in the idea of the consummation: it has to do with final salvation and final judgment on the one hand, and it is personal and cosmic-universal on the other.[30] If we view the eschatological discourse in this light, final salvation is plain, the judgment is assumed; cosmic-universal eschatology is apparent at the beginning and fills the horizon at the *parousia*, and the messianic function of Jesus includes the personal aspect. But Wendland sees the emphasis within the discourse as on the first and last of these features. He affirms: "No single declaration as to the new world is given, and only the dealing of the Son of Man with mankind is depicted, not the dealing of God himself. The personal-soteriological eschatology is the central thing . . . All expectation is directed to the ethical decision: the coming of the Messiah, the judgment and the gift of life."[31]

The comment is just. Mark's restraint in the discourse has often been commented on. Apocalyptic works frequently describe the heavenly world and the world to come, the appearance of God, the judgment of the wicked and reward of the righteous. In these respects the Book of Revelation is typical of apocalypses; the discourse of Mark 13 is wholly atypical, yet it preserves the elements of hope which are essential to a full orbed eschatology.

It is well that Mark has provided us with a discourse that provides a balance which the apocalyptic dimension supplies, for without it our understanding of the eschatology of Jesus would be incomplete. By the same token the representation of the eschatology of Jesus in Mark 13, if divorced from that in the other three Gospels, would be unbalanced. But not even Mark intended it to be read in isolation; it forms the climax of his teaching on the kingdom. A full orbed understanding of the teaching of Jesus, in eschatology as in all other aspects of the revelation of God through him, requires the illumination provided by the Spirit through all four evangelists.

NOTES

1. *The Life of Jesus,* trans. G. Eliot (London: Williams & Norgate, 1935) 98-99.

2. *The Life of Jesus,* 145-46.

3. *Das Leben Jesu für das deutsche Volk bearbeitet* (Leipzig 1864) 237.

4. *Untersuchungen über die evangelische Geschichte* (Freiburg: J. C. B. Mohr, 1864) 121-22.

5. *Zum Verständnis der synoptischen Eschatologie; Markus 13 neu untersucht,* (Gütersloh: Bertelsman, 1938) 54.

6. Ibid 59.

7. *Prophecy Interpreted: The Formation of Some Jewish Apocalyptic Texts and of the Eshatological Discourse Mar 13 Par* (Lund: Gleerup, 1966).

8. *Markus 13 und die Apokalyptik,* (FRLANT 134, Göttingen: Vandenhoeck & Ruprecht , 1984) 13.

9. Ibid, 15.

10. *Documents of the Primitive Church* (New York: Harper & Brothers, 1941) 14-15.

11. So for example L. Gaston, *No Stone on Another, Studies in the Significance of the Fall of Jerusalem in the Synoptic Gospels* (Nov Test S; Leiden: Brill, 1970) 423-28.

12. "Apocalypticism" in *IDB* (1976) 29-34.

13. *The Son of Man in Mark* (Montreal:McGill University Press, 1967) 149; and "Trial and Tribulation in Mark XIII," *BJRL* 65 (1982) 78.

14. "The Kingdom Sayings in Mark," *Forum* 3, 1 (1987) 6.

15. "An Intemperate Case for an Eschatological Jesus," due to appear in *Forum.*

16. "Apocalyptic, Literacy and Canonical Tradition" in *Eschatology and the New Testament*: FS G. R. Beasley-Murray, ed. W. H. Gloer (Peabody, Mass: Hendrikson 1988) 18-19.

17. Ibid, 27.

18. In *Jahrbücher für Deutsche Theologie* 13 (1868) 144-46.

19. See e.g. *Das älteste Evangelium*, (THNT; Göttingen: Vandenhoeck & Ruprecht, 1908) 72-74.

20. *Das Evangelium des Markus* (Leipzig: 1931) 154.

21. *Das Evangelium nach Markus* (EKKNT; Neukirchen: Neukirchener Verlag 1979) 186-88.

22. *Das Evangelium des Markus* (Gütersloh: Mohn, 1979) II, 574.

23. *The Gospel Message of St. Mark* (Oxford: Oxford University Press 1950) 51-54.

24. "The Study of Mark XIII," *BJRL* 56 (1974) 386-87.

25. *Zum Verständnis der synoptische Eschatologie*, 48.

26. "Zum Verhaltnis von Christologie und Eschatologie im Markusevangelium" in *Jesus Christus in Historie und Theologie:* FS H. Conzelmann, ed. G. Strecker (Tübingen: J. B. Mohr, 1975) 400-8.

27. On the interpretation of Luke 17:20-21 see G. R. Beasley-Murray, *Jesus and the Kingdom of God* (Grand Rapids: Eerdmans, 1986) 97-103.

28. *Markus und die Apokalyptik*, 96-102.

29. "Die Rede von der Parusie des Menschensohnes Markus 13" in *Jesus und der Menschensohn*: FS A. Vogtle, ed. R. Pesch & R. Schnackenburg (Freiburg: Herder, 1975) 263-64

30. *Die Eschatologie des Reiches Gottes bei Jesus* (Gütersloh: Bertelsmann, 1931) 245.

31. Ibid. 246.

"THE GOD OF PEACE WILL SHORTLY CRUSH SATAN UNDER YOUR FEET" (Romans 16:20a): The Function of Apocalyptic Eschatology in Paul

DAVID N. SCHOLER

I. INTRODUCTION

In his mature letter (probably A.D. 57) to the Romans Paul writes this "apocalyptic kicker" as part of his conclusion to that letter: "The God of Peace will shortly crush Satan under your feet" (Rom 16:20a).[1] This rather incidental remark indicates that apocalyptic language and thought are "alive and well" in the mature Paul.

Four apocalyptic features can be identified in the saying of Rom 16:20a. First, the battle is conceived of in cosmic terms; it is one between God and Satan. Second, the event is anticipated "shortly." This term is a virtual apocalyptic password, as may be observed from its use in Revelation (1:1 and 22:6; 22:7).[2] Third, connected to the previous observation, is the strong sense of imminence expressed. This is consistent with the perspective of Rom 13:11-14 (especially ". . . For salvation is nearer to us now . . . . The day is near . . . .). Fourth, there may well be here an allusion to Ps 110:1 in the phrase "under your feet." Psalm 110 was viewed in the early church as a messianic/eschatological Psalm (see, e.g., Paul in 1 Cor 15:24-28). Although the majority of commentators see in this phrase an allusion to Gen 3:15, it may be better understood as a community extension (=those in Christ) of the victory guaranteed to the church in the resurrection and confirmation of Jesus Christ as Lord and the one in whom Ps 110:1 is/will be fulfilled. Thus, the apocalyptic function of Rom 16:20a is to provide to the people of God both hope and a sense of group or community empowerment.

Of course, both the definition of the terms apocalypticism and apocalyptic and also the degree to which apocalyptic language and thought are present in Paul are matters of considerable debate. It is the intention of this essay to illumine these questions, with special emphasis on the function of apocalyptic language and concepts in Paul and their significance for the theology of the church today.

The definition of the terminology has been greatly helped by Paul D. Hanson's distinctions and delineations of three terms.[3]

First, apocalypse is defined as a literary genre used often by apocalyptic writers as a means of communicating their ideas. Second, apocalyptic eschatology is a religious perspective on divine plans for the world. Such perspectives do not belong to any one group or ideology. These perspectives are in continuity with prophetic eschatology, but do entail certain clear differences.

In Hanson's words: "The difference involves the degree to which divine plans and acts are interpreted as being effected within the structures of mundane reality and through the agency of human persons."[4] The apocalyptic perspective is that in which the mundane and the human are less involved and/or less significant. Third, apocalypticism is ". . . the symbolic universe in which an apocalyptic movement codifies its identity and interpretation of reality."[5]

Given this conceptual framework, it is clear that the issue for the study of Paul is the matter of apocalyptic eschatology. Paul did not write any apocalypses, and Pauline thought could hardly be characterized fairly as apocalypticism in Hanson's terms. Further delineation of the meaning and character of apocalyptic eschatology is possible and will provide more specific background for approaching Pauline texts. The work especially of John J. Collins, Klaus Koch, J. Christiaan Beker, Wayne Meeks and Christopher Rowland is important for the study of apocalyptic eschatology and its presence and function in Paul.

Klaus Koch has developed eight pointers or identifying marks of Jewish apocalyptic eschatology:[6] (1) ". . . urgent expectation of the impending overthrow of all earthly conditions in the immediate future;" (2) "the end appears as a vast cosmic catastrophe;" (3) "the time of this world is divided into fixed segments. . . ;" (4) ". . . an army of angels and demons is mustered. . . ;" (5) "beyond the catastrophe a new salvation arises, paradisal in character;" (6) "the transition from disaster to final redemption is expected to take place by means of an act issuing from the throne of God;" (7) ". . . a mediator with royal functions is frequently introduced to accomplish and guarantee final redemption;" and (8) "the catchword glory is used wherever the final state of affairs is set apart from the present and whenever a final amalgamation of the earthly and heavenly spheres is prophesied."

Both John J. Collins[7] and J. Christiaan Beker[8] affirm Koch's eight pointers to apocalyptic eschatology. In fact, Beker provides a convenient four point summary of Koch: (l) historical dualism; (2) universal cosmic expectation; (3) the imminent end of the world; and (4) the faithfulness and vindication of God.[9] Collins notes that Koch's points are appropriate for the "historical type" of apocalyptic thought, but that this must not obscure the "heavenly journey type" of apocalyptic literature or thought, an aspect of apocalyptic eschatology particularly illuminated by the work of Christopher Rowland (see the next paragraph). Collins also has a one point "definition" of apocalyptic eschatology: the ". . . hope for the transcendence of death . . . is the distinctive character of apocalyptic over against prophecy."[10]

Christopher Rowland has argued appropriately that the definition of apocalyptic thought should not be too restrictive and has emphasized that the defining element is not so much eschatology as it is essentially about the revelation of divine mysteries, often in visions or "heavenly journeys.[11]

A final, and very helpful, summary of apocalyptic thought is that of Wayne A. Meeks:[12] (1) secrets have been revealed to the author or prophet; (2) these secrets relate to an imminent cosmic transformation and tend to distinguish "this age" from "the age to come;" (3) judgment is central among the events of the end; and (4) the apocalyptic universe consists of three dualities—l) the cosmic duality (heaven/earth); 2) the temporal duality (this age/the age to come); and 3) the social duality (elect/world; righteous/unrighteous; sons of light/sons of darkness).

The degree to which and the way in which Paul's thought involves apocalyptic eschatology, language and concepts has long been a matter of debate. In fact, Leander E. Keck has said that ". . . 'Paul and apocalyptic' defies solution."[13] An excellent survey of the whole issue is given in the recent work of E. Elizabeth Johnson.[14] Keck's "insoluble" to the contrary, Johnson notes that virtually every Pauline scholar (Bultmann excepted) since Schweitzer[15] affirms his insight, to one degree or another, that Paul's thought is clearly indebted to and shaped by Jewish apocalyptic eschatology. In the last decade no one has argued more strongly than J. Christiaan Beker that Paul's thought is basically apocalyptic in character.[16] As will be argued here, "taken with enough grains of salt," Beker is correct.

It is not possible within the limits of this essay to undertake a complete or thorough study of apocalyptic eschatology in Paul's Letters. The selective approach here will focus on Galatians (in my view Paul's earliest Letter and one often excluded from this discussion) and on portions of 1 and 2 Corinthians and Romans. For this study, 1 and 2 Thessalonians, which generally receive the bulk of attention, will not be considered, nor will Philippians or the other later Letters of Paul or his "school" (Colossians, Ephesians and the Pastoral Epistles). This will allow the investigation of the function of apocalyptic eschatology in Paul to proceed with a good span of Paul (Galatians to Romans) and with a focus on some texts not usually considered in this discussion.

II. GALATIANS: THE "NEW CREATION" AS THE FOCUS OF PAUL'S THOUGHT

The concept of the "new creation" is specifically expressed by Paul in Galatians and 2 Corinthians (see Gal 6:15; 5:6; 3:28; 2 Cor 5:16-17; 3:1-18). The "new creation" concept appears to be in these texts the critical point of Paul's theological argumentation and in that sense at least the focus of Paul's thought (or "center" of Paul's "theological structure"). The new creation is clearly an apocalyptic concept and structure. The new creation in Galatians entails the triple dualism of Meeks' definition (noted above): (1) cosmic dualism in 6:14 (world vs. cross); 5:16-17 (flesh vs. Spirit) and 4:24-26 (present Jerusalem vs. Jerusalem above); (2) temporal dualism in 6:15 and 3:24-29; and (3) social dualism in 3:28 and 4:30-31.

Implied throughout the structure of Galatians is the tension of the present/future (already/not yet; this age/the age to come). This is seen especially in 3:1-5 (the reception and power of the Spirit) and in the emphasis of 5:16, 18 and 25 over against 5:5 and 6:8-9 in which the contrast between the present and future is explicit.

It is critical to note that Paul's major defense of his understanding of the gospel/new creation given in Galatians is rooted in his apocalyptic claim to "direct heavenly revelation" (see Rowland above): "For I want you to know . . . that the gospel that was proclaimed by me is not of human origin; for I did not receive it from a human source, nor was I taught it, but I received it through a revelation of Jesus Christ" (1:11-12).[17]

III. 1 CORINTHIANS

1 Corinthians is a Letter midway between Galatians and Romans and one in which the focus is primarily on pastoral and community issues. Nevertheless, this text contains considerable eschatological and apocalyptic data, which can be summarized

here in seven categories.

First, the awareness of the presence and imminent nature of the End is a given. The somewhat incidental remark in 1 Cor 10:11, ". . . on whom the ends of the ages have come" is evidence of both apocalyptic temporal dualism and of the sense of imminence. The argument for celibacy within the believing community in 1 Cor 7:25-35 is undergirded, at least in part, by a three-fold appeal to the sense of apocalyptic urgency and imminence and the presumption of apocalyptic temporal dualism: ". . . in view of the impending crisis . . . " (7:26); ". . . the appointed time has grown short . . . " (7:29); and ". . . the present form of this world is passing away" (7:31).

Second, the whole matter of the understanding and misunderstanding between Paul and the Corinthians of the future resurrection reflects various apocalyptic concerns and understandings (see especially 1 Corinthians 15). Paul argues in 1 Cor 15:12-28 that Christ's resurrection (presupposed as common ground between Paul and the Corinthians in 15:1-11 and 6:12-14) is an apocalyptic reality and guarantee of the future resurrection of those who have died in Christ. The "logic of apocalyptic thought" means that the future event/reality is inevitable given the present reality of Christ's "end time resurrection." Over against the "over realized" eschatology of his opponents in Corinth (see especially 4:8; 15:12; 10:1-5), Paul argues for what Ernst Käsemann has called "eschatological reserve,"[18] which preserves an apocalyptic tension between "this age"/the present and "the age to come"/the future (see 6:12-14; 15:30-34; 13:11-13; 1:7). This tension requires, in Paul's judgment, that believers live now a life of moral responsibility in anticipation of the arrival of "the age to come."

Third, Paul cites an apocalyptic saying[19] in 1 Cor 2:9 in order to explain something of both the cosmic and temporal dualism that underlay the cosmic drama of Christ's death in the context of God's secret and hidden plan (l Cor 2:6-10; note also the use of the term "glory" in 2:8; see Koch's eighth pointer cited earlier). It should be noted that the believing community is understood to be composed of the recipients of God's revelation which provides this understanding.

Fourth, Paul uses an apocalyptic understanding, similar to one expressed in the Jewish apocalypse, *The Testament of Abraham*,[20] of the final judgment in order to comment on the responsibilities of Apollos, himself and other leaders and to issue a warning about the proper care of God's temple = the believers in Corinth! (l Cor 3:10-17). Again, the apocalyptic data is given a "communal/ethical transformation" in its immediate application to the life situation of the believers.

Fifth, Paul uses the apocalyptic idea of the future and final judgment to argue a point with his Corinthian detractors. Paul writes: "Do you not know that the saints will judge the world? . . . . Do you not know that we are to judge angels. . . ?" (1 Cor 6:2-3). The concept of the future apocalyptic judgment, and especially the believers' active role in it, is used by Paul to fault the Corinthians for their failure to exercise appropriate mundane judgments within the church (l Cor 6:1-8).

Sixth, Paul appears to appeal both to apocalyptic social and temporal dualism and to the concept of apocalyptic judgment in order to explain the pressing and disturbing question about the untimely death of certain members of the Corinthian church (l Cor 11:30-32).

Seventh, Paul uses the powerful concept of the transcendence of death (recall Collins' judgment that this is the distinctive character of apocalyptic thought) to press for present faithfulness among the Corinthians and to provide encouragement for all forms of the church's ministries (l Cor 15:35-58).

V. 2 CORINTHIANS

This Letter of Paul, presumably coming not too long after 1 Corinthians, contains two quite different identifiable types of apocalyptic texts: 2 Cor 4:16-5:10 and 12:1-10.

2 Cor 4:16-5:10 builds upon an apocalyptic temporal and cosmic dualism, especially in terms of the "outer nature/inner nature," "slight momentary affliction/eternal weight of glory," "what can be seen/what cannot be seen," and "temporary/eternal" contrasts in 2 Cor 4:16-18. The concept of apocalyptic judgment is also invoked (2 Cor 5:10). All of this is set in a framework of communal/ethical transformation from the "so we do not lose heart" (2 Cor 4:16) to the "so we are always confident" (2 Cor 5:6) to the "we make it our aim to please him" (2 Cor 5:9) to the final "for all of us must appear before the judgment seat of Christ, so that each may receive recompense for what has been done in the body, whether good or evil" (2 Cor 5:10).

The larger context of this section of 2 Corinthians, going back to 2 Cor 3:4-4:6 (see 3:4 "Such is the confidence that we have;" see 5:6), introduces the theme of apocalyptic *glory* (see again Koch's eighth pointer cited earlier): "Now if the ministry of death . . . came in *glory* . . . , a *glory* now set aside, how much more will the ministry of the Spirit come in *glory*? For if there was *glory* in the ministry of condemnation, much more does the ministry of justification abound in *glory*! Indeed, what once had *glory* has lost its *glory* because of the greater *glory*; for if what was set aside came through *glory*, much more has the permanent come in *glory*! Since, then, we have such a hope, we act with great boldness . . . . And all of us, with unveiled faces, seeing the *glory* of the Lord as though reflected in a mirror, are being transformed into the same image from one degree of *glory* to another; for this comes from the Lord, the Spirit . . . . In their case the god of this world has blinded the minds of the unbelievers, to keep them from seeing the light of the gospel of the *glory* of Christ . . . . For it is the God who said, 'Let light shine out of darkness,' who has shone in our hearts to give the light of the knowledge of the *glory* of God in the face of Jesus Christ" (2 Cor 3:7-18; 4:4-6). This apocalyptic concept of glory provides structure for Paul's larger framework of understanding the work of God in Christ.

2 Corinthians also contains an apocalyptic text which belongs to the mystical, heavenly journey category of apocalyptic thought and concepts. In 2 Cor 12:1-10 Paul tells of his (see "me" in 12:7) journey to the third heaven = Paradise.[21] This apocalyptic experience is crucial to Paul's self-understanding as an apostle. The function of this "apocalyptic adventure" for Paul is its legitimation of Paul's apostleship and authority. This is, it may be recalled, similar to the experience and function of Paul's Damascus Road revelation experience as described in Gal 1:11-12. Further, Paul's theological self-understanding of weakness comes out of this critical apocalyptic experience. For Paul, weakness is equivalent to subordination to Christ. And, such submission to Christ is even seen in the context of an apocalyptic cosmic dualism to some degree: Paul's weakness (= submission to Christ's power) is set over against Satan (the thorn in the flesh is a messenger of Satan)

V. ROMANS

Romans 9-11 is the critical, driving concern of the argument in Romans, as the "debate" between Krister Stendahl and W. D. Davies shows.[22] The concern of Romans 9-11 is framed within the issues of apocalyptic eschatology, as has been recently demonstrated so clearly by E. Elizabeth Johnson.[23]

The function of Romans 9-11 is the resolution of divine integrity. Although this text does not concern itself with the typical apocalyptic concern over theodicy in which the apocalyptic community understands itself to be oppressed or persecuted, as Keck observes, [24] it does deal with fundamental apocalyptic issues. In a conceptual crisis parallel to a theodicy, the integrity of God is at stake for Paul. The ultimate resolution for God's integrity is found in part in the affirmation of God's superior wisdom (Rom 11: 33-36), something which may be reflective of a cosmic apocalyptic structure.

Another part of the resolution for God's integrity which is clearly apocalyptic in character is Israel's ultimate salvation (Rom 11:25-26), which is the result of God's irrevocable promise (Rom 11:29) . Israel's ultimate salvation is not only an apocalyptic mystery, it is also an eschatological event.

Romans 9-11, of course, is not the only section of Romans in which apocalyptic ideas occur; some other texts may be briefly noted. Rom 6:1-11 reflects both an apocalyptic cosmic dualism and the apocalyptic transcendence of death. It also contains Paul's eschatological reserve, noticed earlier in 1 Corinthians. Again, the apocalyptic structure is used to encourage communal/ethical behavior of responsible life in Christ.

In Romans 8, after the discussion of the "cosmic dualism" of flesh and Spirit (8:1-16), the focus shifts to the apocalyptic redemption of all creation (8:17-30), with specific attention given to apocalyptic temporal dualism (e.g., "the sufferings of this present time"/"the glory about to be revealed" 8 :18; "what is seen"/"what we do not see" 8:24-25). There is also present in this text the language of glory: ". . . if, in fact, we suffer with him so that we may also be glorified with him" (8:17); ". . . the sufferings of this present time are not worth comparing with the glory about to be revealed to us" (8:18); ". . . that the creation itself will be set free from its bondage to decay and will obtain the freedom of the glory of the children of God" (8:21); and ". . . those whom he justified he also glorified" (8:30). All of this apocalyptically oriented discussion in Romans 8 functions as encouragement for the believers; the closing word is that nothing ". . . will be able to separate us from the love of God in Christ Jesus our Lord" (8:39).

Finally, one may recall Rom 13:11-14 and 16:20a mentioned at the opening of this essay. These texts reflect apocalyptic imminence and both the temporal and cosmic types of apocalyptic dualism. In Rom 13:11-14 the function is clearly to encourage behavior appropriate to life in Christ. Rom 16:20a provides to people of God both hope and a sense of empowerment over against evil and Satan.

VI. CONCLUSIONS

On the basis of the data presented from Galatians, 1 and 2 Corinthians and Romans it is possible to draw some conclusions about Paul's relationship to and use of apocalyptic language and concepts.

Paul's thought is deeply shaped and structured by Jewish apocalyptic categories and themes. As stated earlier, taken with enough grains of salt, Beker is correct, Keck's "insoluble" notwithstanding. Each one of the Pauline texts examined here shows that apocalyptic ideas are part of the warp and woof of the texts and that they are present both implicitly and explicitly. They are used for theological argument, perspective on hope and instruction in behavior. All three of the apocalyptic dualities noted by Meeks are clearly present in Paul: the cosmic duality (e.g., Rom 16:20a; 2 Cor 12:1-10); the temporal duality (e.g., Galatians; 1 Corinthians; 2 Cor 3-4); and the social duality (e.g., Galatians; Rom 13:11-14). Paul's apocalyptic thought is found both in the motifs of end-time concerns (Koch's pointers 1, 3, 5, 6, 7 and 8 are well represented in Paul; pointers 2 and 4 are not) and in the utilization of revelations, mysteries and apocalyptic/mystical experiences (see Rowland and Segal).

Further, however, it must be noted that Paul's apocalyptic structures and ideas, motifs and expressions are deeply[25] modified and/or reconceptualized in the light of his experience of and convictions about Jesus Christ as the fulfillment of God's promises, his understanding of the cross, his belief in the resurrection of Jesus as the guarantee of the end (the so-called "already"), his belief in the presence of the Spirit as guarantee within the believing community and his understanding of the new inclusiveness of the people of God which transcends and replaces the "nationalism" of Jewish apocalyptic thought.

Apocalyptic concepts and structures appear to have four functions in Paul's thought.[26] These functions are both social and theological; it is probably not appropriate to make a dichotomy between these two functional categories, although some recent scholarly traditions have tended to argue or imply that all so-called theological functions are, in fact, only sociologically motivated (or "power politics"). It is critical to recognize the realities of social function, group identity and boundary concerns and "power politics" in understanding the development of theological thought and preferences in the early church. However, it is also critical to give recognition to the realities of theological conviction rooted in understandings of God and the world, of spirit and matter, and of human destiny which, in their own ways, shape the social forms of life and action. Some concepts are rooted in theological world-views of what constituted reality and God's relation to the creation, rather than in only sociological issues and factors.[27]

First, the apocalyptic tradition as used by Paul provides three overarching theological convictions about God and the world which shape the social realities of the early church. 1) There is the conviction of the transcendence of death both in the apocalyptic future and in the present ethical stance of the believers; death has been overcome! 2) The integrity of God's promise to Israel is understood to mean that Israel's salvation has future apocalyptic validity. 3) There is a certain future hope and deliverance for the people of God (the community of faith). This hope is also power or empowerment and has clear sociological implications for group identity, boundaries and commitments in relationship to and/or over against the world apart from the community.

Second, the overwhelming function of apocalyptic thought in Paul and his communities is the ethical transformation of these concepts in the present life and behavior of the community.[28] This means that apocalyptic language and concepts are to function, not as tantalizing speculations about the future nor as means of avoiding issues in the present, but rather as encouragements, directives and sanctions about issues of righteousness and justice for the people of God now.

Third, the apocalyptic traditions, especially those in Galatians and 2 Corinthians, also function to legitimate Paul's apostleship and authority in the church.[29] Probably this function has been significantly abused in the history of the American church in those cases when religious leaders have claimed apocalyptic and eschatological revelation and insight to lead and mislead persons sometimes for reasons of personal power and pride. Such a function could exist legitimately only with extreme caution. It may be wise to let it belong only to Paul in terms of the church's understanding of him as one selected by God to be a vehicle of revelation for the new covenant.

Fourth, Paul's modified or reconceptualized apocalyptic understandings also enable Paul to "redefine" his understanding of scripture and Judaism in the direction of his inclusive, law-free, new creation theology.[30] These understandings form the basis in the history of the Church for understanding the church as the new people of God and for accepting the concept of a canonical New Testament for the life and faith of the church. Tragically, these understandings have also been the alleged basis for the development of Christian anti-semitism. They ought not to be so used; Paul cannot be legitimately invoked for such purposes.

NOTES

1. Biblical translations are from the *New Revised Standard Version* (1989). Assumed here is the integrity of Romans 16 and the view that 16:20 is not a resolution of the situation described in 16:17-18, but is an independent piece of concluding apocalyptic hope (see the commentaries for discussions of these issues).

2. C. E. B. Cranfield, *A Critical and Exegetical Commentary on the Epistle to the Romans,* (ICC; Edinburgh: T. & T. Clark, 1975, 1979) 803, plays down far too much the apocalyptic significance of this term.

3. P. D. Hanson, "Apocalypticism," *The Interpreter's Dictionary of the Bible: Supplementary Volume* (ed. K. Crim; Nashville: Abingdon, 1976) 28-34. See also Hanson's *The Dawn of Apocalyptic* (Philadelphia: Fortress, 1975; 2d ed., 1979).

4. Hanson, "Apocalypticism," 30.

5. Ibid.

6. K. Koch, *The Rediscovery of Apocalyptic: A Polemical Work on a Neglected Area of Biblical Studies and Its Damaging Effects on Theology and Philosophy* SBT, 22 second series (Naperville: Alec R. Allenson, n.d. [1972]) 28-33; reprinted in P. D. Hanson, *Visionaries and their Apocalypses: Edited with an Introduction* (Issues in Religion and Theology 4 (Philadelphia: Fortress/London: SPCK, 1983) 24-29.

7. J. J. Collins, *The Apocalyptic Imagination: An Introduction to the Jewish Matrix of Christianity* (New York: Crossroad, 1984) 10-11.

8. J. C. Beker, *Paul the Apostle: The Triumph of God in Life and Thought* (Philadelphia: Fortress, 1980) 135-36.

9. Ibid for the first three points. The fourth is added in J. C. Beker, *The Triumph of God: The Essence of Paul's Thought* (Minneapolis: Fortress, 1990) 20-21.

10. J. J. Collins, "Apocalyptic Eschatology as the Transcendence of Death," *CBQ* 36 (1974) 21-43; reprinted in P. D. Hanson, *Visionaries,* 61-84 (quotation from page 68).

11. C. Rowland, *The Open Heaven: A Study of Apocalyptic in Judaism and Early Christianity* (New York: Crossroad, 1982) 70-72.

12. W. A. Meeks, "Social Functions of Apocalyptic Language in Pauline Christianity," in *Apocalypticism in the Mediterranean World and the Near East . . . ,* ed. D. Hellholm (Tübingen: J. C. B. Mohr , 1983) 687-705; summary on 689.

13. L. E. Keck, "Paul and Apocalyptic Theology," *Int* 38 (1984), 229-41 (quotation, 229).

14. E. E. Johnson, *The Function of Apocalyptic and Wisdom Traditions in Romans 9-11* (SBLDS 109; Atlanta: Scholars Press, 1989) 4-23. In fact, Johnson finds the apocalyptic interpretation of Paul so strong that she argues in this study that it should be balanced by the wisdom tradition's influence on Paul.

15. A. Schweitzer, *The Mysticism of Paul the Apostle* (New York: Seabury, 1968).

16. In addition to *Paul the Apostle* and *The Triumph of God,,* see also J. C. Beker, *Paul's Apocalyptic Gospel* (Philadelphia: Fortress, 1982).

17. A. F . Segal, *Paul the Convert: The Apostolate and Apostasy of Paul the Pharisee* (New Haven and London: Yale University Press, 1990), although undoubtedly wrong on chronology, rightly emphasizes the mystical (=apocalyptic; see Rowland) character of Paul's Damascus Road revelatory experience.

18. E. Käsemann, *New Testament Questions of Today* (Philadelphia: Fortress, 1969) 132.

19. See G. D. Fee, *The First Epistle to the Corinthians* (NICNT; Grand Rapids: Eerdmans, 1987) 109: "Most likely the 'citation' is an amalgamation of OT texts that had already been joined and reflected on in apocalyptic Judaism . . . . "

20. Ibid, 141-42 .

21. See especially Rowland, *Open Heaven* and Segal, *Paul the Convert.*

22 . See in particular K. Stendahl, *Paul Among Jews and Gentiles and Other Essays* (Philadelphia: Fortress, 1976) and W. D. Davies, "Paul and the People of Israel," *NTS* 24 (1978) 4-39; reprinted in W. D. Davies, *Jewish and Pauline Studies* (Philadelphia: Fortress, 1984) 123-52, 341-56; see especially the very long footnote 32 .

23. Johnson, *The Function of Apocalyptic..*

24. Keck, *Int* 38 (1984) 229-41.

25. Beker, *The Triumph of God*, 21, does grant that Paul "strongly modifies" his apocalyptic heritage.

26. Meeks, "Social Functions," 700, gives his list of the seven social functions of apocalyptic language in Paul: l) to emphasize and legitimate boundaries between the Christian groups and the larger society; 2) to enhance internal cohesion and solidarity; 3) to provide sanctions for normative behavior; 4) to warrant innovations over against the Jewish norms and structures from which Christianity emerged; 5) to resist, on the one hand, deviant behavior that led to disruption of the Christian community; 6) to legitimate the leadership of Paul and his associates against challenges; and 7) to justify radical interpretation of scripture and tradition.

27. See my discussion of these issues in the context of my review of E. Pagels, *The Gnostic Gospels* (New York: Random House, 1979), in *CBQ* 47 (1985) 171-73.

28. This function is basically equivalent to Meeks' functions 1, 2, 3 and 5.

29. This function is basically equivalent to Meeks' function 6.

30. This function is somewhat analogous to Meeks' functions 4 and 7.

Eschatology In The Book Of Revelation

ADELA YARBRO COLLINS

According to the *Oxford Dictionary of the Christian Church*, "eschatology" is the doctrine of the last things. The term connotes the part of systematic theology which deals with the final destiny both of the individual soul and of humankind in general.[1] As the historical critical method became dominant in the nineteenth century, it became apparent that there were gaps between the logical, coherent, systematic doctrines of the Christian churches about the last things and biblical eschatology. In fact, it gradually became clear that there was no unified biblical doctrine of eschatology. Major differences were noted between the prophetic books of the Old Testament, for example, and the point of view presupposed by most of the books of the New Testament. By the end of the nineteenth century, the standard view in Germany was that the eschatology of the New Testament had to be understood against the background of the, in large part, newly rediscovered pseudepigraphical literature. Eventually, the differences between the prophetic books and the later pseudepigraphical and New Testament books came to be expressed in the distinction between "prophetic eschatology" and "apocalyptic eschatology."[2]

According to Paul Hanson, the continuity between the two is shown by their shared view that the future is the context of the divine saving and judging activity. The difference lies in the degree to which the divine activity is perceived as working through the structures, events and persons of the political, historical, and social realm. Prophetic eschatology involves God acting in and through history and humanity, whereas apocalyptic eschatology expects God to deliver the elect from the unjust present order into a new transformed order. Because of their lack of power within political and social institutions and the contrast between brilliant hope and bleak reality, apocalyptists could not envision salvation through the current order. John J. Collins has argued that the essential difference between prophetic and apocalyptic eschatology is that the latter involves "the transcendence of death by the attainment of a higher, angelic form of life."[3]

From both of these perspectives, the Book of Revelation expresses apocalyptic eschatology. According to 2:11, "The one who conquers will surely not be injured by the second death." This promise clearly expresses the hope for a life beyond death. In the message to Sardis, garments have a double significance. On the one hand, they symbolize the character of one's life on earth. Those who have not soiled their garments are the ones who have remained faithful to the word of God and the testimony of Jesus (3:4). In the same verse, white garments also symbolize the state of eschatological salvation: "they will walk with me in white (garments)." In the cultural context of the work, these white garments express in pictorial language the idea that the human body will be transformed into or replaced by a spiritual body. In other words, the faithful human being will be granted a heavenly or angelic mode of existence. Compare also the white garments of the twenty-four elders, who are probably angelic beings modeled on ancient astrological figures, with the white garments of the innumberable multitude "who have come out of the great tribulation" (cf . 4:4 with 7:14) . The last series of visions speaks explicitly about resurrection (20:4-6, 11-16) . The difference between the old order and the new creation can be summarized in the statement "death shall be no more" (21:4).

Similarly, the Book of Revelation presents the resolution of the present crisis as deliverance from the old order and the establishment of a radically new order. The crisis addressed by the book is portrayed, for example, by the vision of the souls under the altar, the vision linked with the fifth seal. These souls ask how long it will be until God will avenge their blood on those who dwell on the earth (6: 9-11) . The resolution of the crisis is depicted in part as the judgment upon those who dwell on the earth in the vision of the sixth seal that involves the collapse of the cosmos, the dissolution of the old order (6:12-17). The fullest description of the passing of the old order is associated with the general resurrection and judgment. When God appears on the great white throne as Judge, earth and heaven flee, for "no place was found for them" (20:11). The description of salvation begins with the words, "And I saw a new heaven and a new earth. For the first heaven and the first earth had passed away and the sea was no more" (21:1). Since the sea symbolized the adversary of God in the ancient combat myth and represented natural and historical forces of disruption, its lack in the new order expresses the profound discontinuity between the old order and the new. The fact that the new Jerusalem comes down from heaven implies that the new order is a divine accomplishment, not a human achievement. It is not the culmination of a historical process; it is a divine gift that replaces that process and makes it superfluous. Human existence is radically different in the new order. Not only is death abolished; there is to be no grief, crying, or distress any more (21:4). Even the natural world will be fundamentally changed. There will be no sun or moon and never again will night fall (21:23; 22:5). The lack of continuity between the old and new order may be correlated with the social position of the author and original audience of the work. The author and some among the audience were probably refugees from the Jewish war with Rome of the late 60s and early 70s. These refugees probably had the legal status of resident aliens with few, if any, privileges. Their Christian faith was likely to make them marginal and powerless in the social life of the cities of the Roman province of Asia.

Alongside the clearly apocalyptic elements just mentioned, there are aspects of Revelation that have led some commentators to speak of it as prophecy. The prologue of the book designates its content as "revelation" (*apokalypsis*) in verse 1 and as "prophecy" in verse 3.[4] The commission that the risen Christ gives to John, "Write therefore what you see, both what is and what is about to happen afterward" (1:19) is a common Hellenistic formula used to describe prophecy. [5] When John is commissioned anew by a mighty angel, he is told explicitly, "You must prophesy again . . . . " (10:11). The words of the revealing angel to John, "I am a fellow servant with you and your brothers the prophets" (22:9), suggest that John too is a prophet. Recent studies have sought to place the author of Revelation and his book in the context of early Christian prophecy. [6]

One could of course argue that the early Christian revival of prophecy is prophecy in a new key, that is, prophecy imbued with apocalyptic eschatology. But there are aspects of the world view and eschatology of Revelation that are remarkably similar to prophetic eschatology, as Paul Hanson describes it. The divine judging activity is portrayed in Revelation as taking place largely through "the structures of mundane reality and through the agency of human persons."[7] The major act of judgment expected in Revelation is the destruction of the city of Rome, the new "Babylon." This destruction is explicitly announced in 14:8, but already hinted at in the first seal: "And behold, a white horse, and the one seated upon it had a bow, and a crown was given to him, and he went forth conquering and in order that he might conquer" (6:2) . In the cultural context, the mounted archer is a clear allusion to the Parthian military force. The positive tone of this picture has led some commentators, ancient and modern, to identify the horseman with Christ. The positive tone, however, is due to the fact that the expected victory of the Parthians over the Romans was viewed favorably by John as vindication of the martyrs and divine judgment upon Rome. Likewise, the sixth trumpet evokes the rivalry between Parthia and Rome, between East and West, and hints that the armies of the East will overcome those of the West: "Release the four angels at the great river Euphrates. And the four angels were released who had been held in readiness . . . , in order that a third of humankind might be killed. And the number of the troops of cavalry was twice ten thousand times ten thousand; I heard their number" (9:14-16) . The picture is no doubt larger than life, but it evokes actual historical and political tensions and suggests divine judgment through human agency.

As noted earlier, the destruction of the city of Rome is announced in 14:8. In the same context, a double vision of judgment is recounted under the images of harvest and vintage (14:14-20) . Toward the end of this vision, the imagery shifts from vintage to battle: "and blood issued forth from the wine press up to the bridles of the horses a thousand six hundred stadia away" (14:20). Although this image may have been a typical one, the context suggests that a potential, but historical battle is alluded to here.[8]

Like the sixth trumpet, the sixth bowl evokes the expectation of a great battle between East and West: "And the sixth (angel) poured his bowl upon the great river Euphrates, and its water dried up in order that a way might be prepared for the kings from the East" (16:12). This image suggests that the battle of Parthia against Rome is a new Exodus! Judgment on Rome is equivalent to salvation of the people of God. This war is spoken of hyperbolically: the unholy trinity will assemble "the kings of the entire inhabited world" for battle (16:14). This universal war is characterized by the use of the traditional notion of "the day of the Lord" as God's judgment. That this war is envisioned as a process within history is suggested by the fact that this universalizing vision of the sixth trumpet is followed once again by the announcement of the destruction of the historical city of Rome in connection with the seventh trumpet (16:19). This destruction is then elaborated in chapters 17 and 18.

Now one could argue that some of the battle imagery in Revelation indeed refers to the expected historical defeat of Rome, but that this event is part of the eschatological woes of the last stage of history, not part of the last things themselves. The truly eschatological judgment is the battle that follows the parousia, the appearance of the risen Christ as a warrior upon a white horse (19:11-21). Some would argue that this scene has nothing to do with an actual military engagement on the plane of history. The weaving together of images and the allusions within Revelation from vision to vision or scene to scene, however, suggest that a real battle is meant even here, at least on one level of meaning. The white horse upon which Christ rides calls to mind the allusion to the Parthians in the first seal. Over against Christ and the heavenly armies, the beast and the kings of the earth are lined up for battle (19:19). As chapters 13 and 17 have indicated, the beast, at least on one level of meaning, represents Rome. "The kings of the earth" call to mind the kings from the East and the kings of the whole inhabited world who are mentioned in the sixth bowl. The kings from the East are at least functionally equivalent to the ten kings mentioned in chapter 17 who ally themselves with the "beast" (17:12-13). Even though the motif of the ten kings derives from Daniel 7, it has a historical referent. Their alliance with the beast evokes an aspect of the Nero legend, according to which Nero would return with Parthian allies to reclaim his throne. Chapter 17 creates a problem for those who would say that the destruction of Rome in Revelation is expected as a historical event, whereas the battle connected with the parousia is strictly eschatological or metahistorical. Chapter 17 depicts the beast and the ten kings making war on the Lamb and his allies in the same terms as it portrays them attacking the "harlot," that is, the city of Rome.

Nevertheless, the notion of the risen Christ engaging in battle with Roman and Parthian armies is not a typically prophetic scenario, unless we assume that the role of Christ is analogous to the angel who brought the plague upon the Assyrian army. The pictures of this battle mix the earthly and the heavenly in a way that is more apocalyptic than prophetic, in Hanson's terms. Similarly, the battle after the millennium has little relation to history. "Gog and Magog," figures with at most a loose connection with history and geography, are stirred up by Satan to attack "the camp of the saints and the beloved city" (20:9). "The beloved city" no doubt refers to Jerusalem, so once again we have a mixing of the historical and geographical with the transcendent or mythical. How these "mixed" visions should be interpreted is a problem to which we shall return. The point I want to make here is that a major part of God's future judging activity is envisioned as taking place through the political structures of this world and through human agency.

But first I would like to discuss the final vision of salvation and its relation to prophetic eschatology. This final vision is found in 21:1-22:5. It owes much in terms of form and content to the prophetic books of the Old Testament. The form is very similar to Ezekiel 40-48 in that a visionary is transported by spiritual means to a high mountain from which he views a new Jerusalem. Both visions are mediated by an angel who measures various parts of the city. The introductory and key theme of the passage in Revelation is based on a theme from Isaiah: "For behold, I create new heavens and a new earth" (Isa 65:17a; 66:22). The passing away of former things also echoes Isaiah (cf. Rev 21:4c with Isa 65:17b), as do the images of God putting an end to death and wiping away human tears (cf. Rev 21:4a and b with Isa 25:7-8). A number of other allusions and common motifs could be mentioned. Among the more important connections is the notion that the new Jerusalem would be adorned with precious stones (cf. Rev 21:18-21 with Isa 54:12). This motif had become traditional, as is indicated by its presence in the literature from Qumran and in Tobit.[9]

But what is significant for our topic is not so much particular motifs as the overall type of eschatology envisaged. In spite of the discontinuity pointed out earlier between the old order and the new in Revelation, some commentators find evidence in this final vision of continuity between the two. For example, they find it significant that the new Jerusalem, God and the Lamb come down to earth, rather than the faithful being taken up into heaven. They emphasize that the final state is pictured in the context of a new earth, rather than in the heavenly or spiritual world. They argue that the use of a city to symbolize the final state is not only an adaptation of tradition, and not only compensation for the lack of ordinary citizenship, but also an affirmation of human history and cultural achievement. Some commentators also conclude that salvation in Revelation is universal; most mean by this primarily that the book envisions the conversion of the nations, including the erstwhile enemies of God, the Lamb and the faithful. Such a theme, if it is really present, could be seen as an adaptation of the universalism of Second Isaiah.

It has long been apparent that there is tension between the historical critical emphasis on the diversity within the Bible and the biblical theological concern to discern "the biblical perspective" or "the biblical message" and to re-express it in a way that is meaningful today. One of the issues that we were invited to consider in this conference is the "conflict" between prophetic and apocalyptic eschatology. We were invited to reflect on the question whether the two are reconcilable. It seems to me that the Book of Revelation is a canonical example of the synthesis of the two views. This conclusion is supported by the observation that the last series of visions incorporates both the prophetic and the apocalyptic view of the End in a new at least quasi-chronological sequence of eschatological events. The prophetic promises are to be fulfilled in the thousand year reign that most commentators rightly take as occurring on earth, even though the text does not explicitly say so (20:4-6). The bolder apocalyptic hopes are then to be fulfilled in the general resurrection (20:11-15), the new creation, and the descent of the new Jerusalem.

A further question that we were encouraged to address is whether one form of eschatology is to be favored over the other. It is clear that the Book of Revelation subordinates the prophetic eschatological perspective to the apocalyptic eschatological perspective. Even the thousand year reign begins with resurrection from the dead. This glorious reign can take place only because Satan will be bound first by an angel. But the question remains whether either approach is relevant to the modern Church.

It could be argued that one eschatological perspective will be favored over the other depending on the philosophical perspective of the individual or group involved. The apocalyptic perspective, with its emphasis on the heavenly world and personal afterlife, may be preferred by traditional Christians who believe in the objective reality of heaven, the immortality of the soul, and the resurrection of the body. The prophetic perspective may appeal more to Christians with a materialist perspective or a perspective like Tillich's "ecstatic naturalism," for whom God is the ground of being and Christian tradition is an adequate symbol-system, not a representation of objective reality. For such Christians it is this world that counts and the prophetic point of view seems more realistic to them. It could also be argued that the choice of one perspective over the other is related to the social situation of the individual or group involved. It is easier for those who are comfortable and feel in control of their lives to identify with the prophetic perspective that finds the acts of God in the historical process. Those who feel oppressed, excluded and powerless are more likely to identify with the often sectarian-like perspective of apocalyptic eschatology.

Perhaps we ought to accept, even affirm, the validity of both perspectives and their diverse interpretations in diverse contexts. They are both biblical after all. The canonical process has preserved strikingly diverse points of view, even though the underlying assumption is that each distinctive piece contributes to the overall design, like the pieces of cloth in a quilt. I will not attempt here to trace the eschatological design in the Bible as a whole, but will return to Revelation to address the question of the significance of eschatology for the modern Church.

As indicated earlier, it is difficult to discern how the parousia of Christ as the divine warrior and the subsequent battle relate to history and geography. When a text is ambiguous, interpretations vary and are determined in large part by the fundamental philosophical perspective of the interpreter and by what the interpreter's community judges to be appropriate modes of interpretation. In dispensationalist circles and in the popular understanding of eschatology shaped by Hal Lindsey and Herbert Armstrong, the historical elements in this vision play the leading role. The expectation of the return of Christ as a historical event reinforces the tendency of such interpreters to assume that the events narrated refer to public events of the historical future. The connection of "the beast" and "the false prophet" (19:19-20) with chapter 13 are duly noted. These figures are understood as individuals or institutions of the immediate future and the language of war and battle is taken not only seriously, but literally. The invitation addressed to the birds "in order that you may eat the flesh of kings and the flesh of military officers and the flesh of the mighty men of war and the flesh of horses and of those who ride them and the flesh of all, both free and slave, both small and great" (19:18) is interpreted to mean that all humanity will be killed in an actual war that will end human history on earth. According to the design that these interpreters find in the Bible as a whole, the faithful Christians will not be killed in this war, since they will already have experienced "the rapture." That is, they will have been taken up into heaven so that they will not need to suffer in the tribulations of the end-time. This notion, as is well known, is based primarily on 1 Thessalonians 4. The great battle described in Revelation 19 then is understood as divine judgment on the ungodly. It is often said in such circles that this final war will break out in the Middle East. It is sometimes specifically associated with the great plain near the ancient city of Megiddo southwest of Mount Carmel. This association is based on Rev 16:16.

A very different interpretation is offered by M. Eugene Boring in his recent commentary on Revelation. It appeared in 1989 in the Interpretation series entitled "A Bible Commentary for Teaching and Preaching." Boring argues that the lack of numbering in the last series of visions (19:11-22:5) shows that they are not related to a strictly chronological progression of the eschatological events.[10] Citing G. B. Caird, he refers to the "kaleidoscopic changes of metaphor" and suggests that this final series of visions is "a tour through an eschatological art gallery in which the theme of God's victory at the end of history is treated in seven different pictures, each complete in itself with its own message and with little concern for chronology."

Boring suggests that the vision of Christ at the parousia might well be called a picture of Jesus the Conquerer. He indeed wears the bloody garments of the divine warrior of Isa 63:1-3, but the blood on his garments is his own. Boring interprets this vision in terms of the vision of the Lamb in Revelation 5: "The death by which he conquers is his own, the once-for-all offering of his life on the cross."[12] There is no violence against enemies here. "This conqueror destroys his enemies, not with a literal sword, but with the sword of his mouth; his only weapon is his word, the Word of God which he himself is (19:13)."[13] According to Boring, the author of Revelation has used the ancient literary form of the combat myth to depict the ultimate victory of God, but has filled it with new content. In the theology of Revelation as a whole, the crucifixion of Jesus is not preliminary to his victory, but *is* his victory. Conquering is dying, Lion is Lamb. The ultimate victory of God is the making effective and manifest to all the reality that has already occurred in history in the death of Jesus.[14]

In interpreting the last battle (19:17-21), Boring divides the military opponents of Christ and his heavenly army into two groups. He designates one group as "rebellious humanity." He argues that the grisly menu of the messianic banquet contains the flesh, not only of the enemies of John and his audience, not only the rich and powerful, the oppressors, but also the little people, including slaves. But, he concludes, the primary opposition is not actual human beings at all, but "the transpersonal powers of evil that have inspired and deceived them, as symbolized by the beast and false prophet."[15] He cites the lack of a literary description of the battle as support for his contention that there is no battle here. The decisive battle was won long ago on the cross.[16]

From the perspective of the critical Biblical scholar, the major weakness of the dispensationalist, popular eschatological view is, of course, its premise that chapters 4-22 describe the immediate future, not from the author's point of view, but from our point of view. The theory that John predicted events that will take place in the late twentieth century—or at whatever the latest new date for the End is—does not fit the critical scholar's view of prophecy, inspiration, or God. This weakness, however, has as its flip side a certain strength. This popular eschatological view takes seriously the predictive character of the language of Revelation, manifest in the statements of urgency at the beginning and end of the book (1:3 and 22:20). It also takes seriously the imagery of battle and the links between chapter 19 and chapters 13 and 17. Another weakness is that this popular view often takes the language too literally. The contrast between the poetic language of Revelation and the pedestrian prose of Hal Lindsey is enough to make a sensitive reader wince.

The strength of Boring's interpretation is that it recognizes that the language is pictorial, rather than propositional. Its weakness is that it does not take the imagery seriously enough. Although Boring is certainly correct that the last series of visions in Revelation do not provide a detailed, systematic doctrine of the last things, his virtual denial of a chronological scheme is not fair to the text. The seven seals, trumpets, and bowls are numbered in part to structure those visions, since they do not have a strong natural coherence. In the last seven visions, one thing follows upon another in a way that makes numbering superfluous.

The question of the metaphoric relation of the Lion and the Lamb goes to the heart of the question of the overall meaning of the Book of Revelation. The metaphor of the Lamb is first introduced in chapter 5. One of the twenty-four elders announces that the Lion of the tribe of Judah, the Root of David, has conquered and is therefore able to open the seals of the scroll (5:5). What John sees next is not a Lion, but "a Lamb standing as if slaughtered, with seven horns and seven eyes . . . ." (5:6). The significance of this scene is made explicit in the new song sung by the four living creatures and the twenty-four elders: "Worthy are you to take the scroll and to open its seals because you were slain and you redeemed for God with your blood (persons) from every tribe and tongue and people and nation and you made them for our God a kingdom and priests and they will reign upon the earth" (5:9-10). The conquest of the Lamb is his death, because through that death a people has been ransomed, has been wrested from the powers of evil and made a priestly kingdom under God's rule. This conquest is not yet the ultimate victory of God, however. I agree with Boring that the ultimate victory of God according to Revelation is the making effective and manifest to all the reality that has already occurred in the death of Jesus. I differ with him on how that process is envisaged.

The death of Jesus, the slaughter of the Lamb, enables him to open the seals of the scroll of destiny; that is, the death of Jesus has made him worthy, as Lord of history, to initiate the eschatological events. The fact that the plagues of the seals and trumpets come from the hand of the Lamb does not make them any less destructive and violent. The culmination of these eschatological events is the eschatological battle described in 19:17-21. The only way that Boring can affirm that there is no battle here, no violence, is to interpret this vision in the most abstract allegorical terms. The forces of evil (the beast and the false prophet) are eliminated from God's creation (thrown into the lake of fire). The human beings who ostensibly die in the slaughter are redeemed (the kings of the earth and the nations reappear in the description of the new Jerusalem). Although Boring characterizes the theory that the Christ of Revelation is first a Lamb, then a Lion, as "a retrogression from a Christian understanding of the meaning of Messiahship to the pre-Christian apocalyptic idea,"[17] the eschatological role of Christ in Revelation 19 is not significantly different from the activity of the Messiah of *4 Ezra*, symbolized by a lion: "he will denounce them for their ungodliness and for their wickedness, . . . and when he has reproved them, then he will destroy them" (12:32-33).[18]

The observation that it is not only the high and mighty that are killed in the last battle, but also the little people, undercuts any simplistic interpretation of Revelation as a book of the poor vis-a-vis the rich or the politically powerless vis-a-vis the powerful oppressors. But it does not refute the theory that it is primarily "the other" from the point of view of Revelation who are judged in this war. Recall that all humanity for Revelation is divided into two groups—those who bear the seal of God and those who bear the mark of the beast. The "other" includes not only the emperor, Roman officials, and the wealthy of the province of Asia. It includes all who accept Rome's claim to ultimate sovereignty and who reject Christian faith as crass superstition or misguided messianism. In John's social world, religious and political allegiances cut across what we would call class lines. The words "and the flesh of all, both free and slave, both small and great" in verse 18 are often taken to mean that all humanity is involved. But verse 19 speaks only of the beast, the kings of the earth, and their armies. The universal language of verse 18 has the rhetorical function of indicating the total destruction of those armies, from the smallest to the greatest.

The conclusion that the lack of a description of a battle indicates that no battle takes place is unwarranted. The lack of description of a battle is a well-known literary and dramatic device. In chapters 17-18 the actual battle is not described, but it is abundantly clear that a battle has taken place. The situation is the same with chapter 19.

The argument that the conquerer "destroys" his enemies, not with a literal sword (violently), but with the sword of his mouth (presumably non-violently), overlooks the ancient conception of the effective word. This ancient conception involved much more than the notion of "performative language" in modern linguistics and philosophy. It is the effective word of the Creator who is also the Destroyer. When Christ appears in this scene as Word of God, it is as the Word of God of the Wisdom of Solomon 18 who makes effective the divine command that the first born of the Egyptians die. Further, the claim that the primary opposition of Christ is not actual human beings at all, but transpersonal powers, does not represent the text fairly. In any case, it makes little difference to those slaughtered on a battlefield that they were secondary targets.

Boring's interpretation of the final battle is supported by his conclusion that Revelation's picture of salvation has universal and inclusive elements. The nations that are "destroyed" in the final battle are redeemed in the new Jerusalem. I cannot resist noting a certain irony in this argument. In the Introduction to the commentary, in the treatment of propositional and pictorial language, Boring states, "Pictorial language can communicate the message expressed by a certain picture, vision, or symbol without affirming all the implications of the message if it were reduced to propositional language."[19] As an example, he cites the picture given in Genesis about Cain marrying and begetting children (Gen 4:17). He rightly points out that any one who asks where Cain got his wife is asking the wrong question. Similarly, logical inferences should not be drawn from the fact that all the green grass is burned up at the sounding of the first trumpet (8:7), yet it reappears in connection with the fifth trumpet (9:4).[20] But in drawing the conclusion that the reappearance of the nations in chapters 21 and 22 means that they have been redeemed, Boring violates the rules he has set down for interpreting pictorial language.

The remark in 21:3, "They will be [God's] peoples," however, seems to support the view that the salvation envisaged is universal. The plural "peoples" suggests that all the nations of the earth will come into right relationship with God. Another important passage is part of the description of the new Jerusalem: "And the nations will walk by its light, and the kings of the earth will bring their glory into it, and its gates will never be closed by day, for there will be no night there, and they will bring the glory and the honor of the nations into it" (21:24-26). Boring interprets this to mean that the kings of the earth and the nations will be citizens of the new Jerusalem. This conclusion goes beyond the text. The idea that the nations will walk by the light of Jerusalem and bring their glory into it does not entail the notion that they will be on an equal footing with those who reign with God and the Lamb (22:5). The passage to which these verses allude includes statements like: "For the nation and kingdom that will not serve you shall perish; . . . The sons of those who oppressed you shall come bending low to you; and all who despised you shall bow at your feet" (Isa 60:12, 14). This is exploitative power in Rollo May's terms, power *over* others. A final passage, however, like the reference to "the peoples of God," does reflect a less self-centered form of power: And the leaves of the tree [of life] were for the healing of the nations" (22:2). Again in Rollo May's terms, this is nurturing power, power that works for the sake of the other.

If the historicizing interpretation of popular eschatology and the allegorizing interpretation of Gene Boring are less than fully satisfactory, is there a mediating interpretation that is more appropriate? I would suggest that such an interpretation is what we should work toward in attempting to express the significance of eschatology for the Church today. The military and political connotations of the vision of the last battle in Rev 19:17-21 are essential to its meaning and its expressive power. We live in a time when any war could be the "last" for the human race and the planet as we know them. I spoke earlier of the mixing of human and heavenly warriors as typically apocalyptic. It seems appropriate to take the heavenly warrior and the beast of Revelation 19 as symbols of transpersonal powers and values, but without divorcing them from history and geography. There is great ethical danger, as well as danger to the discernment of the truth, in identifying one's own ethnic group, nation, or alliance with the risen Christ and the "other" with the beast. Now, in the Fall of 1990, I believe that western propaganda is too easily labeling Saddam Hussein as "the beast" and the western military forces as the armies of heaven. Iraqi propaganda is also one-sided. Without accepting the popular view that Revelation is predicting some specific sequence of events, the consonance of text and history is now especially a possibility. We must keep in mind the awful possibility that a "limited" war in the Middle East could escalate into a world war that could lead to a nuclear death of the planet. From our limited perspective, if it comes to that, it will probably look as though we brought it upon ourselves.

Another way in which this imagery might function is to sensitize us to the role of dualism in human propaganda and conflict so that we can work to mitigate its effects.

Rather than hurtling toward war, confident that we are right, perhaps we could stop and ask why is it that the Iraqis and many other Arabs see us as "the beast." Politically speaking, such discernment is likely to lead toward compromise and thus toward peace. Our politicians and members of the press, as well as educators and ministers, have a responsibility to educate the public and the Church about the point of view of the "other." Spiritually speaking, discerning and correcting our "beast-like" elements is likely to make us better expressions of the Word.

NOTES

1. "Eschatology," *The Oxford Dictionary of the Christian Church,* 2nd rev. ed. F. L. Cross and E. A. Livingstone (New York: Oxford University Press, 1983) 469.

2. See, for example, Paul Hanson, "Apocalypticism," *IDBSup* (1976) 30.

3. John J. Collins, "Apocalyptic Eschatology as the Transcendence of Death," *CBQ* 34 (1974) 43.

4. The content of the Book of Revelation is again described as "prophecy" in 22:7, 10, 18, 19.

5. W. C. van Unnik, "A Formula Describing Prophecy," *NTS* 9 (1963) 86-94.

6. For a summary and assessment of these studies, see Adela Yarbro Collins, *Crisis and Catharsis: The Power of the Apocalypse* (Philadelphia: Westminster, 1984) 34-50.

7. Hanson, "Apocalypticism," 30.

8. The presence of a similar image in *1 Enoch* 100:3 suggests that the picture of blood flowing up to a horse's bridle may have been a typical apocalyptic motif.

9. This motif is reflected in the *Description of the New Jerusalem* in the mention of white stone (5QJN-ar F5 1 1.6), alabaster or white marble and jasper (5QJN-ar F 1 1.7), and a gate of sapphire (2QJN-ar F 3 1.2). See the Introduction, text and translation of this document by Adela Yarbro Collins in the forthcoming comprehensive edition of the Dead Sea Scrolls, edited by J. H. Charlesworth and published by Princeton University Press. See also Tobit 13:16-18.

10. M. Eugene Boring, *Revelation* (Interpretation: A Bible Commentary for Teaching and Preaching; Louisville: John Knox Press, 1989) 194.

11. Ibid. 195.

12. Ibid. 196.

13. Ibid.

14. Ibid. 198.

15. Ibid. 199.

16. Ibid. 199-200.

17. Ibid. 109.

18. For the role of the Messiah, see *4 Ezra* 11-12, especially 11:36-46 and 12:31-34.

19. Boring, *Revelation*, 57.

20. Ibid. 135.

21. Rollo May, *Power and Innocence: A Search for the Sources of Violence* (New York: W. W. Norton & Co., 1972).

FROM STRANGERS TO CITIZENS: ESCHATOLOGY IN THE PATRISTIC ERA

AGNES CUNNINGHAM

> The Church of God which resides as a stranger at Rome to the Church of God which is a stranger at Corinth . . . . May grace and peace from Almighty God flow to you in rich profusion through Jesus Christ![1]

I. INTRODUCTION

This greeting, with which the *First Epistle of Clement to the Corinthians* begins, reflects clearly the sense of "transitoriness and non-citizenship" experienced by Christians at the opening of the patristic era.[2] The followers of Jesus did not belong to this world. They were "sojourners," waiting "in exile" (1 Peter 2:11), aware that the world was "passing away" (1 Cor 7:31). Their hopes were rooted in expectations of another world, in a kingdom already proclaimed, in the glorious, imminent Second Coming of the Lord.

Any attempt to address the question of eschatology in the period known as Christian Antiquity must take into account the attitude of patristic scholars regarding this topic. In fact, although the contributions of the early Fathers to a theology of the End-Time are carefully recorded by a writer such as Quasten,[3] patristic scholars, on the whole have not emphasized this dimension of Christian teaching. Thus, the distinction between "prophetic" and "apocalyptic" eschatology in the patristic age does not seem to have heen a question for serious students of the Church Fathers. Even a document identified as "apocalyptic," *The Shepherd of Hermas*, has been the object of study and analysis by biblical scholars and systematic theologians, rather than by patristic scholars, especially in recent times.

One might well ask, then: Is it possible to investigate the patristic teaching on eschatology? The "otherworldliness" which characterized Christians of the first century and texts such as *I Clement* provide sufficient reason to investigate the eschatological attitudes and teachings of the patristic era. Such validation seems necessary, in light of the fact that eschatology, itself, as Florovsky has pointed out, has long been a neglected field in modern theology.[4] Indeed, he claims, eschatology "cannot be discussed as a special topic" or a "separate article of belief." Rather, it is only in the total perspective of Christian faith that eschatology can be understood. What Florovsky perceives as the "recovery of the eschatological dimension of the Christian faith . . . in contemporary thought" seems to underline von Balthasar's assertion that, "Eschatology is the 'eye of the storm' in the theology of our time."[5]

The "eschatological dimension" of Christian faith in the age of the Fathers of the Church can be found in a number of documents, in what Quasten calls the "eschatological attitude,"[6] and in the development of doctrines concerning the "Last Things." In this paper, I propose to present the major understandings of eschatology as these emerged in Christian Antiquity, from the sub-Apostolic Age into the Golden Age of patristic literature;[7] to investigate the articulation of these understandings by selected theologians or ecclesiastical writers; to suggest implications for Christian faith and life today, as we seek to learn from those early Christian thinkers whom John Henry Newman called"giants." It is on their shoulders we must stand, if we want to see far into that future whose horizons stand visible to the "eyes" of believing hearts.[8]

II. THE APOSTOLIC FATHERS

The age of the Apostolic Fathers,[9] the sub-Apostolic age, is marked by the appearance of documents and writers that reflect the Jewish heritage of Christianity. Christians were not content simply to read, revise and adapt Jewish prayers, liturgical formulas or legislation. They sought to imitate the literary genre with which they had been familiar, before their conversion to the Christian way of life. For this reason, early Christian writings frequently included imitation of the biblical books. This apocryphal literature provides information regarding customs and life in the early Church, as well as the origins of Christian legends and follk stories. It frequently reflects the simple piety of the faithful.

More importantly, it is in much of the Christian apocrypha that characteristics of earlier prophetic, apocalyptic and eschatological writing can be found. For example, among the documents of the sub-Apostolic age, we find the *Epistle of Barnabas*, the *Shepherd of Hermas*, and the *Didaché* to mention only a few. All of these are apocryphal. All of them are marked by a strong eschatological character. Hermas carries a prophetic dimension.[10] All of them show signs of a development and transformation of type that has begun.

There is one predominant eschatological theme which reflects the firm conviction of Christians in the sub-Apostolic age concerning the Second Coming of Christ. The final chapter of the *Didachè* reiterates the expectation of an imminent *parousia*, as certain as the hour of its happening is uncertain. Therefore:

> Watch over your life; your lamps must not go out, nor your loins be ungirded; on the contrary, be ready. You do not know the hour in which Our Lord is coming.[11]

In the same vein, Clement exhorts the Corinthians:

> Take a vine: first it drops its leaves; then a shoot comes, then a leaf, then a flower, after that the sour fruit, then the fully ripe grapes. You see that in a short time the fruit of the tree reaches maturity. In truth his will shall be ful-

> filled quickly and suddenly. . . . He shall come quickly and not linger, and the Lord will come suddenly to his temple. . . .[12]

The intense anticipation of an imminent Second Coming resulted in more than one response on the part of Christians in the sub-Apostolic age. Their eschatology was prophetic, rather than—or, perhaps, as much as it was—apocalyptic. It has also been called "realized."[13] Christians were convinced that they were living in the "last times."[14] The *parousia* had been foretold.[15] Christ was to come again "in majesty and power . . . clothed in purple like a king."[16]

Christians, then, in anticipation of this event, had to be ready, watchful, prepared. The concerns of the *ekklesia* were all *ad intra,* focused on what it meant to be a Christian; what the unity and fidelity of the community were; how to be found waiting for the Lord. There is little, if any, sense of mission, in this early age, apart from the proclamation of the Gospel, at the Lord's command, so that the number of the elect might be complete.[17]

Another characteristic response in this era is demonstrated in the Christian answer to persecution. Where *I Clement* exhorts the Christians in Corinth to live in harmony and unity, in expectation of the *parousia,* Ignatius of Antioch speaks for all those who saw in martyrdom a way to anticipate the End-Time through a death that gave witness to faith in Jesus Christ, Son of God and Savior.[18]

> This is the only favour I ask; that I may be poured as a libation while an altar is still ready. . . . Let me be given to the wild beasts, for by their means I can attain to God. I am God's wheat, and I am being ground by the teeth of the beasts so that I may appear as pure bread. . . . if I suffer, then I am a freedman of Jesus Christ, and shall rise free in him. . . . Permit me to be an imitator of the Passion of my God.[19]

The words of Ignatius are, perhaps, the most dramatic expression of the eschatological dimension that can be found in the *Acts of the Martyrs* or other accounts of the manner in which Christians gave witness under persecution to their convictions about entry into another world through suffering and death, "for the sake of the Name," as they so often exclaimed. Thus, the phenomenon of martyrdom in the early Church, along with a lively expectation of an imminent Second Coming and an intense concern for matters *ad intra,* that is, within the Christian community itself, becomes an expression of an *eschatological attitude* that prevailed during the sub-Apostolic Age. The following era would see the development of several *eschatological theories,* all of them marked by a strong apocalyptic character.

III. ESCHATOLOGICAL THEORIES IN THE PATRISTIC AGE

With the appearance of the Apologists in the second century, a new generation of Christians appeared in the Church. These converts, unlike those who had preceded them, came from advantaged positions of influence, wealth or power in the Roman Empire. Many were professional philosophers or rhetoricians. They were eager and competent to assume the task they set for themselves: the defense of Christianity against attacks and accusations from the imperial government, from Jews and pagans.[20] They made use of their knowledge of the law, the Old Testament, the Greek philosophies to present the teachings of the Gospel and to argue for the Christian way of life. It is with the Apologists that the eschatological theory of the millennium comes into Christianity.

A. Millenarianism

The theory of the thousand-year duration of an intermediate messianic reign was not unknown in Judaism. There were, in Jewish eschatology, speculations about a future messianic kingdom that would consist of a sabbath of one thousand years.[21] Christian converts from Judaism would have been familiar with this theory. Apologists, like Justin, who studied the Hebrew Scriptures so that he might proclaim the Gospel persuasively to the Jews, found a biblical basis for millenarianism as an explanation of the eschatological beliefs of the Christians. In the *Dialogue with Trypho*,[22] Justin affirmed:

> I and every other completely orthodox Christian feel certain that there will be a resurrection of the flesh, followed by a thousand years in the rebuilt, embellished, and enlarged city of Jerusalem, as was announced by the Prophets Ezechiel, Isaias and the others.[23]

Millenarianism was consonant with several other beliefs of second-century Christians. A gradual and increasingly certain awareness of a delay in the Lord's Second Coming had to be addressed. If the Lord was not to come as soon as had been expected, it must be so that salvation might be made available to all peoples. Universal salvation was to be possible through an expansion of the *ekklesia*.

With these insights, a sense of mission *ad extra* came to the Church. It was necessary to convince the imperial government of the value of Christianity and the rights of Christians, as citizens, to the protection of the State. It was important to demonstrate to Jews that everything foretold by the Prophets had been fulfilled in Jesus Christ. It was urgent that the Greeks understood that the Truth, Beauty and Goodness promised, but never fulfilled, by their greatest philosophers, had been realized in the Gospel.

> Everything that the philosophers and legislators discovered and expressed well, they accomplished through their discovery and contemplation of some part of the Logos. But, since they did not have a full knowledge of the Logos, which is Christ, they often contradicted themselves. . . . The truths which men in all lands have rightly spoken belong to us Christians.[24]

Another proponent of millenarianism or chiliasm, as it was also called, was Irenaeus of Lyons. In Book Five of his anti-Gnostic work, *Adversus haereses*, Irenaeus states his view of the end of the world:

> For in as many days as this world was made, in so many thousand years shall it be concluded. . . . For the day of the Lord is as a thousand years.[25]
> . . . [W]hen this Antichrist shall have devastated all things in this world, he will reign for three years and six months, and sit in the temple at Jerusalem; and then the Lord will come from heaven in the clouds, in the glory of the Father, sending this man and those who are following him into the lake of fire; but bringing in for the righteous the times of the kingdom, that is, the rest, the hallowed seventh day.[26]

Irenaeus, the "man of Tradition,"[27] claimed to teach only what he had heard as having been proclaimed "from the beginning." He attributes his knowledge of the thousand-year reign to Papias and a "group of 'elders'." This time of peace granted to the just has been foreseen so that they might better prepare for the greater fulfillment that is to come.

Millenarianism perdured throughout the patristic era, and evidence of it can be found, in minor ecclesiastical writers, even into the sixth century.[28] However, although all expressions of the chiliastic tradition are based especially on the Book of Revelation, chapters twenty and twenty-one,[29] interpretation of that material differs. Writers both use and reject allegorical understandings of the "earthly kingdom" and a time of peace prior to the general resurrection and final judgment.[30] Millenarianism, and, with it, a strong apocalypticism were the objects of renewed interest as changing conditions in the empire and in the Church influenced the character of Christian hope.

B. The Theory of Recapitulation

Still another eschatological theory emerged in the second century, from the great bishop of Lugdunum in Gaul, Irenaeus. In his efforts to "unmask and overthrow the pretended but false" teachings of the Gnostics, Irenaeus developed a theological worldview based on Paul's proclamation of the "headship" of Christ:

> God has given us the wisdom to understand fully the mystery, the plan he was pleased to decree in Christ, to be carried out in the fullness of time: namely, to bring all things in the heavens and on earth into one under Christ's headship (Ephesians 1:10).

Recapitulation has been called the heart of Irenaeus's theology. His vision is of a Christ who comes to "restore," "renew," "consummate," "sum up," "have pre-eminence," "take to himself the primacy," "appoint himself head," "draw all things to himself," that is, "recapitulate" God's plan of salvation. Christ is, indeed, that "true man" who fulfills the purpose God originally had for all of creation. In Christ, all of human history, all of human experience, all humankind are purified, restored, made whole and renewed. The sin of Adam is "reversed," "undone." Through the Incarnation, Christ

> . . . summed up in himself the long line of the human race, procuring for us a comprehensive salvation, that we might recover in Christ Jesus what in Adam we had lost. . . .[31]

Recapitulation, as an eschatological theory, embraces all the mysteries of Divine Revelation. Faith and reason come together, for Irenaeus, in a theological method that begins in the Scriptures and the Apostolic Tradition and seeks, through all the means available to human intelligence, to understand the truths that have been "handed on" in the "rule of faith," "from the beginning."

> Thus the end is joined with the beginning and we are shown that it is he who has summed up in himself all the nations descended from Adam who are dispersed throughout the world, and all men of different languages. Together with Adam he has summed up all generations.[32]

Through the theory of recapitulation, Irenaeus gives us what might be called a cosmic eschatology, where all of time, space, humanity and created reality are brought into one in Christ:

> All things are yours, whether it be Paul, or Apollos, or Cephas, or the world, or life, or death, or the present, or the future: all these are yours, and you are Christ's and Christ is God's (1 Cor 3:21-23).

C. Apocatastasis

The eschatological theory developed by Irenaeus was based on one of several scriptural terms associated, at times, with Greek Christian reform vocabulary. Another biblical word which carried both reform and restoration ideas is apocatastasis (Matthew 17: 11; Mark 9:12; Acts 1:6, 3:21). The concept of restoration, or renewal, as found in patristic literature, can be traced to pagan cosmological and eschatological ideas. It is not surprising that the word would be adopted by Origen, the first great Christian biblical scholar and theologian.

Origen's theory of apocatastasis reflects both his eschatological doctrine and his extraordinary gift for theological speculation.[33] Certain apocalyptic characteristics are absent from Origen's eschatology. He does not submit to the notion of any *eternal* hell-fire or everlasting punishment. The great, final eschatologiccal "restoration" was to bring about a state of bliss, following a "purifying fire" experienced by sinners after death. In Origen's view, all sinners are to be saved. Satan and his demons will be purified. Holy souls will be admitted to "paradise," which Origen thought of as "a kind of school" where every earthly problem was to be solved by God.

> The end and consummation of the world will be granted; and then each being will undergo the punishment which his sins have merited. . . . We suppose that the goodness of God will restore the whole creation to unity in the end, through his Christ. . . . Meanwhile, both in time and in eternity all these beings are dealt with in due order and proportion according to their deserts. . . . In the end "God will be all in all." . . . When it is said that "the last enemy" shall be destroyed, it is not to be understood as meaning his substance, which is God's creation, but that his purpose and hostile will perishes, . . . ceasing to be an enemy and ceasing to be death. [34]

Only after the realization of this universal "salvation," Origen teaches, will Christ's Second Coming take place. Then, the resurrection of human beings will follow; all will be restored in "spiritual" bodies.

> . . . what at first was flesh [formed] out of earthly soil, and was afterwards dissolved by death, and again reduced to dust and ashes, will be again raised from the earth, and shall after this, according to the merits of the indwelling soul, advance to the glory of a spiritual body.[35]

The eschatological teaching as presented by Origen in the theory of apocatastasis is closely related to his doctrine of creation and reflects the influences of Platonic philosophy. Prior to the creation of this world, there had been other worlds. In the world preceding ours, pre-existent human souls were spirits who, because of "sin," were condemned to reside in material bodies. After this world there will be others, since the final apocatastasis will come only after a series of cycles of "corruption and restoration."

There are two points to be made about this teaching. In the first place, Origen, despite his expressed rejection of philosophy as an adequate vehicle for the transmission of Christian thought, shows signs of a definite influence of philosophy in his theology. As a student of Ammonius Saccas and a fellow-student of Plotinus, Origen was introduced to Neo-Platonism. Thus, a strong belief in a succession of multiple worlds appears in his eschatology. Secondly, Origen's teaching of successive stages of "corruption and restoration" is closely linked to his conviction of the spiritual freedom that allows a soul to turn to evil from good, under the direction of its free intentions. At the expense of defending the freedom of the created spirit which could choose evil, even after an intermediate "End- Time" experience, Origen developed a "progressive" eschatological theory that had to be rejected by the Church.

> There were ages before our own and there will be others after it. . . . And when death shall no longer anywhere exist, nor the sting of death, nor any evil at all, then verily God will be "all in all."[36]

The eschatologicaal theory of apocatastasis was taught after Origen by other theologians, particularly, by Gregory of Nyssa. Gregory, however, did not accept the teaching of a purely spiritual state, either before or after life on earth. Neither did he teach the theory of successive cycles of corruption and restoration. Gregory did affirm the possibility of a spiritual "restoration" of Paradise in the Christian who seeks God, through a life of spiritual purification and renunciation of things which are "less good" than purely spiritual realities.

> It is indeed possible for us to return to the original beatitude, if we now will run backward on the same road which we had followed when we were ejected from Paradise together with our forefather [Adam]. . . . [R]eason leads those who sever all other ties on behalf of Christ to leave behind first, marriage, . . . then to withdraw from the hard work of the soil in which man was placed after sin; . . . next . . . to divest themselves of the wisdom of the flesh and to renounce all the secrets of shamefulness . . . and to have as counsellor . . . the precept of God only.[37]

Despite the fascination that apocatastasis held for some theologians who subscribed to the teachings of Origen, it was increasingly regarded as erroneous, from the fourth century on. It was condemned in A.D. 543 by an edict of Justinian and, again, in A.D. 553, at the Second Council of Constantinople.[38] Origen and his "impious writings" were specifically mentioned along with other "heretics" in the eleventh canon of the Council, as were his eschatological teachings in a number of the "fifteen anathemas" against him, attributed to the Fathers of the fifth ecumenical Council.

Scholars have disagreed about the intention of the canon regarding Origen as well as about the authenticity of the anathemas against him. Nevertheless, apocatastasis failed to survive as an accepted eschatological theory throughout the remainder of the patristic age. Millenarianism, too, had lost support during the third and fourth centuries, as the Church progressed through continued expansion in the Roman world and through the development of theological thought and doctrinal clarification.[39]The theory of recapitulation taught by Irenaeus came to be recognized as the organizing principle of his theology, rather than as a uniquely eschatological doctrine. Later eschatological theories particularly addressed the nature of the resurrection of the body, the *parousia*, judgment and everlasting life.

D. The Teaching of Augustine

Augustine of Hippo has been credited with having contributed most importantly to later eschatological doctrines, especially in the West.[40] With his unique and blessed genius, Augustine

> . . . established that balance between God's grace and man's will, between mystery and ethos, which was to become the theological substratum of all Christian reform movements in the West for a thousand years. He did so by stressing the role of the divine reformer Christ over that of man the reformer and, on the other hand, by insisting on the necessity of continuous reform in human life.[41]

The whole aim of Augustine's spiritual life was "to know God and the soul."[42] His deepest thoughts on the "first and last things" were the fruit of his prayer.[43] Attracted by millenarianism at one time, he later rejected it in favor of an allegorical interpretation of the scriptural text. He understood that Revelation 20:3 represented the present age of the Church.

> . . . the Church, even in this world, here and now, is the kingdom of Christ and the kingdom of heaven. Here and now Christ's saints reign with Him, although not in the way they are destined to reign hereafter.[44]

Augustine's eschatological doctrine is found in his great work, *The City of God.* In his commentary on the Apocalypse of John the Evangelist, he refutes Millenarianism and sets forth his understanding of the "two resurrections," the devil's binding and the intervening thousand years.[45]

> There are people who claim that the idea of resurrection applies only to bodies and that the first resurrection, as well as the secord, is to be a corporeal one. . . . Well, they have St. Paul against them, for he spoke of the soul's resurrection. . . .[46]
>
> The Devil's binding has been a fact from the day the Church began to expand beyond Judea into nation after nation. . . . The Devil is bound whenever men are converted to the faith from the infidelity in which he possessed them, and there will certainly be conversions until the end of time. . . .[47]
>
> The "thousand years" may mean either what remains of the thousand years that make up the "sixth day," or the entire course of time this world has still to go.[48]

Augustine's "city of God" is an eschatological society. It is completely detached from temporal, political society, even though it is present in this world. This "city of God" belongs to an "order" superior to earthly cities, but it is still to be found in the movement of human history, announcing the glorious coming of the Son of Man in his body which is the Church.

Augustine defended the resurrection of the body; insisted that the eternal punishment proclaimed in Scripture should be understood to be just that; affirmed that the blessed in heaven will behold God, "made known to and be perceived by us, in many ways."[49] Eternal beatitude, according to Augustine, will be both social and christological in character.[50] Finally, it can be said that Augustine

> . . . bears witness to the faith of Christians that, notwithstanding all appearances, human history does not consist of a series of repetitive patterns, but marks a sure, if unsteady advance to an ultimate goal. As such, it has a beginning, a middle, and an end.[51]

It is with Augustine's teaching on eschatology that the transition from "strangers" to "citizens," highlighted in the title of this paper can be said to have taken place. In his work, *The City of God*, Augustine addresses the subject of the *eschaton* as that "seventh day" of rest in which we shall be filled with the peace of knowing that the Lord, indeed, is God (XX, 30):

> On that day, we shall rest and see, see and love, love and praise, for this is to be the end without the end of all our living, that Kingdom without end, the real goal of our present life (ibid.).

The "present life" finds us in a more ambiguous situation. As Gilson has stated:

> It is not a question of determining whether a man lives or does not live in one of the societies into which the world is actually inevitably divided, but whether he himself defines his last end as on earth or in heaven. In the first case, he is a citizen of the earthly city; in the second, of the heavenly city.[52]

These words echo Augustine's comparison of the "homes of unbelieving men" with "families which live according to faith":

> Both types of homes and their masters have this in common, that they must use things essential to this mortal life. . . . For, as mortal life is the same for all there ought to be common cause between the two cities in what concerns our purely human living (XIX, 17).

For Augustine, the two cities are "linked and fused together, only to be separated at the Last Judgment" (I, 35). Thus, human society as a whole is not to be identified with the earthly city, nor is the Church to be confused with the City of God. In human society, as in the Church, there can and will be found those who desire and seek to be exclusively of the earth, as well as those whose hearts are set on Heaven. Christians, citizens of the City of God, can never be citizens of the earthly city, but they can belong to and participate in all the activities of human society on this earth.

IV. THE APOCALYPTIC DIMENSION OF PATRISTIC ESCHATOLOGY

To what extent can it be said that Christian eschatology in the patristic age is apocalyptic, rather than prophetic? Actually, the question has not been explored to any great extent in classical patristic studies. Patrologists have tended to understand "prophecy," "apocalypticism" and eschatology in discrete categories, following definitions that are not always germane to others—biblical scholars, historians or systematic theologians. In general, the prophetic element in Christian antiquity has been associated with the question of community organization and ministry. Apocalyptic has been restricted to the consideration of apocalyptic apocrypha. Eschatology, on the contrary, has figured largely in Christian thought, from the earliest convictions regarding an imminent Second Coming to later developments in theological reflection on salvation, beatitude and the "Last Things."

It cannot be denied, as McGinn has pointed out, that "Christianity was born apocalyptic."[53] He claims, further, that "apocalyptic hopes . . . have never been absent from" Christian belief. In his review of apocalyptic in the patristic era,[54] McGinn traces the changes in Christian usages and expressions of this literary genre and classical apocalypticism. While it seems that the apocalyptic movement did not long perdure as such into the age of the early Church Fathers, signs of adaptation in themes and vocabulary did not disappear.

McGinn identifies three themes which reflect the apocalyptic dimension in patristic literature: the Antichrist; the ages of the world; the millennium. Two of these have been referred to earlier in this paper. The Antichrist theme, according to McGinn, paralleled the development of Christology. This would be a topic worth exploring at another time, since it falls outside the limits of this study. Both Irenaeus, in Book Five of the *Adversus haereses,* and Hippolytus, in the first complete treatise on the Antichrist ("On Christ and Antichrist"), discuss this theme in apocalyptic terms.

Apocalypticism underwent several moments of renewal throughout the patristic era. In the third century, the great North African theologian, Tertullian, gave signs of acquaintance with and interest in certain apocalyptic themes. Between the third and fifth centuries, other apocalyptic "renewals" occurred, although the recognition of Christianity as the religion of the empire gave priority to anti-apocalyptic themes. Eusebius of Caesarea, in loyalty to and support of Constantine, seemed ready to equate the Roman Empire with the kingdom of God.

Two major Latin, western Fathers, Jerome and Augustine, strongly opposed apocalypticism. Jerome, through his endeavors in biblical translation and exegesis, rejected earlier, less scholarly interpretation of and commentaries on Scripture. Augustine's monumental work, *The City of God,* contributed to an anti-apocalyptic posture that was to influence even medieval eschatology. At the same time, as McGinn points out, it was largely through Jerome and Augustine, along with still another emergence of renewed interest late in the fourth century, that apocalyptic was transmitted to the Middle Ages.

Underlying the history of apocalyptic in the patristic era is the question of biblical exegesis. The "Scriptures" known by the Christians of that age were the writings of the First Covenant, the Hebrew Scriptures. The story of the formation of the New Testament Canon is not germane to the topic addressed by this paper. What is germane is the impact on patristic eschatology of the various "writings" that emerged in Christian Antiquity. Apocryphal, Gnostic and Montanist "Scriptures" developed alongside the documents that came to be recognized as "canonical" writings of the Second Covenant. Other works, initially included in the canon, but later excluded, carried their influences as well.

Methods of reading and interpreting the Scriptures changed and evolved also. One has only to compare the use of biblical texts in a document such as *I Clement* with the exegesis that appeared later in the schools of Alexandria and Antioch to recognize this fact. From simple citation as authority to allegorical and fourth-century "scientific" and neo-allegorical methods, a full range of exegetical methods were used by the Fathers, in their efforts to proclaim the revealed Word.

Eschatology was only one area of Christian theology affected by patristic exegesis. In every instance, the underlying purpose was not too unlike the one for which, Paul taught, spiritual gifts are necessary in the Church: "To each person the manifestation of the Spirit is given for the common good" (1 Cor 12:7). What, then, we might ask, is the relation between eschatology, as we have seen it in the patristic era, and the life of the Church, the Body of Christ, the community of faith?

V. ESCHATOLOGY AND THE CHRISTIAN LIFE

The better we come to know the Fathers of the Church, the more we appreciate all that their teachings have to say to us. They were, first of all, men of faith: theologians, yes, but believers and pastors. Their faith led them, through theological research and reflection, to an encounter with Mystery: the mystery that can be described in Rudolph Otto's words as, "*tremendum et fascinans*." They sought to articulate a doctrine of Trinity or Incarnation in ways that proclaimed not only the salvation, but even the "divinization" of every human being. Their recourse to the allegorical interpretation of the Scriptures is one example that persuades us of their conviction that every Christian in every age is called to the spiritual reality of holiness.

The Fathers of the Church perceived the Church as the Body of Christ, a community assembled in faith, love, worship and witness to their commitment to the Lord Jesus. Eschatology, then, becomes an essential element in the life of every Christian. It is revelatory of spiritual values, and that, for several reasons.[55]

In the first place, all our eschatological expectations are overshadowed by the "eschatological drama" of Calvary. God's Reign is assured, indeed it is already accomplished, through the Cross. This "realized eschatology" is imperfect in human history. We know struggle and suffering. We share in the glory and power of the Risen Christ only through sharing in the Cross.

The life of the Christian is a life of faith: "Now we see indistinctly, as in a mirror" (1 Cor 13:12). The eschaton, when it is fully realized, will mean an end to struggle, suffering, sorrow and sin. Unlimited horizons will open before us. We shall see, then, clearly, "face to face." In the meantime, we—members of the Lord's Body, the Church—are called to proclaim that the world is oriented not to catastrophe and disaster, but to final transformation, assumed in the victory of a peace that is not the world's to give. That is the reason for our search to live a life worthy of the Gospel: a life of hope, love, service, and the transformation of suffering and evil through faith and worship. These values are our heritage from the earliest centuries of Christianity. If a general review of eschatology in the patristic era can enable and inspire us to pursue this ideal, it will have been worth the time and the effort.

NOTES

1. Clement of Rome. "The First Epistle to the Corinthians" (trans. and ann., J. A. Kleist). (Ancient Christian Writers; 1. (Westminster, Maryland: The Newman Bookshop, 1946) salutation, 9.

2. The patristic age is commonly understood to have begun *circa* A.D. 95; it continued, in the West, until the death of Gregory the Great (A.D. 608) and, in the East, until the death of John Damascene (A.D. 759). Historians do not always agree with patrologists on these dates.

3. Johannes Quasten, *Patrology*. (Utrecht-Antwerp: Spectrum Publishers) I, 35.

4. G. Florovsky, "The Last Things and the Last Events" in *Creation and Redemption* (Belmont, Massachusetts: Nordland Publishing Company, 1976) 243.

5. Florovsky, *Creation and Redemption, III,* 245.

6. Quasten,*Patrology*, I, 35.

7. The sub-Apostolic age is, generally, understood to include the late first and early second centuries of the Christian era. The Golden Age of patristic literature occurred in the fourth and first half of the fifth centuries.

8. "The eyes of the heart" is a common patristic expression.

9. The term, "Apostolic Fathers," refers to Christian writers who had personally known the Apostles or had been instructed by a disciple of one or another of the Apostles.

10. Cf. J. Danielou and H. Marrou. *The Christian Centuries*, vol. 1: *The First Six Hundred Years* (trans., V. Cronin) (London: Darton, Longman and Todd, 1964) 52.

11. Cf. Quasten, op. cit., I, 36.

12. *I Clement,* XXIII.

13. Cf. "Eschatology" in Encyclopedia of Early Christianity, ed. E. Ferguson (New York, London: Garland Publishing, 1990) 310.

14. J. N. D. Kelly. *Early Christian Doctrines.* (New York, London: Harper & Row, 1960) 462. Kelly cites several patristic texts to demonstrate his statement.

15. Cf. *Didachè*, 16.

16. Kelly, *Doctrines.*, 463.

17. This is a constant theme in *The Shepherd of Hermas*. It explains, for example, why the "building of the tower" (a symbol of the Church) is delayed.

18. The phrase, *Jesus Christ, Son of God, Savior,* as quoted by such diverse personalities as Constantine and Augustine, was the meaning of the acrostic found in early Christianity: (ICTHYS = fish). It is found in the Christian *Sibylline Oracles* and became the inspiration for much of early Christian art.

19. "To the Romans," 2:2; 4:1; 3; 6:3.

20. Cf. Quasten,*Patrology*, I, 186-188.

21. "Eschatologie," Galot, Jean, *Dictionnaire de Spiritualité*, IV, 1; col. 1044.

22. Cf. *Dialogue with Trypho,* 7 and 8.

23. Ibid., 80.

24. *Apologia* II, XIII.

25. *Adversus haereses* V, 28, 3.

26. Ibid., V, 30, 4.

27. This title is attributed to Irenaeus, because of his teaching on the Apostolic Tradition.

28. Cf. "Chiliasm," *Encyclopedia of Early Christianity*; 194.

29. Ibid., 193ff.; also , "Revelation, Book of," 782-783.

30. Ibid., 193-196.

31. *Adversus haereses* III, 18,1.

32. Ibid., III, 22, 3.
33. Quasten, *Patrology* , II;. 87.
34. *De principiis* I, VI, 1, 4, 5.
35. Ibid., III, VI, 3.
36. Ibid., also, III,V, 3.
37. *De virginitate* 12, 13.
38. *The Seven Ecumenical Councils,* Nicene and Post-Nicene Fathers (Second Series); 299-323.
39. Galot,"Eschatologie," col. 1046.
40. *Encyclopedia of Early Christianity,* 313.
41. Cf. G. B. Ladner, *The Idea of Reform* ((New York, Evanston, and London: Harper & Row, Publishers) 43, 71.
42. Ibid., 110.
43. Ibid., 106.
44. *De civltate Dei* XX, 9.
45. Ibid., XX, 7.
46. Ibid., XX, 10.
47. Ibid., XX, 8.
48. Ibid., XX, 7.
49. Ibid., XXII, 29.
50. Cf. ibid., XIX, 5, 13; XXII, 30, 4.
51. Quoted in Jaroslav Pelikan, *The Shape of Death* (London: MacMillan 1962), 48.
52. Saint Augustine, *The City of God,* Books I-VII in *Fathers of the Church,* 8 (New York: Fathers of the Church, Inc., 1950) "Foreword," by E. Gilson, lxii.
53. B. McGinn, *Visions of the End* (New York: Columbia University Press, 1979) 11.
54. Ibid., 14-27. I have found this material helpful for my discussion of an apocalyptic dimension to theories of eschatology in the patristic age.
55. Cf. Galot, *"Eschatologie,"* cols. 1053ff., for a full development of these ideas.

Happily At The Edge Of The Abyss: Popular Premillennialism In America

TIMOTHY P. WEBER

In the late summer of 1990, three popular Bible teachers sat together in a rather garish-looking television studio discussing the Scriptures and current events. Behind them was a large map of the Middle East; and in their hands were well-worn black leather Bibles. For over an hour and a half, Hal Lindsey, Chuck Smith, and Chuck Missler[1] traversed both testaments to prove that the crisis caused by Iraq's invasion of Kuwait fit perfectly into the End Times scenario predicted by the Bible centuries ago. With blinding speed, they assembled an elaborate jigsaw puzzle with pieces from Ezekiel, Daniel, Isaiah, Jeremiah, Joel, Nahum, Zechariah, Micah, Matthew, Luke, 1 and 2 Thessalonians, 2 Peter, and Revelation. At times it was hard to tell if the three men were happy or sad about the rapid approach of Armageddon. They rejoiced that history was following the biblical script; but they also grieved over the coming catastrophe. Clearly, the three Bible teachers wanted to move people to action and commitment in light of the future. Chuck Smith urged sinners to repent now so that they will escape the tribulation later. Chuck Missler told the audience to rearrange their personal priorities and announced that he had decided to lay aside his business interests to devote his full energies to spread the news of Christ's imminent return. After surveying the evidence, Hal Lindsey declared this generation to be the last before Jesus comes and asked his viewers the most important question of all: "If Jesus were to come tonight to rapture the Church, would you be ready?"[2]

As we put our heads together to study prophetic and apocalyptic eschatology, we would do well to remember the people who anchor their religious lives on biblical prophecy. According to C. K. Barrett, editor of the *World Christian Encyclopedia,* there are currently about sixteen million premillennialists in the United States,[3] most of whom are dispensationalists like the three Bible teachers mentioned above. Such numbers make premillennialists a force to be reckoned with in American religion. If grouped together, they would become the largest Protestant "denomination" in the United States.

According to dispensationalists, the Scriptures contain a precise outline of the End, a kind of "history before it happens." For them the Bible is a complex code that, if deciphered correctly, predicts the future with absolute accuracy. Needless to say, when such people seek the prophetic significance of current events, they do not beat a path to our door. They tune in their favorite television preacher or head for the nearest Christian bookstore to buy easy-to-read books that explain in detail how the texts and our times fit together. In short, most students of prophecy prefer teachers much like themselves who can unravel it in ways that even common people can understand. While scholars deliberate, their popular Bible teachers deliver. While academicians complicate matters with their sophisticated exegesis, their preachers simplify the meaning of complex texts. At least that is the way it looks to many people in the pew.

At the risk of laboring the point, the fact is that if we were to add up *all* the sales of *all* the books written by *all* the scholars at this symposium and multiply them by fifty or even one hundred, we would not come close to the eighteen million copies of Hal Lindsey's *The Late Great Planet Earth* that have been sold since 1970.[4] I make these observations not to deprecate what we do here, but to remind us what we are up against.

Given their impressive size and this symposium's topic, dispensationalists deserve our attention: where do they come from; what do they believe; and how are they coping during these apocalyptic times?

I. THE HISTORY AND HERMENEUTIC OF DISPENSATIONALISM

During and after the French Revolution, there was a revival of millenarian concerns in England and the United States. Many people believed that such a calamitous event must have prophetic significance and searched the Scriptures high and low to find it. As they studied the prophecies, they became convinced that Jesus was coming soon to establish his millennial kingdom on the earth and that signs of his return were abundant.

Not all millenarians interpreted the Bible in the same way. Historicist premillennialists believed that biblical prophecies of the "last days" were intended to provide an overview of the entire church age. Historicists believed that they could find prophetic fulfillments throughout church history and by means of biblical numerology predict the date of Christ's return.[5] America's best-known historicist premillennialist was William Miller (1792-1849) who worked his "millennial arithmetic" until he became certain that Jesus would return on October 22, 1844. Such specificity produced some understandable fanaticism among his evangelical followers, the so-called Millerites, and set them up for the "Great Disappointment" when Jesus did not arrive on schedule. Miller's failure discredited his hermeneutic and split the Millerites into a number of Adventist groups.[6]

Futurist premillennialists, on the other hand, fared much better. They expected prophecies of the last days to be fulfilled shortly before the Second Coming. Even before Miller figured a date for Christ's return, John Nelson Darby (1800-1882), a disgruntled priest in the Church of Ireland, came up with his own system. Darby argued that the key to biblical interpretation was recognizing that God dealt with humanity in different ways during different eras or dispensations. According to C. I. Scofield, one of Darby's later American followers, "these periods are marked off in Scripture by some change in God's method of dealing with mankind, in respect to two questions: of sin, and of man's responsibility. Each of the dispensations may be regarded as a new test of the natural man, and each ends in judgment – marking his utter failure in every dispensation."[7] Following Darby's lead, Scofield counted seven dispensations: innocence (before the Fall); conscience (Fall to Noah); human government (flood to the call of Abraham); promise (Abraham to the Exodus); law (Mt. Sinai through the earthly ministry of Christ), church (Pentecost to the Second Coming), kingdom (the millennium). This version of "progressive revelation" helped dispensationalists explain the complexities and apparent contradictions in the way God dealt with humanity.

Darby was not the first to divide history into eras or to claim that his approach was based on a literal interpretation of the Bible; but he did break new ground in the way he separated Israel and the Church into two totally distinct peoples of God, each with its own divine program. Israel was God's earthly people; and the Church was God's heavenly people. Prophecies about one could not refer to the other; and God dealt with only one group at a time. For Darby, "rightly dividing the word of truth" meant keeping the two peoples and their programs clearly differentiated.

In practice, Darby made God's dealings with Israel the key to his hermeneutic. The divine plan for the Jews was spelled out in a series of divine covenants with Abraham, Moses, and David. God promised to make Israel the chosen people and to establish Messiah on David's throne forever.[9] Darby found a key part of this plan spelled out in Daniel 7-9. There will be Gentile domination over the house of Israel until the "times of the Gentiles" are concluded, then a Gentile ruler will issue a decree to rebuild fallen Jerusalem. Seventy weeks later Messiah will come. More specifically, during the first seven weeks, the city will be rebuilt; in the sixty-ninth week, Messiah will come, but be "cut off;" and in the seventieth week, an evil ruler will try to destroy the Jews. Following the seventieth week, Messiah will return, destroy his people's persecutor, and set up David's throne forever.

Darby believed that Daniel's prophecy was fulfilled literally in the history of Israel and the coming of Christ. To make the prophecy come out correctly, he turned Daniel's seventy weeks into seventy weeks of years (or 490 years) and thereby showed that Christ's death on the cross (Messiah's "cutting off") occurred 483 years (sixty-nine "weeks") after Artaxerxes' decree to rebuild Jerusalem's fallen walls (Neh.2:1-8).[10]

This scenario posed a problem: Why did not Messiah return seven years later to set up his kingdom? Darby found the answer in his "postponement theory." Because first-century Jews did not accept Jesus as their Messiah, God canceled his return and created a new people—the Church. Thus normal prophetic time is suspended until God finishes forming the new "heavenly people."[11] Another question arose: How or when will God restart the prophetic clock? Darby located the answer in the "pretribulation rapture" of the Church. According to his basic hermeneutic, God worked with only one people at a time. Thus in order to resume dealing with Israel, God had to stop dealing with the Church. Thus Darby identified Daniel's seventieth week with the "great tribulation" described in Matt 24, 2 Thess 2, and most of Revelation and concluded that before any prophesied events can take place, God must "rapture" the Church out of the earth, as described in 1 Thess 4:13-17. With the Church thus removed, Daniel's seventieth week can begin, followed seven years later by Christ's return to establish his kingdom. The pretribulation rapture quickly became dispensationalism's most distinctive and compelling doctrine.

Followers of Darby, then, viewed Christ's return in two stages: before the tribulation, Jesus will return *for* his saints (the rapture); after the tribulation, he will return *with* his saints (the Second Coming *per se*). Because we are in suspended prophetic time, there are no predicted events between the present and the rapture. Therefore, at any time Jesus may return to rapture the Church.[12]

Darby became a leader in the separatistic Plymouth Brethren, where, despite considerable opposition from other futurist premillennialists, dispensationalism took root. He made a few trips to North America after the Civil War and won over a number of influential Baptist, Presbyterian, and Congregational clergy. At first dispensationalists did not have an easy time in the evangelical denominations. Since Millerism had made premillennialism of any kind rather suspect, dispensationalists often had to fend off charges of heresy from fellow evangelicals, most of whom preferred a *postmillennial* understanding of the Bible. Eventually, however, when conservative evangelicals formed defensive alliances against the spread of liberalism, they reluctantly included the new premillennialists. Though many conservative evangelical leaders considered dispensationalism a bit quirky, they found common ground with dispensationalists who stood for an inspired and authoritative Bible, supported evangelism and foreign missions, and retained a commitment to historic Christian orthodoxy.[13]

In the long run, the success of the movement did not depend on the grudging tolerance of a few leading conservatives. Dispensationalists quickly learned how to make converts and gain influence. They sponsored Bible and Prophetic Conferences, published numerous magazines and journals, and virtually took over the Bible institutes, which sent enthusiastic advocates into churches, mission agencies, and other evangelical enterprises. The Scofield Reference Bible (1909), whose notes explained the Scriptures from the dispensational perspective, exuded authority and credibility and became the wedge into new constituencies.

Furthermore, the times seemed to be on their side. The old postmillennial expectation of the Christianization of the world before Christ's return seemed hopelessly naive at the end of the nineteenth century. From the evangelical perspective, American society was falling apart, not inching its way toward some Golden Age. Consequently, premillennialists who were ridiculed for their pessimism before the Civil War were given a more respectful hearing later on. Many evangelicals who were ready to give up on the world found in dispensationalism a convincing explanation for the decline of civilization and a reassuring hope for the future.

By the end of World War I, which dispensationalists were able to fit into their scenario with considerable accuracy,[14] the movement was firmly established among Pentecostals and the people who were starting to call themselves Fundamentalists. By the 1930s separatistic fundamentalism had developed its own churches, publishing houses, schools, and missionary agencies,[15] thereby providing dispensationalism its own religious subculture where it perpetuated itself without any help or approval from the outside. In other words, while dispensationalism had almost universal support within militant fundamentalism, not many other people knew or cared much about it.

II. DISPENSATIONALISM AND POPULAR CULTURE

The isolation of dispensationalism in separatistic fundamentalism explains in part why so many people were surprised by the popularity of Hal Lindsey's *The Late Great Planet Earth* (1970). Lindsey's was the first premillennialist book to be marketed successfully in "secular" bookstores, supermarkets, and drugstores. The book caused a sensation among people who had never come across premillennialism before.[16] What most Americans did not understand was that *The Late Great Planet Earth* was merely an updated version of the prophetic scenario that dispensationalists had been teaching for over a hundred years.

Lindsey set out to show that world events were moving toward Christ's Second Coming. Though dispensationalists in the last century had understood the Bible correctly, without the existence of the state of Israel in Palestine, there was no realistic way for end-time prophecies to be fulfilled. For Lindsey the rebirth of Israel in 1948 was directly tied to Jesus' parable of the fig tree, which most premillennialists took as a symbol for Israel. "From the fig tree learn its lesson: as soon as its branch becomes tender and puts forth its leaves, you know that summer is near. So also, when you see all these things, you know that he [the Son of Man] is near, at the very gates. Truly, I say to you, this generation will not pass away till all these things take place" (Matt 24:32-34). Once Israel is established, all other prophesied events will occur within a single generation, which Lindsey took as "something like forty years." Thus, counting from the founding o£ Israel in 1948, Christ should return to set up his kingdom by about 1988. Clearly the founding of Israel "has now set the stage for the other predicted signs to develop in history. It is like the key piece of a jigsaw puzzle being found and then having the many adjacent pieces fall into place."[17]

Drawing heavily on Daniel 11, Ezekiel 37-39, and Revelation, Lindsey's jigsaw looked as up-to-date as the morning newspaper. Sometime before 1988 the Israelis will sign a security pact with the Antichrist, the head of the European Common Market (the reorganized Roman Empire), and rebuild their temple in the Holy Land. After three and a half years, the Antichrist will break the treaty, enter the Jerusalem temple, declare himself to be God, and persecute all those who refuse to worship him and receive his mark on their foreheads. Shortly after this treachery, a northern confederation of nations made up of the Soviet Union, its Eastern European allies (including Germany), and Iran will join with an Arab-African confederacy consisting of Egypt, Libya, and the other Arab states to launch a devastating attack on Israel. This move will prompt the intervention of the Antichrist's Common Market and the "kings of the east" with their 200-million-man army, which Lindsey took as Red China. As western and eastern forces move toward Palestine, the Red Army will try to destroy the Jewish population once and for all. To preserve Israel, God will pour out fire and brimstone (probably a nuclear attack) and destroy the Russian northern confederacy. After that, Antichrist's forces will do battle with the kings of the east at Armageddon. A nuclear exchange will obliterate the world's major cities and in Palestine the blood will flow as high as the horses' bridles. Before the nations completely destroy each other, Jesus Christ will return, wipe out the surviving armies, take Antichrist into custody, and set up his millennial kingdom at Jerusalem.[18] Though the predictions of coming events were dire indeed, Lindsey assured his readers that those who have trusted in Christ for salvation wlll be raptured to heaven before Antichrist is revealed and the tribulation begins. Lindsey believed that world conditions made his scenario highly probable.

Despite Lindsey's seriousness, many people did not get out of the book what he thought he put into it. Some folks saw *The Late Great Planet Earth* as an example of the public's taste for the bizarre and offbeat. After all, Lindsey's book was published at a time when America was rediscovering the supernatural and paranormal. In many bookstores, shelf-stockers who had never seen a book on Bible prophecy before often did not know what to do with it. Where does it belong, in the religion section or someplace else? Given the book's sensationalistic style, the question was entirely appropriate. Frequently, the book ended up alongside some of popular culture's latest fads: astrology, ESP, UFOs, pyramid-power, out-of-body experiences, parapsychology, and the occult. The uninitiated might easily mistake it for pseudo-science, science fiction, or a variation on other gloom-and-doom books about the environment or the economy. Even some Christians who knew the prophetic genre well could not easily tell the difference between Lindsey's book and Erik Von Daniken's *Chariots of the Gods* or Immanuel Velikovsky's *Worlds in Collision*.[19]

Social critics and satirists found the interest in Bible prophecy irresistible and often had fun at premillennialism's expense. In the late 1980s, for example, *Harper's* magazine ran a long piece on "Packaging Christ's Second Coming," which contained a complete media strategy, suggestions for a sixty-second T.V. spot, wardrobe guidelines for the returning Jesus, and a proposed opening monologue for Christ's guest appearance on "Saturday Night Live." Plans for a new mass-market edition of the New Testament entitled *He's Back* included a back-cover blurb by Donald Trump: "I think of Jesus Christ as my close personal friend, and this book shows why He is regarded as the ultimate mover and shaker. I look forward to working with Him on the problems that beset New York City and the country when He's settled in."[20]

Sometimes premillennialists trivialized their own message by boiling it down to bumper stickers: "Beam Me Up, Jesus," "In Case of Rapture, This Car Will Be Driverless," and "Jesus Is Coming Soon—and When He Gets Here He's Going to Be Ticked Off." Lindsey undercut his own credibility by predicting that the so-called "Jupiter effect" (a rare alignment of planets) will touch off "history's greatest outbreak of earthquakes" in 1982 and that UFOs, which are actually spacecraft under the control of demons, will land soon on the earth for a "close encounter of the third kind."[21]

Sensationalism aside, dispensationalists were masters of mass communication. During the 1970s they produced a number of Hollywood-type dramatic films with titles like *A Thief in the Night, A Distant Thunder, Image of the Beast, The Rapture,* and *The Road to Armageddon* for use in churches, schools and other places. Virtually all of the electronic church's biggest names preached the premillennialist gospel, including Pat Robertson, Jerry Falwell, Paul Crouch, Jimmy Swaggart, Oral Roberts, Rex Humbard, Kenneth Copeland, and Jim Bakker. A staple in Christian television scheduling is the "Bible prophecy in the news" program. Charles Taylor's "Today in Bible Prophecy" is widely syndicated. Stuart McBirnie, president of the unaccredited California Graduate School of Theology, produces his own "News Commentary." "Jack Van Impe Presents" is carried by over a hundred stations world-wide and is devoted to an analysis of the news from a dispensational perspective. Much of the program is spent promoting Van Impe's "shocking" videotapes ("Russia, World War III, and Armageddon," "America in Prophecy: The Decline and Fall of the American Empire," and "The 90s, Startling End-Time Signs and Your Future") and his magazine *Perhaps Today*. Ray Brubaker hosts "God's News Behind the News" and offers his own magazine *Reflections on the News*. Hal Lindsey is a regular guest on Paul Crouch's Trinity Broadcasting Network, has his own Saturday morning radio program in Los Angeles, and publishes *Countdown News Journal,* which interested persons may order by calling his toll-free number, 1-800-Titus 3:5. No longer content to be on the fringes of American religion, dispensationalists learned how to use every up-to-date method to get their message out.

Not everyone received the premillennialist message with open arms. There was a backlash against the movement. By the early 1980s, many leading dispensationalist Bible teachers were coopted by the New Christian Right, whose concern over the demise of traditional values, the public crusades for feminism and homosexual rights, abortion on demand, and the corruption of public institutions matched dispensationalism's teachings about the decline of civilization before the Second Coming. Many observers feared that premillennialism was becoming too closely tied to reactionary politics.[22]

There was reason for concern. During the 1970s, Lindsey addressed groups of military planners at the American Air War College and the Pentagon on how Bible prophecy related to the Middle East and World War III. Unlike most Christian books, *The Late Great Planet Earth* was translated into Hebrew and published in Israel, where Lindsey said it "caught on like wildfire. A great many copies circulated among military men and government officials as well."[23]

By 1980 Lindsey was ready to enter the political fray. His *The 1980's: Countdown to Armageddon* was an affirmation and update of *The Late Great Planet Earth*; but it also contained a recognizable right-wing political agenda. In his first book, Lindsey stated that by the time Antichrist is revealed, the U.S. will be a second-rate power with no major military or political role to play in the events leading up to Armageddon. He maintained that position in *The 1980's*, but seemed unwilling to live with it. He condemned the weak-kneed liberals who had allowed Soviet expansion around the world and blamed America's slipping prestige on the Council of Foreign Relations and the Trilateral Commission.[24] He traced America's domestic troubles all the way back to FDR's New Deal and suggested that Americans "need to clean house in Washington, and elect a Congress and a President who believe in the capitalist system."[25] Though America's decline is unstoppable, right-thinking people might slow it down: "If some critical and difficult choices are made by the American people right now, it is possible to see the U.S. remain a world power."[26] If conservatives regain control, "America will survive this perilous situation and endure until the Lord comes to evacuate His people."[27] While they cannot change the divine scenario, some dispensationalists hoped to postpone its worst aspects until after the rapture. In this way, premillennialists like Jerry Falwell, Tim LaHaye, and their colleagues in the New Christian Right could push their political programs without compromising their dispensational beliefs.

In the early 1980s the public became aware of the presence of premillennialists in high places. In February, 1981, while testifying before the House Interior Committee, Secretary of the Interior James Watt was asked if he believed that we should leave some of our resources for our children. "Absolutely," Watt replied, "That is the delicate balance the Secretary of the Interior must have, to be steward for the natural resources for this generation as well as future generations. I do not know how many future generations we can count on before the Lord returns, whatever it is we have to manage with a skill to have the resources needed for future generations." The press had a field day with Watt's reference to the Second Coming and usually failed to mention the Secretary's stress on "balance" and being ready for the future. The widespread impression was that Watt's belief in Christ's return precluded any concern for preserving resources for the long-haul.[28] The connection between premillennialism and right-wing politics got even more attention during the 1984 presidential election, when President Ronald Reagan's dispensational views came to light. In April a widely-circulated article in *The Washington Post* asked, "Does Reagan Expect a Nuclear Armageddon?" and answered it in the affirmative.[29] Shortly thereafter, 175 public radio stations carried a documentary on "Ronald Reagan and the Politics of Armageddon."[30] In October the Christic Institute of Washington D.C.

held a news conference and charged that premillennialism was having a deleterious effect on American foreign policy.[31] The next evening, during the second presidential debate, Marvin Kalb of NBC News asked Reagan, "Do you feel that we are now heading perhaps for some kind of nuclear Armageddon, and do you feel that this country and the world could survive that kind of calamity?" Obviously no prophecy pundit himself, Reagan replied that "no one knows whether Armageddon is 1,000 years away or the day after tomorrow" and that he had "never seriously warned and said we must plan according to Armageddon." Nevertheless, he said that he had "philosophical discussions" with various theologians who believed that "the prophecies are coming together that portend that."[32]

That exchange sent journalists and political analysts scurrying for more information on Armageddon and Bible prophecy. *Time*, *Newsweek*, and newspapers coast to coast carried articles on premillennialism.[33] Virtually all of these articles looked for links between Reagan's dispensationalism and his handling of the on-going Middle East crisis and the Soviet Union, which he had labelled the "Evil Empire." Some speculated that dispensationalists might view any effort to prevent a nuclear holocaust as an attempt to thwart God's purposes and suggested that if Reagan and his fellow premillennialists believed that God will rapture the faithful before the bombs fly, there was little urgency to end the arms race.[34] Critics feared that premillennialists' growing political clout might make Armageddon a self-fulfilling prophecy.

The political implications of premillennialism have always been more complicated than that, however. Some dispensationalists have preferred evangelism to politics, following D. L. Moody's old advice: "I look on this world as a wrecked vessel. God has given me a life-boat, and said to me, 'Moody, save all you can.'. . .This world is getting darker and darker; its ruin is coming nearer and nearer. If you have any friends on this wreck unsaved, you had better lose no time in getting them off."[35] While some dispensationalists rejected political involvement, others decided to give the devil as much trouble as possible by engaging in certain kinds of political activity.[36] In the 1980s, when so many fundamentalists rediscovered their political voice, a significant number of premillennialists chose the second option. At any rate, the critics were mostly correct: in the eighties premillennialists turned their essentially religious concerns into powerful political protest.

III. DISPENSATIONALISM AND THE PERSIAN GULF CRISIS

Despite their considerable political power, by the end of the decade, dispensationalists were fast losing their credibility as end-times experts. The rapid transformation of Eastern Europe in 1989-1990 was incompatible with their expectations.

For over a century, Russia stood center-stage in their prophetic play. As head of the northern confederacy, Russia and its allies will eventually attack Israel and precipitate Armageddon. The Communist Revolution, the expansion of the Soviet Union into Eastern Europe after World War II, the Cold War, and the nuclear arms race made this role plausible. Lindsey, for example, viewed Soviet strength with alarm and believed its invasion of Afghanistan was the first step toward the subjugation of Iran (part of the northern confederacy) and control of the Persian Gulf.[37]

By the summer of 1989, such predictions seemed very unlikely. Within a few months, the northern confederacy fell apart. The Soviet "empire" crumbled and due to its enormous economic and ethnic problems at home, many wondered if the Soviet Union itself could survive. Germany (Gomer, according to the dispensational understanding of Ezekiel 38), reunited and joined the western European community. Afghanistan ended in a defeat for the Soviets, not a stepping stone to other conquests. None of these events fit the predictions of dispensationalism. For the first time since World War I, the dispensational scheme was in danger of blatant and undeniable disconfirmation.

How did dispensationalists respond to these events? For the most part, they denied that they were significant. Jack Van Impe, Hal Lindsey, Stuart McBirnie, et al, discounted *glasnost* and *perestroika* as deceptive ploys to throw the western powers off guard. Once the Soviets rebuilt their economy with western help, they will again flex their muscles and reorganize the northern confederacy. The "new world order" is only a temporary glitch. "Don't be deceived by news accounts," the Bible teachers assured, "it's all going to happen exactly the way God said it would." [38]

Dispensationalists stood firm in their state of denial until the Iraqi army invaded Kuwait in August, 1990. The crisis in the Persian Gulf was like a shot of vitamin B-12 for the Bible teachers. Zondervan Publishers reported an 83 percent sales increase of *The Late Great Planet Earth*; and Scripture Press, another publisher of prophetic books, acknowledged brisk sales of the more scholarly *Prophecy Knowledge Handbook* by John Walvoord, chancellor of Dallas Theological Seminary, whose updated-1974 book on *Armageddon, Oil and the Middle East Crisis* was being reissued.[39] The message was clear: Saddam Hussein is not the Antichrist and Armageddon will not occur in the Persian Gulf. But the current crisis is thrusting the nations into their predicted configurations and putting Israel into the kind of peril that will lead directly to the End. All of the teachers knew that time is short and that the rapture is imminent. Lindsey predicted that the Second Coming will occur within a few years. Van Impe promised Armageddon by 1996 based on a numerological argument from the second century that human history will last 6,000 years because God created the universe in six days and "with the Lord a day is like a thousand years" (2 Peter 3:8). Because Van Impe believed that creation occurred in 4004 B.C. (Bishop Ussher's calculation), 1996 will mark the end of the sixth millennium.[40] The fulfillment of biblical prophecy was so obvious that Lindsey did not understand how anyone could miss it.[41]

It is difficult not being a bit cynical about dispensationalism's current confidence. Before the August, 1990 invasion, no Bible teacher had much to say about Iraq. In *The Late Great Planet Earth*, Lindsey virtually ignored it; and in *The 1980s* he mentioned it only in passing: Iraq will probably merge with Syria and restore its broken relationship with the Soviet Union.[42] He wrote nothing about an Iraqi war with Iran or an Iraqi conquest of Kuwait.

Since the invasion, however, many popular Bible teachers have discovered Iraq's place in prophecy. Traditionally, dispensationalists understood "Babylon" as Rome and the "Great Whore of Babylon" as the apostate religion that served the Antichrist (Revelation 17). Lindsey, for example, described the false religion of the Last Days as a combination of astrology, mind-expansion, witchcraft, ecumenism, and drugs.[43] But after the crisis in the Persian Gulf, he suggested that we should take a more literal approach: Babylon, the ancient city, is being rebuilt in the desert by Saddam Hussein.[44] Jack Van Impe suggested that since Babylon was conquered by the Medo-Persian Empire in the 6th century B.C., Iraq is really part of Iran (Persia, Ezek 38:5) and thus part of the northern confederacy, which will soon be reconstituted.[45] To supporters, such adjustments make the Bible teachers appear "flexible" and open to new truth; to others, they seem opportunistic, willing to do or say anything to make their system come out right. There is something disingenuous about finding a place for Iraq in end-time events now when they never saw it before.

IV. AN EVALUATION OF POPULAR DISPENSATIONALISM

Opportunistic or not, dispensationalist Bible teachers are able to convince millions of people that they handle the Scriptures respectfully and well. At a time when most "mainline" scholars or preachers all but ignore prophetic and apocalyptic biblical texts or downplay any modern application of their message, dispensationalists pay close attention. To many people their approach appears straightforward, literal, and concrete; and in those emphases reside much of dispensationalism's broad appeal.[46]

Premillennialism makes difficult texts accessible by historicizing nearly everything. Apocalyptic texts are "true" because they refer to real people and places. Dispensationalists do not leave apocalyptic symbols floating in space; they insist on bringing them down to earth. This commitment to concreteness comes from their belief that the Christian faith is historical through and through. God created a real world; Adam and Eve had a real fall into sin; God called a real man named Abraham and made him the father of Israel. God became incarnate in a real person who died for our sins and rose from the dead. The drama of redemption, then, is played out from beginning to end in time and space. Therefore, Jesus must be vindicated on the earth, where he was first denied. In other words, there is a historical symmetry to dispensational eschatology. Redemption is not complete until Jesus vanquishes his foes on the earth and restores creation.

This approach to the Bible underscores the populist character of dispensationalism, which became known in America when the Bible seemed to be suffering at the hands of experts. In the late nineteenth century, biblical higher critics cast doubts on older notions of biblical inspiration, authority, and accuracy and seemed to imply that ordinary believers could not understand the Bible for themselves. According to the new scholarship, a literalistic, common-sense hermeneutic was dangerous and misleading. People must accept the "assured results" of higher criticism and not read the Bible through the cloudy lenses of their own times and experience.

Many rank-and-file Christians considered this the worst kind of elitism; and dispensationalists capitalized on their deep resentments. In 1909 A.T. Pierson stated their objections clearly: "like Romanism, [higher criticism] practically removes the Word of God from the common people by assuming that only scholars can interpret it; while Rome puts a priest between a man and the Word, criticism puts an educated expositor between the believer and his Bible."[47] Dispensationalists insisted that people could still read the Bible for themselves. All they needed was common sense, a reverent spirit, and a willingness to dig in. Besides, untutored believers often had what the experts did not: the help of the indwelling Holy Spirit. Dispensational Bible institutes pioneered and promoted do-it-yourself Bible study methods that assured that virtually anyone could glean from Scripture what God intended.[48]

This populism is still strong in dispensationalist circles, as seen in an advertisement for Tim LaHaye's new book *How to Study Bible Prophecy for Yourself*. "Most of us think that it takes a special education to break the biblical code on prophecy. Not so, says popular author Tim LaHaye. . . . Discover the basic principles and biblical parameters of New Testament prophecy . . . then use them to reach your own conclusions regarding things to come."[49]

Of course, most dispensationalists do not interpret the Bihle for themselves. Despite the assurances of their teachers, few people can maneuver the dispensationalism system without extensive help. The hermeneutic is not simple; and most advocates must rely on their teachers for the details. Like it or not, dispensationalists have their own experts who stand between the Bible and the common believer. Popular Bible teachers are the higher critics of dispensationalism who explain to laypeople what they could never figure out on their own. Those teachers who can assemble the prophetic puzzle are recognized as authorities. In populist movements, the audience is sovereign. The people determine the experts by buying their books or donating to their television ministries.

In the last analysis, one must question dispensationalism's approach to Scripture. The popular Bible teachers interpret prophetic and apocalyptic texts as slightly embellished historical narratives whose meanings are obvious. This literalism allows them to "level out" all biblical texts by paying little attention to their original historical and literary contexts. Ironically, their critics charge, dispensationalists mishandle the texts they so deeply revere.[50] Even dispensationalist scholars, most of whom teach or were trained at Dallas Seminary, have begun to modify basic elements of their system, including the absolute separation of Israel and the Church and the postponement theory.[51] Popular teachers notwithstanding, dispensationalism may be unraveling at the highest levels of its support.

There is also something disturbing about the way dispensationalists fit people and nations into their scenario. There is no room for doubt in their system; and they never seem to question their standing among the righteous remnant. One suspects that alongside their professed confidence in God's ability to fulfil all the prophecies is a need to deny and finally control what often looks like the hiddenness and unpredictability of God. Dispensationalism's God is allowed few surprises. From one perspective, popular premillennialism may be seen as a way of bringing God and the chaos of the world under tight control.[52]

Despite these shortcomings, dispensationalism reaches people where they live. Millions of people woke up this morning honestly wondering if Jesus will come today; and many young people tonight will make ethical decisions by asking themselves, "Do I really want to he doing *that* when Jesus comes?" Dispensationalism has turned some people into evangelists and foreign missionaries and helped others to take seriously the question posed in 2 Peter: "Since everything will be destroyed in this way, what kind of people ought you to be? You ought to live holy and godly lives as you look forward to the day of God and speed its coming" (3:11-12).[53]

Dispensationalists are currently riding high, though their specificity also puts them in some danger of public embarrassment. But dispensationalists have always been willing to take risks. Though the world teeters on the edge of the abyss, they have reason to feel euphoric. The inspired Scriptures assure them that all will be well, that Jesus is coming soon to rapture them from danger and bring all things to their preordained end. In the 1990s, happiness is knowing that even chaos is under God's control.

NOTES

1. Hal Lindsey is the author of *The Late Great Planet Earth* and other prophetic books; Chuck Smith is the founding pastor of Calvary Chapel in Costa Mesa, California, and a widely-read author of prophetic themes; and Chuck Missler is a businessman and computer expert who is a teacher at Smith's Calvary Chapel.

2. Hal Lindsey, Chuck Smith, and Chuck Missler on "Praise the Lord," Trinity Broadcasting Network, Sept. 5, 1990.

3. Don Lattin, "The End of the World," *The San Francisco Chronicle*, October 9, 1988, *This World*, 9. This figure seems reasonable in light of the forty or fifty million Evangelicals in the U.S. One student of American premillennialism estimated the number of premillennialists at eight million; but I have argued that they may be twice that many. See Dwight Wilson, *Armageddon Now!* (Grand Rapids: Baker Book House, 1977), p. 12 and Timothy P. Weber, *Living in the Shadow of the Second Coming: American Premillennialism, 1875-1982* (Chicago: University of Chicago Press, 1987), note 1, p. 274.

4. Hal Lindsey, *The Late Great Planet Earth* (Grand Rapids: Zondervan, 1970). In 1980 Lindsey claimed that 30 million had read the book: Hal Lindsey, *The 1980s: Countdown to Armageddon* (King of Prussia, Penn.: Westgate Press, 1980), 11.

5. For a helpful overview of this millenarian revival, see Ernest R. Sandeen, *The Roots of Fundamentalism: British and American Millenarianism, 1800-1930* (Chicago: University of Chicago Press, 1970).

6. On the Millerites see Ronald Numbers and Jonathan Butler, eds., *The Disappointed: Millerism and Millenarianism in the Nineteenth Century* (Bloomington, Ind.: Indiana University Press, 1987); David Rowe, *Thunder and Trumpets* (Chico, Calif.: Scholars Press, 1985); Ruth Alden Doan, *The Miller Heresy, Millennialism, and American Culture* (Philadelphia: Temple University Press, 1987).

7. C. I. Scofield, *Rightly Dividing the Word of Truth* (Oakland, Calif.: Western Book and Tract Company, n.d.), 18.

8. Charles C. Ryrie, *Dispensationalism Today* (Chicago: Moody Press, 1965), 66-78 .

9. John Nelson Darby, "The Covenants," *Collected Works*, ed. William Kelly, 34 vols. (London: G. Morrish, 1967), 3:75.

10. Weber, 18-19.

11. C. H. Mackintosh, *Papers on the Lord's Coming* (Chicago: Bible Institute Colportage Association, n.d.), 101-102.

12. John Walvoord, *The Rapture Question* (Findlay, Ohio: Dunham Publishing Co., 1957).

13. Weber, 29-32.

14. Ibid., 105-127.

15. George Marsden, *Fundamentalism and Amerlcan Culture* (New York: Oxford University Press, 1980); Joel Carpenter, "A Shelter in the Time of Storm: Fundamentalist Institutions and the Rise of Evangelical Protestantism, 1929-1942," *Church History* 49 (1980), 62-75 .

16. No study of which I am aware has documented who the eighteen million people were who bought Lindsey's book. But if Barrett's estimation of sixteen million premillennialists is correct, then it stands to reason that somebody outside the movement was reading it.

17. Lindsey, *Late Great Planet Earth*, 53-58.

18. Ibid., 146-179.

19. Robert M. Price, "The Paper Back Apocalypse," *The Wlttenburg Door*, Oct./Nov. 1981, 3-5.

20. "He's Back," *Harper's*, April 1989, 47-55.

21. Lindsey, *The 1980s*, 30-34.

22. E.g., Erling Jorstad, *The Politics of Doomsday: Fundamentalists of the Far Right* (Nashville: Abingdon Press, 1970): Flo Conway and Jim Siegelman, *Holy Terror: The Fundamentalist War on America's Freedoms in Religion, Politics and Our Private Lives* (Garden City, N.Y.: Doubleday, 1982); Carol Flake, *Redemptorama: Culture, Politics, and the New Evangelicalism* (Garden City, N.Y.: Anchor Press, 1984); A. G. Mojtabai, *Blessed Assurance. At Home with the Bomb in Amarillo, Texas* (Boston: Houghton Mifflin, 1986); Grace Halsell, *Prophecy and Politics: Militant Evangelists on the Road to Nuclear War* (Westport, Conn.: Lawrence Hill, 1986); and Michael D'Antonio, *Fall from Grace. The Failed Crusade of the Christian Right* (New York: Farrar, Straus, Giroux, 1989).

23. Lindsey, *The 1980's*, 3-7.

24. Ibid., 138.

25. Ibid., 161.

26. Ibid., 146.

27. Ibid., 176.

28. David Douglas, "God, the World and James Watt," *Christianity and Crisis* 41 (Oct. 5, 1981), 258, 269-270.

29. Ronnie Dugger, "Does Reagan Expect a Nuclear Armageddon?" *The Washington Post*, April 8, 1984, C1, C4.

30. Joe Cuomo, "Ronald Reagan and the Politics of Armageddon," produced at WBAI Radio, New York City, 1984.

31. John Herbers, "Armageddon View Prompts a Debate," *The New York Times*, October 24, 1984, A1, A25. Miles Harvey, "Religious Authorities Ask Reagan, Mondale to Repudiate 'Armageddon Ideology' on Nuclear War, " *Los Angeles Times*, October 24, 1984, part 1.

32. "Washington Diarist: The End is Nigh, " *The New Republic*, November 12, 1984, 50.

33. Richard Ostling, "Armageddon and the End Times," *Time*, November 5, 1984, 73; Kenneth L. Woodward, "Arguing Armageddon," *Newsweek*, November 5, 1984, 91; Walter Goodman, "Religious Debate Fueled by Politics," *The New York Times*, October 28, 1984; "The end is near," *The Tribune* (Oakland, CA), October 23, 1984, B8; Andrew Lang, "The politics of Armageddon, " Convergence: Report from the Christic Institute, Fall 1984, 3, 12, 16.

34. Michael Barkun, "Nuclear War and Millenarian Symbols: Premillennialists Confront the Bomb," a paper delivered at the annual meeting of the Society for the Scientific Study of Religion, October, 1985.

35. D. L. Moody, *New Sermons* (New York: Henry S. Goodspeed, 1880), 535.

36. Weber, 82-104, 234-237.

37. Lindsey, *The 1980s*, 50, 74.

38. "Jack Van Impe Presents," Trinity Broadcasting Network, Sept. 5, 1990; Lindsey, "Praise the Lord," Trinity Broadcasting Network, Sept . 5, 1990 .

39. Michael Hirsley and Jorge Casuso, "Mideast Crisis Sparks Talk of Armageddon," *Chicago Tribune*, Oct. 14, 1990, section 1, 1, 24.

40. Ibid.

41. "Praise the Lord," Trinity Broadcasting Network, October 3, 1990,

42. Lindsey, *The 1980s*, 68, 74.

43. Lindsey, *The Late Great Planet Earth*, 114-134.

44. Lindsey, "Praise the Lord," Trinity Broadcasting Network, Sept. 5, 1990.

45. "Jack Van Impe Presents," Trinity Broadcasting Network, Oct. 8, 1990.

46. William Martin, "Waiting for the End," *The Atlantic* (June 1982), 31—37.

47. A. T. Pierson, "Antagonism to the Bible," *Our Hope* 15 (January 1909), 475.

48. Timothy P. Weber, "The Two-Edged Sword: The Fundamentalist Use of the Bible," in *The Bible in America: Essays in Cultural History*, eds. Nathan O. Hatch and Mark A. Noll (New York: Oxford University Press, 1982), 101-120.

49. *Moody Monthly* (September 1990), 91:44. Tim LaHaye, *How to Study Bible Prophecy for Yourself* (Eugene, Ore.: Harvest Home Publishers. 1990).

50. For example, Daniel P. Fuller, *Gospel and Law: Contrast or Continuum?* (Grand Rapids:

Eerdmans, 1980); Anthony Hoekema, *The Bible and the Future* (Grand Rapids: Eerdmans, 1979); George E. Ladd, *The Blessed Hope* (Grand Rapids: Eerdmans, 1956); Vern S. Poythress, *Understanding Dispensationalists* (Grand Rapids: Zondervan, 1987).

51. Craig Blaising, "Doctrinal Development in Orthodoxy," *Bibliotheca Sacra* 145 (1988) 133-140; Craig Blaising, "Development of Dispensationalism by Contemporary Dispensationalists," ibid., 254-280; Robert Saucy, "The Crucial Issue Between Dispensational and Non-Dispensational Systems," *Criswell Theological Review* 1 (1986), 149-165.

52. Douglas W. Frank, *Less Than Conquerors* (Grand Rapids: Eerdmans, 1986), pp. 60-102. See also Robert Jay Lifton and Charles B. Strozier, "Waiting for Armageddon," *New York Times Book Review*, August 12, 1990, 1, 24-25.

53. My book *Living in the Shadow of the Second Coming* explores the personal, social, political, and religious consequences of believing in the premillennial Second Coming.

Eschatology And Systematics

GABRIEL FACKRE

Currently the field of systematics is as diverse as the systematicians wielding their pens or changing their disks. As such, no definitive perspective on eschatology can be forthcoming. While it is tempting to settle for a survey of the variety of competing views, a believer in the presence of the Spirit in the life of the church will look for evidence of some continuing and coherent eschatological witness. Indeed, there are such refrains in both classical and contemporary theology, and this essay will attempt to identify them.

"Prophetic" and "apocalyptic" are not terms that frame the topic of eschatology in systematic/dogmatic inquiry. More familiar are such categories as Edmund Fortman's "pilgrim state," "interim state," and "final state," or Dale Moody's personal, historical and cosmic futures.[1] The reason for the typological difference lies in the function and warrants of systematics. As a discipline, it seeks to formulate the faith of the Christian community in response to the issues and idiom of its time and place. And as church dogmatics, its touchstones of authority include Scripture read through the lens of Christ and the Gospel, and the long tradition of the church that has identified and developed certain decisive themes. Prophetic/apocalyptic as a field of investigation in Old Testament scholarship is, indeed, contributory to the systematics task. [2] Further, the terms refer in contemporary theological discourse to vigorous points of view which systematic inquiry must engage. We shall deal with these phenomena in specific sections here. And throughout, wherever the intramundane or supramundane aspects which they symbolize are addressed, they will not be far from mind. But eschatology as a theological locus will be examined under more encompassing rubrics.

I. DEFINITIONS AND DISTINCTIONS

In the older systematics, eschatology is the doctrine of "last things."[3] Focussed on the cosmic consummation of God's purposes, it also deals with the destiny of the individual from death onward toward that finale. While these issues continue to be integral to eschatology, biblical studies and theological reconsiderations have expanded the horizon to include all aspects of the "future of God," social and historical as well as cosmic and personal.[4] Existentialist efforts to collapse all futurity into the the claims of divine immediacy have had little effect on systematic restatements.

Eschatology is the Christian doctrine of the future. Following the tradition as read through narrative eyes, it deals with the End of the Story—its purpose and conclusion. Its sub-sections are:

A. The ultimate future, or "last things," as those biblical themes that have come to the fore in ecumenical tradition: the resurrection of the dead, the return of Christ, the final judgment and everlasting life.

B. The penultimate future, or "next-to-last things," with specific reference to:

1. historical sign
2. post-mortem existence

On the boundary between penultimate and ultimate futures are features of eschatology treated (gingerly) by Reformed dogmatics as "diagnostic signs."[5] In contrast to the classical motifs which treat the what of the matter, these entail its how, when and where. While meager and ambiguous biblical warrants preclude ecumenical consensus, their persistence and attraction in popular piety make them also fit subjects for systematics.

An "eschatological proviso" stands over all theological discourse about the End. Biblical portrayal of what is to be, especially its transcendent aspects, is in images laden with mystery. As stained glass windows they are translucent not transparent. They do not give us a God's eye view of the Not Yet, but rather invite worship. Eschatological doctrine lets in enough light for us to to read our hymnals and sing praise to the "immortal, invisible, God only wise, in light inaccessible hid from our eyes."

II. THE ULTIMATE FUTURE

The heart of Christian hope is the fulfillment of God's purpose to be "all in all" (1 Cor 15:28). We employ the ancient creeds' four phrases as rubrics for eschatological ultimacy. First, an observation on the relation of the classical schema to some contemporary issues.

An eschatology implies an ethic.[6] Highly individualistic views of the End are regularly allied with a moral stance devoid of social and systemic mandates. And those that find no place for the renovation of nature will have little ecological concern. The striking thing about classical eschatology is its full orb, including as it does personal, social and cosmic fulfillment, with is correlative ethical imperatives.

With our raised awareness of perils to the environment, theologians and church bodies are giving attention to the "integrity of creation."[7] Thus the eschatological vision of a "new heaven and a new earth" comes into focus. In the section on Everlasting Life, its scope and implications will be explored. However, as with many claimants for priority on the Church's agenda, ecological theology may fall prey to the very reductionism it seeks to challenge. Hence, the needed theological reclamation of the whole created order may lead to blurring the line between nature and human nature or the dismissing of classical Christianity as "anthropocentrism."[8]

Eschatology is both a corrective to a too simple historicism and a reminder of the historical character of Christian faith. Eschatological Scripture, cosmic in scope, does not diminish the place of human beings in the scheme of things. Indeed, three of the four major motifs have to do with with human destiny and accountability (including our stewardship of creation). The "resurrection of the dead" is the first of these.

A. The Resurrection of the Dead

In the New Testament, the final resurrection is the raising from the dead of all the departed to join the living in the Great Assize. As such, the tradition speaks of a "general resurrection." No one is excluded. "Do not be astonished at this; for the hour is coming when all who are in their graves will hear his voice and will come out" (John 5:28).[9] (See also Matt 24:30-31, 25:31-36; Acts 24:15; 1 Cor 6:2-3, 15:23-24, 51-52; 2 Cor 5:10; Rom. 2:6; 1 Thess 4:1; 2 Thess 1:5-10; Rev 1:7; 20:11-13). Such radical accountability leaves no room for theories that would temper the winds to the shorn sheep (for example, "annihilationism"). Ecumenical eschatology is tough Love.

The resurrection of the dead is the "resurrection of the body" (Apostles Creed). Mid-century biblical studies, and then "neo-orthodox theology," were marked by a polemic against Enlightenment reduction of the Christian hope to "immortality of the soul."[10] Again, the ethical import of eschatology played its part, for a solely spiritual future was criticized as giving support to apolitical pieties and moralities. But the biblical evidence weighed in as decisive, both the psychosomatic nature of persons in biblical anthropology and the New Testament evidence for the fulness of the resurrection hope for believers (1 Cor 15:34-53). While "flesh and blood cannot inherit the kingdom of God" (1 Cor 15:50), corporeal continuity as well as discontinuity is maintained in both Scripture and tradition, with Paul's suggestive phrase "spiritual body" (1 Cor 15:44) being stumbling but suggestive.

A christological hermeneutic will find in Christ's own resurrection the prototype of Christian hope. So Paul himself argues (1 Cor 15:1-11), and so it is elsewhere presupposed that Christ is "the first-born from the dead" (Col 1:18). The continuity-discontinuity suggested by Paul's description is reflected in the risen Christ's ordinary (Matt 28:9; Luke 24:3-43; John 20:24-28; Acts 1:4; 10:4) yet extraordinary (Matt. 28:9; Mark 16:19; Luke 24:31, 36-37, 51, John 20:17, 19) state.

In its eagerness to relate to contemporary questions, eschatology can be tempted to accommodate to cultural interests and premises. Thus current interest in the details of life after death as found in reports of persons revived after clinical demise, New Age scenarios and the eschatologies of religions of the far East may prompt the search for equivalent disclosures from Christian sources. So Fortman infers "four supernatural qualities" from our projected existence as spiritual bodies: "impassability," "splendor," "subtility," and an "agility" of the risen body that would enable the blessed "to move easily from place to place perhaps from planet to planet, from star to star, with the speed of thought. And thus the wide expanse of the universe, the remotest recesses of the starry skies would be accessible to the risen bodies of the blessed."[11] Here Calvin's wise words are in order:

> For though we are truly told that the kingdom of God will be full of light, and gladness and felicity, and glory, yet the things meant by these words remain most remote from sense, and as it were involved in enigma, until the day arrives on which he will manifest his glory to us face to face....The more necessary is it for us to cultivate sobriety in this matter, lest unmindful of our feeble capacity, we presume to take too lofty a flight, and be overwhelmed by the brightness of the celestial glory.[12]

B. The Return of Christ

The "return of Christ" has been a special point of contention in 20th century eschatology. Biblical imagery replete with vertical ascents and descents has been the natural target of Enlightenment critique. Thus premodern portrayals are demythologized, with existential, secular, or "spiritual" substitutions and translations proposed. This has provoked, in turn, sharp rebuttals that have ranked geographic interpretations of the *parousia* as an article on which the Church stands or falls.[13]

Better understandings of biblical genre, and the realization that a fundamental *theological* assertion is being made in the New Testament accounts of Christ's return, have pushed the discussion past modernist-fundamentalist foci.

Thus the prominent creedal declaration, "He will come again. . . ." in the narrative flow of Christian faith means that the crucifixion is not the final historical destiny of Jesus Christ. God has the last Word in the victorious return of Christ to the terrain on which the powers and principalities appeared before to have worked their will. That Word is not only the risen Christ known to the eye of faith, but the *returned* Christ disclosed to the eschatological eye of sight before whom "every knee should bow, in heaven and on earth and under the earth, and every tongue confess that Jesus is Lord, to the glory of God the Father" (Phil 2:10). The doctrinal importance of the second advent is established by the many references to it in the New Testament canon: Matt 24:30; 26:64; Luke 21:27; Acts 1:11; 3: 20-21; 1 Cor 4: 5; 15:23; 2 Cor 1:14; Phil 1:6,;2:16; 3:20; Col 3:4, 1 Thess 1:10; 2:19; 3:13; 4:15-17; 2 Thess 1:7; 1 Tim 4:14, 2 Tim.4:8; Titus 2:13; 1 Peter 1:5-7; 4:4 ,5, 13; 2 Peter 1:16; 3:3-10, 12; Heb 9:28 and Revelation *passim*.

Circling about the core theological affirmation *that* Christ will come again are many of the earlier mentioned "when," "where," and "how" questions. We shall turn to specifics of apocalyptic after surveying the eschatological centralities.

While the resurrection of Christ is the foundation of Christian hope, the return of Christ is its capstone. Here the portent that points to the coming of Shalom is validated and the promise of the reign of God is fulfilled. As such, the energizing power of hope is secured by the *parousia*. The importance of this for both the nurture of the faithful and the mission of the Church cannot be underestimated. Despair paralyzes, but hope mobilizes.[14] This vindicating hope has special bearing on the spiritual estate of victims everywhere. To believe that the powers of this world have met their match in Jesus Christ is to empty them now of their presumed invulnerability. So the wisdom of Karl Barth's counsel to British Christians beset by the Nazi juggernaut.

> For Jesus Christ, according to the teaching of the whole New Testament, has already borne away sin and destroyed death. So also has He already (Col 2:15) completely disarmed those "principalities and powers" and made a spectacle of them in his own triumph in order to finally tread them down under his feet on the day of his coming again (1 Cor. 15:15). We Christians. . . . have no right whatsoever to fear or respect them or resign ourselves to the fact that they are spreading throughout the world as though they knew neither bounds nor lord. . . and if we did not, for Christ's sake, come to grips spiritedly and resolutely with these evil spirits.[15]

Already under our second rubric, we hear anticipations of a third: He shall come again--"to *judge* the quick and the dead."

C. Final Judgment

1. *Accountability and Acceptance*

Talk of judgment comes hard today. "Self-esteem" is orthodoxy and the language of sin is suspect.[16] Classical eschatology collides head-on with the conventional wisdom. All human beings must face ultimate scrutiny before the all-seeing Eye.

Final accountability and the *parousia* are linked in the creeds and confessions of the Church. So the gaze that falls upon us is that of Jesus Christ. "For all of us must appear before the judgment seat of Christ, so that each may receive recompense for what has been done in the body, whether good or evil" (2 Cor 5:10).

In this tribunal the standard is rigorous. We face the bar of Agape. Who can stand before this withering love? Its radiance lays open our lives, for when "the Lord comes (he) will bring to light the things now hidden in darkness. . ." (1 Cor.5:4). Love pours hot coals on our sin.

The One we confront in the light of the final Day is the same we know in the Word incarnate. And that means "God did not send the Son into the world to condemn the world, but in order that the world might be saved through him" (John 3:17). Agape hurts, but it also heals. Jesus Christ is our Advocate as well as our Judge (1 John 2:1). All are found wanting by the light and fire of absolute Love. All are offered forgiveness by its boundlessness. Our works do not save, now or then. All we have, then and now, is faith in the mercy of God—effected and made known in the Work of Christ. Before Christ, here or hereafter, we are saved by grace through faith. "Those who believe in him are not condemned . . . " (John 3:18).

2. *Pluralism and Particularity*

The eschatological news of *solus Christus, sola gratia, sola fide,* as good as it is, brings with it yet other modern quandaries. Contemporary pluralism declares: What arrogance! With our knowledge of the high religions, the awareness of the multitudes who never hear of the presumed Savior, the virtues found in others that exceed the evidences of them in Christian lives, etc., the imperial claims of Christianity must go into the melting. So pluralist proposals abound: 1. The *solas* of Scripture are metaphorical self-defintion, Christian "love-talk" not truth claims, with salvation, here or hereafter, dependent not on Christ but on our commitment to the holy or the good. 2. All are saved through the latter, but each religion makes its noetic contribution to a global faith. 3. All are saved through the latter, with Christianity given the clearest disclosure of the same. 4. All are offered salvation through Christ alone, and can receive it outside the visible Church as "anonymous Christians" through faithfulness to the truth found in their religion or conscience. 5. All are saved through the atoning Work of Christ alone, but must yet be told of the same in Christian mission. And more.[17]

In varying degrees, pluralist perspectives on final judgment qualify or eliminate one or more of three Christian nonnegotiables: the decisive *deed* of God in Christ, the definitive *disclosure* of God in Christ, the singular *deliverance* offered by God through faith in

Christ. Jesus Christ is the *way* God made into the world, the *truth* revealed to it and the *life* shared with it (John 14:6). [18]

As with other theological encounters with culture, eschatology must be prepared to stand against modernity's orthodoxies. However, it must also re-examine its inherited formulations in the light of contextual challenges (as warranted by the catalytic function of "general revelation" in human experience) to see if past cultural assumptions have distorted its witness. In that reappraisal, a case can be made that the "gospel was proclaimed even to the dead" (1 Peter 4:6)—to those who know only the covenant with Noah (1 Peter 3:19-20). In this eschatological encounter with Christ, eternal life is offered through the knowledge of Christ given then to all who did not hear the Word in this life. Prompted by the experience of pluralism in the earliest centuries and since, especially in epochs of missionary outreach, theologians have struggled with these Petrine texts and others with affinities to them (Eph 4: 8-9; John 5:25-29; Matt 8:11; 12:40; Luke 13:28-30; Heb 9:15; Rom 10:7; Rev 21:25), putting forward theories of "second probation," "final decision," etc., that question an older imperialism, but not at the price of the soteriological nonnegotiables. The modern experience of "plural shock," with its proneness to christological heart failure makes this struggle more urgent than ever.[19]

3. *The Sheep and the Goats*

Judgment would seem to entail a "Yes" and a "No." But God's ways are not necessarily our ways, say some in the church debate on the outcome of final adjudication. What are the alternatives?

The majority opinion in Christian history is clearly the belief in a two-fold destination of those who stand before the Judge. "He will separate people one from another as a shepherd separates the sheep from the goats, and he will put the sheep at his right hand and the goats at the left" (Matt. 25:32-33). And there is the echo of this throughout the New Testament (Matt 10:28; Luke 16:19-31; John 3:36; 5:25-29; 2 Thess 1:9; Heb 6:8; 9:27; Rev 14:10-11).

Does "double destination" (and "double predestination") show the marks of the age in which it took form as doctrine? Its correlation with retributive judicial theory and vindictive penal practice certainly suggests just that. What would judgment mean if these culture-relative features of received teaching were to be rejected?

A minority opinion has a ready answer: No one is found wanting. So it is "God our Savior who desires everyone to be saved and to come to the knowledge of the truth" (Titus 2:4). What God wills, God does. In the period when "universalism" came to prominence, the rationale varied: Human nature is sound, not deserving of judgment; God is loving, so the divine nature precludes judgment.

Does the dogma of "single destination" show the marks of the age in which it took shape? Its correlation with the premises of the Enlightenment is striking, both with regard to our presumed virtue and God's indulgence.

A third opinion, harder to state and drawn to paradox, strives to honor the biblical data cited by both of the alternatives, to read it canonically in the light of the sweep of the Scripture's epic, and to relate but not capitulate to the questions and sensibilities of our own time and place. So it is said that judgment as punishment is real and lasting to those who refuse the offer of grace. But in the long story of God's dealings with us, and in a textual strand that reflects that eschatologically (Matt 19:28; John 12:32; Acts 3:21; 1 Cor

3:13-15;15:22-28;Eph 1:9-10; Phil 2:10-11; 1 Tim 2:4; 2 Peter 3:9,13), judgment/punishment is rehabilitative not retributive. The fires of God's love cleanse. The traditional Roman Catholic doctrine of purgatory obscures this biblical motif by inordinate elaboration in schemas of meritorious prayer for the dead and in the limitation of cleansing to those with venial sins. Our third scenario holds that judgment can be purgative for all sinners, lasting but not necessarily everlasting. The "can be" and "not necessarily" integral to this view mean that "rehabilitation" is not an ideology borrowed from this culture (albeit a penal theory fast disappearing in a period of revived retributionism) and announced now as eschatologically definitive. Rather, it represents a modest possibility warranted by the Story's trajectory and some strands of Scripture. Given the ambiguity of the textual material, and the prerogative of Christ, not Christian opinion, to make the *final* judgment, the third, and here preferred, scenario remains an *article of hope,* not an article of faith.[20]

A. Everlasting Life

We use the creed's language for our final theme and interpret it in the light of the drama moving to its conclusion. "Life" as purposed for the world reflects its origins in the triune reality of Life Together. God wills the world to be together with its Creator and within itself. Life is the *koinonia* of all the parties to God's purposes, and death is their separation. The fulfillment of creation, therefore, is a liberation from slavery to the fissiparous powers of sin and evil and thus a reconciliation of an alienated nature, human nature and supernature. As noted earlier, our eschatology both reflects and directs ethical commitments and the life of piety.

The visions of the End in the Apocalypse of John express the fulness of the final reconciliation so we use this book to describe this last stained glass window.

1. *Nature*

"I saw a new heaven and a new earth" (Rev 21:1). A redeemed nature receives first mention in the great chapter that reviews the eschatological manifold. Even the seas are not forgotten (Rev 21:1). The City of God is made of the new earth's finest ornaments—jasper, sapphire, onyx, agate, emerald and pure gold (Rev 21:19-21). And the Redeemer is nature's vulnerable creature, now victorious, the Lamb who takes away the sins of the world (Rev 21:9, 14, 23, 27).

The chapter that follows begins also with the revivification of nature. From the very throne of God flows "the river of the water of life" (Rev 22:1). And the "tree of life" flowers on either side of the river "with its twelve kinds of fruits" (Rev 22:2). Indeed, a reconciled nature is integral to the redemption of history, for "the leaves of the trees are for the healing of the nations" (Rev. 22:2).

Nature comes into its own as a creation destined to give glory to its Creator. No longer groaning in travail (Rom 8:22), it now sings its Maker's praises: "I heard every creature in heaven and on earth and under the earth and in the sea, and all that is in them, singing with full voice, To the one seated on the throne and to the Lamb be blessing and honor and glory and might forever and ever! And the four living creatures said Amen!" (Rev 5:13-14). So the rift between nature and God, as well as the alienations within its own being, is put behind.

Revelation's portrayal of nature's glorification continues and completes the prophetic vision of nature's true End. So the eschatological healing of nature's fractures are anticipated in the Isaianic corpus:

1) The separations within nature are ended—"the wolf shall live with the lamb, the leopard shall lie down with the kid. . . " (Isa 11:6).

2) The enmity between nature and humans is overcome—"the nursing child shall play over the hole of the asp, the weaned child shall put its hand in the adder's den" (Isa 11:8).

3) The alienation between nature and God is gone—"the mountains and the hills before you shall burst into song, and all the trees of the field shall clap their hands. Instead of the thorn shall come up the cypress; instead of the brier shall come up the myrtle . . ." (Isa 55:12-13).

At mid-point between prophetic forecast and apocalyptic climax, the incarnate Word embodies and teaches the restoration of nature's brokenness. Thus the healing ministry of Jesus demonstrates the firstfruits of a new creation, for "Jesus went about. . . curing every disease and every sickness" (Matt 9:35). In his teaching ministry, Christ points to God's gracious clothing of the natural world, while at the same time placing nature below humanity in the ordering of creation (Matt 6:28-30). And in the physical resurrection of Christ the natural contingency of human life is given its full due.

The biblical characterization of the End has to do with the *telos* as well as *finis* of creation; believers in that purpose will understand their vocation as the ennoblement in kind of the created order. An ecological ethic, therefore, is inseparable from eschatological vision. The perils to the environment now entering too tardily into our consciousness make us alert to aspects of eschatology formerly neglected, and with it the ecological imperative. Passion for the rehabiliation of our streams and skies and the respect for "all creatures great and small," constitute a morality that cannot sustain itself without the partnership of a Franciscan piety that keeps company with brother sun and sister moon.

2. *Human Nature*

Our irregular juxtaposition of "human nature" and "nature" is calculated to underscore the inextricability of human beings and the natural order. "We are bodies," as Feuerbach was at pains to point out . But we "do not live by bread alone," an anthropological fact lost upon materialisms, historical or otherwise. Eschatology links humanity with the rest of creation in its assertion of the resurrection of the body. But "everlasting life" has to do as well with the fulfillment of the *imago Dei* as well as human creatureliness—and both in all their ramifications. To this human fulness of life we now turn, again with issues of morality and piety in mind.

a. Personal Life Everlasting

"Blessed are the pure in heart, for they shall see God" (Matt 5:8). Christian hope for the individual is the healing of the ruptured relationship with God. Separation of the self from God is death, existence in the night of sin. The new unity with God, is life eternal, living in the Day and thus "seeing the Light." A long Christian tradition has described this new sight as the *visio Dei*.

John employs the same light and sight imagery in describing the beatific vision: "At once I was in the spirit, and there in heaven stood a throne, with one seated on the throne! And the one seated there looks like jasper and carnelian, and around the throne is a rainbow that looks like emerald . . . . Then I saw . . . .Then I saw . . . . Then I looked . . . . Then I saw . . . . " (Rev 4: 2-3; Rev. 5:1, 6, 11; 6:1). So we read of the unveiling (*apokalypsis*) of mysteries of the believer's life with God, when "his servants will worship him; they will see his face, and his name will be upon their foreheads. And there will be no more night; they need no light of lamp or sun, for the Lord God will be their light, and they will reign forever and ever" (Rev 22: 3-5).

The sanctity of individual life in the here and now is confirmed by this luminescence. And a spirituality that lives by this love and faith sees "in a mirror dimly" in the hope of seeing God "face to face" (1 Cor 13:12).

b. Corporate Life Everlasting

To see in the Light is to see *by* the Light. Vertical and horizontal relationships are inseparable. The radiance of God opens our eyes to the others who surround the throne: "The nations will walk by its light, and the kings of the earth will bring their glory into it" (Rev 21:24). The metaphors of human life together include the interpersonal but go beyond it to describe the unity-to-be in transpersonal, structural terms as well. Political, social, and economic powers are no more estranged from and invisible to one another. Nations and regents become agents of reconciliation instead of instruments of alienation.

A controlling image of a world redeemed is that of a new city. The seer is shown "the holy city Jerusalem coming down out of heaven from God. It has the glory of God and a radiance like a very rare jewel, like jasper, clear as crystal" (Rev 21:10-11). The urban imagery of Revelation is matched by the political figures of the new realm—kingdom, commonwealth, country found throughout Scripture. So that no etherealizaion happens to this ultimate hope Jesus himself prays for the coming of this rule of God "on earth as it is in heaven" (Matt 6:10).

The continuity of apocalypse and prophecy is apparent once again. In the arrival of the new realm of righteousness, peace and freedom are heard echoes of the beating of swords into plowshares and spears into pruning hooks. And reflections are to be seen as well in this renovated commonwealth of the end of oppression and the fall of the mighty. Shalom shall be!

A social ethic with egalitarian mandates is the natural partner of such an eschatological vision. Finally both are grounded in the trinitarian Life Together whose co-equal Persons will for the world the Shalom God is.

3 *Supernature*

We have already met the outcropping of the Powers and Principalities as they make themselves known in the orders and institutions of history, and as they also move ineluctably toward the final liberation from bondage to sin.[21] But the thrones and authorities of this world are not reducible to their empirical manifestations. Shrouded in the mystery of their special workings, the elemental spirits of the universe, the angels, archangels and rulers of the air were made to be messengers of God and servants of Christ. So it shall be in the *eschaton*, however much these powers also shared in the world's rebellion and fall. Indeed, their resistance continues to the very end, for "war broke out in heaven" and "the dragon and his angels fought back" (Rev 12:7). But the outcome is assured and "they were defeated, and there was no longer any place for them in heaven" (Rev 12:8).

In the End the angels too gather around the throne of God. In the vision of John they "fell on their faces before the throne and worshiped God, singing 'Amen! Blessing and glory and wisdom and thanksgiving and honor and power and might be to our God forever and ever! Amen' " (Rev 7:11-12). And they live out their calling, messengers of the consummation itself with the Word, "Come gather for the great supper of God"! (Rev 19:17).

In a world like ours, too ready to believe in the hegemony of astral forces, the threat of demonic and satanic powers, the sway of the goddess Fortuna and the ranging about of sundry other rulers of the nether world, eschatology is the good news that Christ has already disarmed these presumed authorities "in order finally to tread them down under his feet on the day of His coming again (1 Cor15:15)."[22] Here eschatological piety frees the believer from the widespread anxieties over the unknown, with its confidence that the future belongs to the powers of Life not death.

As Moltmann has helped us to see, every eschatological indicative has its corresponding ethical imperative. The visions of the End make us restless with the status quo.[23] "Amen. Come, Lord Jesus!" (Rev 22:20).

III. APOCALYPTIC

The prophetic-apocalyptic tandem in Old Testament context identifies the latter as the supramundane end of eschatology. In that sense, we have already dealt extensively with apocalyptic in our four motifs of the ultimate future. And in exploring the ethical imperatives associated with these ultimacies, we have touched regularly on areas of prophetic and terrestrial hope. In this section, we examine apocalyptic in its narrower meaning. As such, it has to do with the *immediacy* of trans-historical expectation and the *intricacy* of its disclosure. As noted earlier, apocalyptic eschatology is interpretation of the ultimate future that focuses on a series of subsidiary questions: the detailed "when" of its immediacy, and the elaborate "who," "how," and "where" of its intricacies. Apocalpytic seers furnish us, accordingly, with a *timetable, playbill, chart,* and *map* of Things to Come.

The most vigorous apocalyptic readings of eschatology with which systematic theology has dealt, is an imminent premillennialism. With advocates as early as the second century, and appearing from time to time throughout Christian history, [24] it has today a vocal and volatile following.[25] Best-known because of its television, radio and Christian bookstore clientele are the pre-tribulational premillennialists, although post-tribulational premillennialism has a zealous following along with its firm criticism and even "exposures" of "pre-trib" proposals. [26] All proponents of apocalyptic eschatology can find stretches of Scripture to support their claims. We examine briefly one version of pre-tribulational premillennialism using its characteristic genre, a "Destiny Chart."[27]

"Bible Prophecy" begins its visualization of the End in 1948 with the return of the Jews to their homeland and the establishment of the state of Israel (Matt 3:12). In the ensuing years, "the beginning of sorrows," the informed interpreter follows the news of the Middle East, Europe and elsewhere, the "ten nations" that begin to unite, the rise of secular humanism, the coming of natural disasters, etc. (Mark 13:4-13; Rev 17:12-13). As the days darken, the believer prepares for the Rapture, the occasion of Christ's initial return *for* his church, gathering them "in the air" to secure them in heaven against the coming times of anguish (1 Cor 15:51-53). Then the seven year drama of the Great Tribulation unfolds, with the revelation of the Antichrist, the conversion of many Jews, the beast-king's guarantee of Israel's security and the occurance of World War III with Arab-Russian onslaught against Israel and nuclear holocaust (Rev 6:2; 13:1,;17:3). At the Tribulation's midpoint, believers martyred ascend to Christ, then Satan is cast out of heaven, indwells the slain Antichrist and slays the saints still left and the 144,000 Jewish witnesses (Rev 12:7-9, 13:3,7; 14:1-4). Following these and other untoward events, the Tribulation ends with the return of Christ *with* his saints to wage the final battle of Armageddon and Satan cast into the bottomless pit and the beast and false prophets thrown into the lake of fire (Rev 19:11-21; 20:1-2). So comes a thousand years of "righteous rule" with peace and plenty. In this time the saints will repopulate the earth, Israel will receive back its land, a purified temple worship will be restored and Christ will rule the world from David's throne in Jerusalem (Rev 20 :1-6). At the end of the millennium, Satan returns, a final insurrection takes place and is turned back with Satan cast permanently into the lake of fire (Rev 20: 7-10). The judgment throne of Christ is set up and unbelievers are sent to the lake of fire (Rev 20:11-15). The old earth and heaven are then destroyed, a new Jerusalem appears on a new earth and heaven and the saints dwell in blessedness with Christ for eternity (Rev 21-22).

Apocalyptic invites controversy among its adherents as well as with its amillennial and postmillennial foes. [28] A major division within its ranks is that between the dispensationalism of the Scofield Bible and "historic premillennialism" with its diminished Jewish nationalism and post-tribulation framework. Our Destiny Chart is a dispensationalist variant.

"Pre-trib" "pre-mil" apocalyptic, theologically considered, (much assessment from outside its ranks is psychological and sociological—a haven for the fearful, opiate of the masses, etc.),[29] evidences both strengths and weaknesses. On the plus side, it takes seriously the apocalyptic literature in the two Testaments, especially Daniel and Revelation, attempting to find some contemporary Word in them. And it does so in the spirit of high drama that marks the Christian story, providing a framework for interpreting events and giving a "theology of hope" to the hopeless. Further, the *political* apocalypticism of the Christian Right propels its advocates into the public arena with a level of commitment that puts conventional Church activists to shame.

Whatever the theological merits of contemporary apocalyptic, it must finally be judged wanting. Its hermeneutic excludes both canonical and critical components.[30] In the former case, it does not weigh the meaning and role of apocalyptic texts in the light of the full canon, its center and substance in Jesus Christ and the Gospel, and the Bible's pervasive eschatological modesty (1 Thess 5:1-2; Acts 1:7; Matt 24:36; Mark 13:32). Fifteen verses in a figural book (Revelation 20) interpreted grammatical-historically on their own terms are not sufficient warrant for a major Christian doctrine. In the latter case, contemporary apocalyptic is innocent of the historical circumstances and literary genre necessary to decipher textual intent. Ironically, Armageddon eschatology allows the experience of modernity—contemporary political commitments and discernments, with their psycholgical and sociological propellants—to control the reading of Scripture, a secular humanism that is the very foe against which it struggles. Furthermore, when the radical polarities that mark apocalyptic are translated into political programs they encourage a

Manichaean reading of that order, juxtaposing the armies of night and the legions of light, with attendant self-righteous fury, and lack of personal and institutional self-criticism.[31]

A theological rather than geographic reading of apocalyptic can honor its intent by seeing in its rich imagery themes that cohere with the Story:

1) The millennium is a symbol of the confidence that approximations of the goal of Shalom are historical possibilities.

2) The Antichrist is a reminder that evil continues until the end of time, and thus theories of automatic progress and utopian expectation are illusory.

3) The Christian understanding of history is a drama with a plot that proceeds over time and place through conflict to resolution.

4) The purposes of God are cosmic in scope including nature, humanity and supernature.

5) Israel has a special place in the divine plan, its covenant not being abrogated with the coming of Christ.[32]

6) Hope energizes and eschatological hope has political impetus and implications.

IV. THE PENULTIMATE FUTURE

The End began with the coming of the Kingdom in the life, death and resurrection of Jesus Christ. The New Testament paradox of the Already-Not Yet means that Christian hope is focussed between the times as well as beyond them. This "pareschatology" fills the whole horizon, promising signs of the consummation in next-to-last things *within* history and after death.[33] We shall explore the penultimate future under these two headings.

A. Historical Expectation

The inauguration of the Realm of God in the Person and Work of Christ brings with it anticipations of the Eschaton. Treated systematically, the eschatological signs correspond to the four great visions of the End. Thus

1) "life"—eternal life—begins now, a refrain of the Johannine literature. Wherever true life—personal, social, cosmic—manifests itself, there the Future is at work.

2) While the public rule of Christ awaits the consummation (the "return of Christ"), Christ reigns even now, the source of new life in all its expressions.

3) The tribunal of Christ at the last Day pre-exists in the judgment rendered now by the Lord of history.

4) The bodiliness that marks the resurrection fulfillment of God's purposes for us, has its earnest in the divine care for the earthy underside of human existence.

At this point the Old Testament tradition of "prophetic eschatology" makes its greatest contribution to systematic inquiry. Already it has been functioning tacitly in the discernment of ethical imperatives and historical implications present in the four motifs of the ultimate future. Marcionite readings of these themes have been a constant temptation in traditional eschatology, but are corrected by a canonical hermeneutic with its crucial prophetic tradition. But here in the specific attention given to historical hope, the implicit becomes explicit. Not to be ignored in this appropriation of prophetic eschatology is the catalysis of twentieth century experience and its consequences in the earlier social gospel movement and in current liberation and political theologies.

An indication of the prophetic legacy within the church's eschatology can be seen in its lections. We use as our framework its advent readings, trifocular in nature dealing with the longing for Christ's first and second coming, but also for his appearance and power in the bringing of righteousness, peace and justice in our historical future.[34]

At every point in the Isaianic writings, the coming of historical shalom is promised. The eighth century poet-seer points to the time when "they shall beat their swords into plowshares and their spears into pruning hooks; nation shall not lift up sword against nation, neither shall they learn war any more" (Isa 2:4). Hope means expectation of a ruler who "with righteousness. . . shall judge the poor, and decide with equity for the meek of the earth . . ." (Isa 11:4). The refrain continues in the "Babylonian Isaiah" called to speak a tender word to those in exile: "Cry to her that she has served her term . . . The glory of the Lord shall be revealed, and the people shall see it together . . ." (Isa 40:2, 5). And the Isaiah heritage persists into the period of the rebuilt Temple with a priestly Israel called "to bring good news to the oppressed, to proclaim liberty to the captives, and release to the prisoners" (Isa 61:1). Throughout, life in the world to come means an intra-historical expectation and imperative, with *bodies* fed, clothed and freed from prison and war, a prophetic hope integral to Christian preaching and teaching.

The prophet lost no time in calling to account those who brought hunger and captivity, the mighty who lived by the sword and spear. *Judgment* resounds in the lectionary readings: "He shall judge between the nations, and arbitrate for many peoples . . . . " (Isa 2:4). And that judgment entails accountability for the unjust: "He will come with vengeance, with terrible recompense . . . . the haunt of jackals shall become a swamp . . . . " (Isa 35:4,7). Along with the good news to the oppressed comes the bad news of "the day of vengeance of our God" (Isa 61:2).

Life in prophetic eschatology includes the renewal of nature as well as history. Thus the lections remind us that "the wolf shall live with the lamb, the leopard shall lie down with the kid" (Isa 11:6) and "the wilderness and the dry land shall be glad, the desert shall rejoice and blossom. . . ." (Isa 35:1) The expected restoration of nature includes its harmony with humanity for "the nursing child shall play over the hole of the asp . . . . " (Isa 11:8).

While we have drawn only on Isaiah lections, their companion prophetic texts sound the same notes: So Jer. 33:14: "I will cause a righteous Branch to spring up for David; and he shall execute justice and righteousness in the land." And Zeph 3: 15: "The king of Israel, the Lord is in your midst; you shall fear disaster no more." And Malachi 3:2: "But who can endure the day of his coming, and who can stand when he appears? For he is like a refiner's fire and like fullers' soap." And Micah 4:3-4: "Nation shall not lift up sword against nation, neither shall they learn war anymore, but they shall sit under their own vine and fig trees, and no one shall make them afraid."

The use of these stretches of prophetic eschatology in the Advent season in conjunction with New Testament readings, of course, implies a Christological interpretation of Old Testament hopes. So the Lukan context of Isaiah 61 with Jesus' declaration: "Today this scripture has been fulfilled in your hearing" (Luke 4:21). But the development of lectionary readings since the inception of the Advent season in the sixth century indicate the adding of the second to first advent interpretation (not the replacement one by the other), and their further widening to the promises of glory in the historical future—our triple lens. Yet Christian eyes do read the prophetic hopes for history as under the aegis of Christ. As the Lord of history, he hurls the mighty from their seats and exalts those of low degree, releases the captive, brings justice and makes peace. He *is* our Shalom. Hence the fourth eschatological theme also finds its place in historical expectation: the present regency of Christ anticipatory of his return.

Prophetic eschatology roots Christian hope firmly in history. All the political, social and economic implications of "apocalyptic eschatology," both broadly and narrowly understood, are explicitly stated in this aspect of penultimacy. Ahistorical eschatologies, both within and without the church, are thus called into question. Christian hope mobilizes believers for action in history to participate in those portents of Shalom that Christ the Prophet—as well as Priest and King—brings to be among us.

Historical hope is personal as well as corporate. Classical theology customarily explores it under the topic of subjective soteriology. "Sanctification" in the *ordo salutis* is, in fact, a form of this-worldly expectation, and thus an aspect of the penultimate future. We note it in passing, having given primary attention to the corporate themes in the prophetic tradition. In our final section, however, we do return to the individual dimension of eschatology.

Prophetic eschatology makes its telling contribution to this doctrine, but standing alone it does less than justice to the Christian canon. A full understanding of eschatology situates its themes between the four visions of the ultimate future and the pareschatological expectation of life after death.

3. Post-Mortem Hope

We come lastly to what may be the culture's first interest in the End, either by its attraction to imports from the far East, or by a secular rebuff of the same. Do we cease to be? Or make our transmigratory way through many lives to final peace? Or . . . ? And popular Christianity has its reponse in kind with talk of a soul that makes its eternal flight to God after the body's last breath.

Speculative eschatology eager to connect with New Age interests and pluralist spiritualities incorporates reincarnation themes and "bardo world" theories.[35] Others seeking to be faithful to a unitive biblical anthropology disavow soul separations, deny the "intermediate state" and defend "soul sleep" or immediate death-into-the-End hypotheses.[36]

A systematic statement about the death state will be in harmony with other eschatological affirmations. Two themes earlier developed have special bearing: 1) The fundamental orientation of all Christian hope, including penultimate expectations, to the ultimate future--resurrection, return, judgment, everlasting life. 2) The encounter with Christ integral to soteriology. As the meager New Testament evidence about the "how" of post-mortem reality is ambiguous (for example, the "awake texts--Luke 16:19-31, 23:43; Rev 6:9, and the "asleep texts"—Luke 8:52; 1 Cor 15:20; 2 Peter 3:4), theological coherence becomes a critical test. We shall pursue these two lines in search of it.

a. Christian Hope

As anticipations of the four visions of the End are found in our historical journey, so we look for them in the interim state also. Everlasting life is not reserved for the eschatological finale but begins for the believer in this world. So the witness of John to "eternal life" (John 3:36; 5:24; 6:40). And with it, Paul's confidence that nothing "will be able to separate us from the love of God in Christ Jesus our Lord" (Rom 8:38). Whatever transpires between our death and Last Things, the bond is unbreakable.

But more can be said about the tie that binds. If the resurrection of the body is in the picture of historical hope, can it be excised from the trans-historical hope of the death state? As the bodies God wills to be made whole in this world are the anticipations of their final state, the same is true of any interim embodiment. It is murky what this might mean, given the dust to which we return. Yet "this mortal body puts on immortality" (1 Cor 15:53). The earnest of the End seems to signify that at death "this perishable body puts on imperishability" (1 Cor 15:53).

Our forebears, less self-conscious about the invasion of Greek categories, were content to speak of the soul separating from the body in the intermediate state.[37] But the biblical "soul" is not some invisible entity we "have," as in all dualisms, but something we *are*. An individual as soul is a person-in-relation-to-God. In that sense, we do "have" a soul—a relationship to God, singular to each of us. That unique bond is not severed by death, so it is proper to speak of the soul continuing after the body dies. But that immortal soul is not removed from the mortal body for that body has now "put on immortality" on its way to fulfillment. We are on the grounds of theological inference, to be walked upon with proper hesitation.

Judgment too is not confined to the End. In history we know it, and beyond the grave we face it (Heb 9:27). These are provisional judgments, portents of the Final Assize.

As the return is foreshadowed by Christ's regency in life, so that rule extends beyond death's doors. We meet our Lord at our departure. But this fourth theme is better addressed in our final attempt at systematic inference.

1. *Encounter with Christ*

Jesus Christ is the Hound of Heaven. Like the woman's quest for the lost coin, Christ's pursuit is implacable (Lk 15: 8-10). We have spoken of his search beyond death for those who have not known him in life (1 Peter 3:19; 4:6). And his fiery love that cleanses, purifies in eternity as well as time, is a Christian hope (1 Cor 3:15). Just so, the return of Christ is anticipated by his presence in the place of the dead as it pre-exists in portent in the Easter illumined world. Nothing can stand between us and Jesus Christ, "neither death, nor life . . . nor things present, nor things to come . . . " (Rom 8:38).

As with apocalyptic, so with the post-mortem world, our commentary has been reserved about "how," "when," and "where" questons. *That* we shall have to do with Christ, resurrection, judgment and everlasting life in their firstfruits is the Word we hear spoken. The rest is a whisper.

V. CONCLUSION

The contribution of systematics to eschatology is its effort to discern the patterns of Christian hope in Scripture and tradition, and to provide therein resources for teaching and preaching in a given time and place. Its gift is also its peril. Systematic theology is regularly tempted to find order where there is none and to take texts hostage to its schemes. Mea culpa. That's why the systematician needs the biblical scholar, and why the best theology is done in community. May the conversation go forward, "as each part . . . working properly, promotes the body's growth in building itself up in love" (Eph 4:16).

NOTES

1. Edmund Fortman, *Everlasting Life After Death.* (New York: Alba House, 1976) *passim.*; Dale Moody, *The Word of Truth* (Grand Rapids: Eerdmans, 1981) 481-594.

2. As in Gerhard von Rad, *Old Testament Theology,* vol 2: *The Theology of Israel's Prophetic Traditions.,* trans by M. G. Stalker (New York: Harper & Row, 1965) 301-308. On the issue of usage, see also "Eschatology," *Eerdmans' Bible Dictionary.*(Grand Rapids: Eerdmans , 1987) 347-349.

3. C. Hodge, *Systematic Theology,* vol. III (New York: Scribner, Armstrong, and Co., 1874) 713-880; Augustus Hopkins Strong, *Systematic Theology: A Compendium* (New York: Fleming H. Revell , 1907) 981-1056.

4. So C. Braaten's *The Future of God* (New York: Harper & Row, 1969). Behind much contemporary stretching of the horizons is Jürgen Moltmann's *Theology of Hope.,* trans. by J. Leitch. (New York: Harper & Row, 1967) and Gustavo Gutierrez, *A Theology of Liberation.,* trans. and ed. by C. Inda and J. Eagleson (Maryknoll ,N.Y.: Orbis, 1971)

5. As in H. Heppe, *Reformed Dogmatics.,* rev. and ed. by E Bizer, trans. by G. T. Thompson, foreword by Karl Barth (Grand Rapids: Baker Book House, 1978) 697f.

6. The refrain of James Luther Adams' presidential address to the American Theological Society, 1974.

7. A World Council of Churches theme in its Canberra assembly, 1991.

8. A case in point being James Carpenter's *Nature and Grace.* (NewYork: Crossroad, 1988) *passim.*

9. All biblical quotations are from *The Holy Bible*: New Revised Standard Version (New York: Oxford University Press, 1989).

10. In this connection see O Cullmann's well-known work, *Immortality of the Soul or Resurrection of the Dead?* (New York: Macmillan , 1958).

11. Fortman, *Everlasting Life* , 249.

12. John Calvin, *Institutes of the Christian Religion,* vol. 2, trans. by Henry Beveridge (Grand Rapids: Eerdmans Publishing Co., 1957) 273-274.

13. As in the volumes on *The Fundamentals,* 1909-1915.

14. So J. Moltmann, *passim.*

15. Karl Barth, *A Letter to Great Britain from Switzerland.* (London: Sheldon Press, 1941) 10.

16. See K. Menninger, *Whatever Became of Sin*? (New York: Hawthorn Books, 1973).

17. The various options are reviewed in the author's *The Christian Story,* vol. 2, *Authority: Scripture in the Church for the World.* (Grand Rapids: Eerdmans 1987) 306-316.

18. Ibid., 254-340.

19. Ibid., 286-296. For a discussion of this issue in contemporary theology, see John Macquarrie, *Christian Hope.* (New York: Seabury, 1978) 121-127 and Russell Aldwinckle, *Death in the Secular City* (Grand Rapids: Eerdmans P 1974) 136-143. On the idea of "final decision," held by an increasing number of Roman Catholic theologians, see Fortman, *Everlasting Life* 78-87,

20. Karl Barth's view as set forth in *Church Dogmatics,* IV, 3, First Half, trans. and ed. by G. W. Bromiley and T. F. Torrance (Edinburgh: T.& T. Clark, 1961) 477-478.

21. For a searching exploration of the empirical underside of "powers and principalities" see Walter Wink, *Naming the Powers,* vol 1, (Philadelphia: Fortress Press, 1984) and *Unmasking the*

Powers, vol. 2, (Philadelphia: Fortress Press).

22. Barth, *A Letter to Great Britain from Switzerland*, 10.

23. As in Jürgen Moltmann's various eschatological works: *Theology of Hope*, *The Experiment Hope*, trans. and ed. with foreword by M. D. Meeks (Philadelphia: Fortress Press, 1975), *Religion, Revolution and the Future* , trans. by M. D Meeks (New York: Charles Scribners' Sons, 1969), *The Future of Creation.*, trans. by M. Kohl (Philadelphia: Fortress Press, 1979).

24. For a review of the same see B. Hebblethwaite, *The Christian Hope* (Grand Rapids: Eerdmans 1984) 43-198.

25. In addition to Hal Lindsey's best-selling work, *The Late Great Planet Earth*, see *There's a New World Coming: "A Prophetic Odyssey"* (Santa Ana, Cal.: Vision House Publishers, 1973). For a sample of TV evangelist (and political fundamentalist) eschatology, see Pat Roberston, *Answer to 200 of Life's most Probing Questions* (Nashville: Thomas Nelson Publishers, 1984) 151-164 and *passim.*

26. D. MacPherson's *The Great Rapture Hoax* (New Puritan Library, 1983) is an attack on pre-tribulational theories, tracing the origins of John Nelson Darby's thought on the rapture to the 1830 "revelations" of one Margaret Macdonald in Scotland. A major defense of "pre-tribulation rapturism" and associated theories of the tribulation, see J. D Pentecost, *Things to Come* (Grand Rapids: Zondervan, 1967) 193-369.

27. Charles R. Taylor, *The Destiny Chart* (Cypress, Cal.: Today in Bible Prophecy, 1978).

28. M.. Erickson reviews the alternatives in *Contemporary Options in Eschatology: A Study of the Millennium* (Grand Rapids: Baker Book House, 1977). An illuminating exchange among advocates of four different millennial views appears in the Christianity Today Institute's essay, "Our future Hope: Eschatology and its Role in the Church," *Christianity Today* (February 6, 1987) 1- I- 12- I.

29. Robert Jay Lifton and Charles B. Strozier, "Waiting for Armaged" in *The New York Times Book Review* (August 12, 1990) 1, 24-25 is typical of secular psycho-social analysis, and is innocent of the distinctions among evangelicals and of the divisions within millennial camps.

30. See Fackre, *The Christian Story*, vol. 2, op. cit., 157-253 for a view of the common, critical, canonical and contextual senses of Scripture.

31. A criticism developed by the writer in *The Religious Right and Christian Faith.*(Grand Rapids: Eerdmans , 1982) *passim.*

32. See the volume on recent church statements on the relation of Christian faith to Judaism, particularly their "anti-supersessionist" direction, World Council of Churches, *The Theology of the Churches and the Jewish People* (Geneva: WCC Publications, 1988).

33. The word is introduced by John Hick in his wide-ranging survey of the views of world religions on life after death, and his attempt (ill-conceived, in the writer's view) to state a "global theology" of pareschatology/eschatology. See *Death and Eternal Life* (New York: Harper & Row, 1976) 22-23.

34. The material that follows summarizes research done for exegesis of Advent texts in "Vision of Shalom and Hope of Glory," in Dieter Hessel, editor, *Social Themes of the Christian Year: A Commentary on the Lectionary* (Philadelphia: The Geneva Press, 1983) 32-39.

35. So Hick, 400-404.

36. Hans Schwarz argues that "Regardless of when we cross this line we will appear on 'the other side' at the 'same moment' as everyone else." *On the Way to the Future*, Revised Edition (Minneapolis: Augsburg Publishing House, 1979) 233. Werner Elert holds that before the End the one who dies is "in the eternal memory of God, who will not forget him on the Last Day." *Last Things*, trans. by M. Bertram, ed. by R. F. Nordern (St. Louis: Concordia Publishing House, 1974) 42.

37. Heppe, *Reformed Dogmatics*, 695-696.

Professors of Biblical Theology

Have you considered using the issues of EX AUDITU as basic resources for your Seminars in Biblical Theology?

EX AUDITU Vol. 1 (1985) consists of selected articles presenting the issues inherent in the theological interpretation of Scripture.

EX AUDITU Vol. 2 (1986) discusses the theme: "Church and State Relationship." In addition there are two lead articles, one by Peter Stuhlmacher on "EX AUDITU and the Theological Interpretation of Holy Scripture," and the second by Ben F. Meyer on "The Primacy of Consent and the Uses of Suspicion."

EX AUDITU Vol. 3 (1987). The theme is: "Creation."

EX AUDITU Vol. 4 (1988). The theme is: "The Church and Israel (Romans 9-11)."

EX AUDITU Vol. 5 (1989). The theme is: "What is Salvation?"

EX AUDITU Vol. 6 (1990). The theme is: "Prophetic and/or Apocalyptic Eschatology."

EX AUDITU Vol. 7 (1991) to be published in the Spring of 1992 will be on the theme: "Christology and Incarnation."

Ten copies or more may be purchasedfor $10.00 per copy from:

Pickwick Publications
4137 Timberlane Drive
Allison Park, PA 15101-2932

ETHICS AND ESCHATOLOGY

JOHN H. YODER

"Ethics" is not an independent mode of access to the understanding of either ancient documents or ancient ideas; it is rather one subdiscipline of theology. It has to be constructed on the foundations laid by the community's prior history. In the mix of the disciplines it needs to listen to those other specialists who read texts in their settings. For that reason preparing this text prior to the North Park event was somewhat anomalous; I shall take the liberty to add references from the symposium to the definitive text.

We have been working intensively these days at the challenges of genre analysis, considering "prophecy," "apocalypse" and "eschatology" as each describing a kind of literature or a kind of world view. A large literature, much of it written by colleagues present in this meeting, has been pursuing those themes, often seeking to adjudicate which is prior to the others or which is the broader. I expressly prescind from offering an answer of my own to those questions, and of course I must proceed without adjudicating even for myself the issues that literature presents, and in ignorance of the progress which this symposium might have made toward some agreed readings. I must therefore be resigned to a very coarse formulation of the hermeneutic issues posed to us by the witness of these strange and distant voices. Within these limits, rather than assuming that apocalyptic is a subset of prophecy, or vice versa, I shall use the still coarser metaphor of "vision" to group the testimonies I am attempting to honor.

In terms of the sociology of knowledge, the role of "scriptures" is to bring to bear on the present the identity-bearing resources which a community brings from its prior story. Canonical Scripture, or any other kind of normative appeal from outside one's own setting, can challenge the self-evident quality of our present world. A text from another time, especially one which summons our attention by its differentness, inserts into our present setting a fulcrum capable of being leaned on to pry us away from the assumption that the world as we see it is the only way it can be.

Instead of asking as we usually do what problems are posed for us by the way the world, as it is assumed by the ancient literature to be, differs from ours, I therefore suggest that we try turning the question around. After all, they were here first. It is we who claim to be their heirs, not the other way 'round.

To discern what apocalypse does for us—perhaps also with regard to worship, or ecclesiology, or soteriology, but at least with regard to ethics[1]—we need therefore to center our attention not on the immediate sense of distance with which particular assumptions of moral relevance strike us, as for instance the rewarding of continence in Revelation 14 or the judgment on merchants in chapter 18. We should ask rather about the over-all cosmological and eschatological frame of reference within which value judgments occur. My role in this symposium is not the advocacy of specific moral choices, nor the elaboration of a basis for moral guidance as a part of catechesis or pastoral care.[2] I speak here of ethics as the architectonics of moral choice,[3] concerned less with what we should decide and do than with how we think about deciding and doing. I should attend more to dissimilarity than to resonance; more to what is hard for us moderns to appropriate empathetically than to what seems self-evidently clear to us.

Many of the sub-disciplines which aid us in interpreting the Scriptures may, when taken in isolation, fall short of aiding the texts to discharge that function. One instance, which enormously preoccupied generations of scholars, especially protestants, was the debate of high scholasticism about the unique epistemological status of "Scripture" as a kind of propositions different from other propositions because of their having been written uniquely under "inspiration." From this were derived further fruitless debates about "inerrancy" or "infallibility," just as fruitless as the related Roman Catholic handling of the authority of the episcopal and papal magisterium.

It begins to seem that fine-grained discussions about genre are beginning in a similar way to spin off, beyond their contribution to the utility of texts to edify the church, into becoming a discipline which runs on for its own sake.[4] In any case *my* task cannot be to review here the differences between apocalypse and prophecy, as if getting each text in the proper generic slot[5] were prerequisite to its speaking to us. For most of my present purposes, the challenges they raise are the same. For that reason I shall group them all as "seers."

My procedure shall then be to seek to note some of the major ways in which the ancient seers' world differed from ours, in order to discern which of those can yield usable leverage capable of contributing moral insight to believers in our age. The inventory cannot be thorough; I shall seek to name a few of the most weighty differences.

I. POWER AND CAUSATION

Our modern (or post-modern) world view differs from that of the first-century seers in that we take for granted a deterministic, even mechanistic vision of human affairs. From the micro level where DNA analysis explains more and more of who we are, to the macro level where statistics on resource depletion and global warming describe changes which no one can control, we assume our universe to be one massive causal nexus with no loopholes.

In the middle range between the molecules and the greenhouse effect, we do still speak meaningfully of human agency, but the psychological and social sciences which deal with those activities are no less deterministic. That is what they mean by being called sciences.[6] They make no new room for "freedom" or for "God."

The simple word for one of the philosophical problems this poses is "divine agency." The ancient seers—no less than the historians and the sages, the folklorists and the kings[7]—assumed that God or the gods act in the same world where men and women do, and in ways that are analogous to the ways men and women act, only bigger.

When Isaiah, extrapolating from the experience of JWHW war, called on the king to eschew military alliances, it was because God would protect Israel in other ways, as their national historical memory told them. When prophets from Jeremiah onward called world Jewry to adjust to the end of (what our age calls) statehood in favor of nationhood in disaspora, the reason was that God would guide them in that new mission and sometimes enable them to prosper. In that setting, under those assumptions, "expect a miracle; you need not do it, because JHWH will" was a rational moral argument

It is by no means the case that the modern cultural problematic of "divine agency" obtains *only* in the field of ethics. The credibility of god language is no greater in the realms of conversion, prayer, sacrament or doxology. Yet it is in the field of ethics, singularly, that it will make a difference in the historical process.

Within the subculture of ethics, "divine agency" has classically been testified to as working in two ways. Sometimes it is because God is doing something that we do not do it.[8] Ahaz should not rely on alliances to defend Jerusalem because God will defend Jerusalem. The Christians at Rome should not avenge themselves, because God has reserved that role to himself (Rom 12:19). Other times, it is because God is doing something, because it is his nature to do that kind of thing, that we should do it too in the confidence that it is worthwhile to do.

For a millennium and a half, Western moral thought has been making some broad assumptions about our setting, which could not have been made before the fourth century. They represent a kind of fulfilled apocalyptic. The special role of the ruler is itself a part of the changing history of Christian eschatology. When in the century stretching from Eusebius to Augustine Christian thought adjusted to the changes which Constantine had symbolized, the way to say that was to juxtapose the new era with the millennium of chapter 20 of John's Apocalypse, when "the great serpent, who is the Devil and Satan,"is chained for a thousand years and the saints with Christ will rule on earth. It is obviously a fact (in the fourth century) that Christians have ceased to be the persecuted and have become the persecutors, and that fact is assumed obviously to be a change for the better. This providentially transformed social setting makes fundamental differences for ethics.[9]

Thereby I have identified backhandedly one of the sources of our own world view, specifically at the points where it differs from that of the ancient seers.

This newness of world view can be broken down into several components. One is the providential place of the power-bearer, already alluded to, to which I shall return. It is assumed, at least since Eusebius, that the frame of reference of ethical deliberation is that of the person with power; the king deciding whether to wage an unjust war, the merchant deciding whether to set a fair price, the head of household deciding whether to beat his wife or his child, the wealthy person deciding whether to lend at interest. The action is to be evaluated not by whether it keeps the rules, or by whether it resonates with the grace of God, or by whether it exemplifies virtue, or whether it coheres with the salvation story, but by whether, when carried out, when generalized through the ruler's power, it will produce the best possible outcomes.

Modern analysts of moral logic call this "consequentialism," the moral validation of a choice or an action by its results. Ethical theory can analyse its self-evident strengths and its less obvious weaknesses.[10] What we seldom analyse is the *Sitz in Leben* of consequentialism. Evaluating means by ends is only self-evident when two assumptions obtain; a) that the social system of causation is a transparent nexus of connections, comparable to a machine whose shafts and cogwheels interact in reliable ways, so that the results of one's decision and action can be calculated; and b) that the actor whose decision we are evaluating has power.

We are seldom reminded that these two assumptions (actually three, as we shall soon see) obtain, even for us, only seldom and very imperfectly. The socio-political nexus is by no means subject to exhaustive analysis as a machine, when there are multiple actors, some of whom have a stake in interfering with one anothers' intentions or denying one anothers' rights. Neither the social scientist nor the politician really knows what will in fact result from this or that choice. Even the historian, after the fact, is at a loss in the face of some major events to "explain" why what in fact happened happened.

I was one of a tableful of faculty colleagues privileged to host at Notre Dame, early in 1989, the first sociologist from the Soviet Union to visit our university. We plied him with questions about whether *perestroika* was going to work. He answered that it was not within his competence to say, since the sociologist is a scientist, and scientists deal with what can be generalized and replicated. Michael Gorbachev not only cannot be replicated; he cannot be explained. In terms of social science, he could not have happened. Politics is the art of the possible; history on the other hand is the realm of the unique, sometimes the impossible.

The first characteristic I ascribed to consequentialistic reasoning was its assumptions about causation Secondly, then, it makes important assumptions about information, which are a part of the causation picture, but constitute an independent source of uncertainty. In order to make decisions on the basis of preferable outcomes, one must know the facts of the case, exhaustively and accurately. There may be simple settings where such highly accurate knowledge exists, about what will be the outcome if I do this instead of that; but hardly can that obtain in modern social conflicts. Some facts are so complex as to be unknowable; some are the object of secrecy, or of disinformation.

A third characteristic of consequential justifications of actions, the one I began with, is the assumption that the actor disposes of power, so that he or she or they can in fact "make a difference." The Western experience of ethics in inseparable from the assumption that the behavior whose rightness one seeks to illuminate is that of the bearers of power. If someone challenges the morality of violence, the counter-question is: "should we disarm the police? Should Churchill have let Hitler overrun the world?" If the question is the sacredness of fetal life, the "strong" answer is the one declaring abortion a crime. Rulers are the prototypical moral agents; if an act is immoral it must be sanctioned civilly. If the rulers do not punish an act, it is "condoned" i.e. not *really* wrong.

Fifteen years ago I was visiting a small Roman Catholic theological seminary in South Africa, discussing the moral resources for nonviolent social struggle, a vision which was born in that country in the work of Gandhi. One of the students immediately appealed to the action of John F. Kennedy in the 1962 Cuban missile crisis, as having proven the rightness of armed conflict. What is striking is not the status of the arguments for or against violence,[11] or for or against the American policies in 1962, but the assumption made by a poor black man in South Africa that the settings in which the President of the United States makes decisions are more paradigmatic than his own. Even the weakest of us would rather daydream about what they would do if they were President than struggle with what to do at the bottom of the pile.[12]

Apocalyptic and prophetic literature does us the service of ignoring and thereby striking down our confidence in system-immanent causal explanations for the past, and, even more, in system-immanent causal descriptions of how the future is sure to unfold from the choice we are just now making. It reminds us of a world view in which the cosmos was not all knowable; where transcendence could be expressed in terms of divine (or demonic) agency within the real world, rather than being restricted to some other dimension. That frees us for the possibility that other than consequential modes of moral reasoning—founded for instance in virtue, in motivation, in obedience to *halakah* —not subject to being set aside on consequentialist grounds, might be admitted.

The specific "other mode of moral reasoning" that is the most evident is *hope.* When we make the ancient world an odd subset of our own, the strangeness of the literature of "vision" is easily classified in terms of social or psychological pathology. It is explained as compensating for weakness, fear, and defeat. It can be compared to schizophrenia; one reads of "culture shock" and "social powerlessness" as explanations. Parallels can be sought in the "ghost dances" which signalled the breakdown of the original American culture, or the "cargo cults" which arise on the frontier between traditional and imperial culture in Africa or Southeast Asia. Such comparisons to modern pathologies are not utterly erratic, but they do not capture what was essential to the biblical seers. The odd visions generally cited from our century as approximate analogies seldom render their communities more viable. The biblical seers were not compensating for desperation—at least they did not say they were. They said they were engaging in doxology, restating in a new setting their proclamation of the resurrection. They were testifying that the powers of oppression were swallowed up in God's larger story, whereas our modern explanations try to do it the other way 'round, by subsuming God talk in our own visions of human dignity and therapy.

II. POWERLESSNESS AND SURVIVAL

"Be faithful unto death; I will give you the crown of life." "Faithfulness" in this setting included for the beleaguered first-century believers much that we would call "ethical" by way of truth-telling, promise-keeping, sexual purity, et cetera, yet the primordial ethical obligation is the cohesion of the believing community in the face of the pressures working against its identity. Sometimes those pressures pushed toward dilution of identity from inside through schism or speculation. Sometimes they threatened destruction from outside through banishment or martyrdom. In either case the first imperative is to discern the temptation to deny the faith, and not to yield to it. The strategies of identity maintenance which we may call "exclusiveness" when we see them in a modern sect have a different meaning in a clandestine synagogue. The claim to be the only bearers of truth, which is ecumenical bad manners in our pluralistic and tolerant setting, is a simple fact when (in your eyes) your survival is the only way for the honor of the only true God to be upheld in your corner of Asia Minor.

But it is not enough to affirm the value of survival; death too is a part of victory. The crucifixion of Jesus, described by the evangelists as model for the readiness of his disciples to suffer, is transmuted in the fist vision of John into the sovereignty of the slain lamb as key to the cosmic mystery. The reason John is told not to weep is that the death of the lamb has purchased a new people to share in his reign; they share in his cosmic rule by participating in his historic martyrdom. Martyrdom is not defeat but victory. It is victory not merely in the stoic sense of internal dignity, the integrity of the one who can keep "hanging in there" whatever the cost; it is in fact what moves the world. Any claimed "pragmatic" or "realistic" claim to validate particular behaviors by their results must collide with this testimony.

This is far from being an odd and obsolete world view. It is the kind of revisioning of the world which has just redrawn the map of Europe. Vaclav Havel the phenomenologist playwright and Lech Walesa the populist electrician have just set aside the Stalinism into which Roosevelt and Churchill at Yalta had sold their peoples, and in which Westen politics of the era of Dulles had sealed them. They achieved this not by negotiating more shrewdly between the superpowers, but by deconstructing the way both sides have been insisting on seeing the problem. Havel's message is that truth-telling from below is a weapon.[13] It is what Latin American thinkers are beginning to speak of as the "epistemological privilege of the poor." From below is the best way to see reality not only because there are more people down there, so that if you can properly manipulate their votes or risk their bodies, you can get into power and do good from above;[14] it is that seeing things from below is to see them for what they really are.[15]

Before we leave the theme of the power of the "powerless," it is worth repeating that the original move in the direction of over-valuing empire was itself not a value-free reading on the simple realities of the world "out there," but an apocalyptic response to the phenomenon of Constantine. Satan was not really bound and thrown into a pit by the Edict of Milan. Sin was not really suppressed. Constantine did not really inaugurate a qualitatively new era in the nature of the empire. Yet the imagery of the millennium began to be used. Let it therefore not be wrongly thought that only underdogs used the idioms of apocalypse. So did Constantine and Charlemagne. So did Ronald Reagan.

It is not false when people who call themselves "realists," from Machiavelli to Klausewitz to Reinhold Niebuhr, tell us that power comes from the barrel of a gun. That is one kind of power; but the alternative is not weakness but other kinds of power.[16] It is not that the seers compensate for their being in fact incapacitated, by dreaming vindictively about cosmic catastrophe; it is that to be disarmed after the mode of Christ is to be endowed with the power of truth-telling (recently renamed "consciousness-raising") and community-building, for which the metaphors of cosmic conflict are most apt because they break the frame of normalcy.

III. REJOICING IN BABYLON'S FALL?

I should name at this point the question put to us by our protected cultural style, which has taught us how gentleness fosters wholesome social process. We are uncomfortable with the avowal of anger, or the appearance of rejoicing at the evil people's getting what they deserve. I share that discomfort; but if we are to be doing ethics across the centuries rather than etiquette in polite society, there need to be some qualifications to our haste to disavow vindictiveness.

1) Rejoicing in the downfall of evil people is not a peculiarity of apocalyptic literature; it is just as prominent in the Psalms.

2) Avowing this visceral dimension may be one way to discipline it; I am not sure that people who shout do one another more harm than people who lower their voices. Part of our genteel revulsion at the language of anger may well be the way colder-blooded nordic cultures convince themselves that we are superior to the more expressive Mediterraneans.

3) More important; with our nordic coolness of blood and of language, we are quite capable of enormous cruelty. It is hardly morally better that we are dispassionate about incinerating Hiroshima or that we are quiet as we go about depriving our country's children of health care or schooling. The overt anger of Psalm 137 or of Revelation 18 leaves the door (or should I say the wound?) open for a continuing dialogue with the

message of the cross, as the ennoblement of empire since Eusebius does not.

4) The believers, the addressees of John's epistle, are not called on to join in the carnage, nor is the destruction in the visions wreaked by the people of God. Their role is martyrdom.

5) What the great throng in heaven rejoices in (Revelation 19) is the victory of God; that this is concretized in the downfall of the evil empire and the suffering of its supporters is not the theme of rejoicing, but it is accepted as part of the cost of the victory. The general human appetite to see evil people ill-treated in return seems to me not to be compatible with some other components of the Gospel, but my judgments on that matter are not a legitimate screen through which to ask what the ancient seers have to tell me about the downfall of oppressors.

Thereby the question is not resolved: Is it right for us to rejoice in evil's being punished? A world in which evil would not call down destruction on itself would in any case not be a better world.

IV. THE OPEN FUTURE

I have already referred to the deterministic world view as one component of the assumption that historical movement is mostly the work of powerful people. For the consequentialism which justifies the compromises of powerful people to make sense, one must assume a fully known causal nexus; otherwise one cannot argue to justify this or that sacrifice of one value for another, the breaking of this rule for the sake of that objective. The structural pastoral attention to the pros and cons of particular decisions, which in the age of Pascal gave to Jesuits and to "casuistry" a bad name, began with the assumption that there was a closed system with only two choices, each costly, neither one compatible with all of one's moral imperatives. The quandary became the paradigm for moral discourse. Hard cases on the edge of ordinary experience became the way to test the reach of one's principles. *Exceptio probat,* the exception tests the rule.

This is not the place to look at all of the limitations of the quandaristic approach to moral analysis or moral education.[17] What I attend to here is the axiom of the closed moral nexus, with two and only two choices, both of them bad. This assumes the closed world view from which the seers' vision not only of divine agency but even of human agency calls us to be freed. There are other choices; some foreseeable and others not. If we call those other possibilities "miracle" our contemporaries will sneer; but we can also call them creativity or surprise.[18] The closed nexus breaks down as soon as there are more parties to the process, each with some degree of unpredictability if not freedom.

I am not sure what value to give another kind of argument which some thinkers in the realm of science and religion take quite seriously; namely the way in which the natural sciences today are painting a less orderly, less machine-like picture of things, with Heisenbergian uncertainty about measuring subatomic particles, or with turbulence in fluid systems, or with fits and starts in species evolution. I am not sure that such loosening of the mechanistic vision by the natural scientists makes room for human or even divine freedom, but it certainly is compatible with our refusing to let a hopeless dilemma be the last word. If the cosmos is not closed, then what seemed *prima facie* to be the lesser evil may well not be the least evil.

There is yet another way in which contemporary thought is retreiving, not always very carefully, an apocalyptic style. Human intervention can so interfere with the ecosphere as to make the world uninhabitable. Jonathan Schell's *The Fate of the Earth* predicted that history as we know it would be ended by a nuclear exchange; others had said it of the way the arms race had changed the world, even without war. Others have discerned the "end of history as we now know it" in the collapse of the Soviet Empire, or in the end of the abiliy of ideologies to convince, or in the overloading of the ecosphere. Ethical sobriety demands that we take all of these new thresholds seriously; but is that eschatology?

The notion that system-immanent thought has declared itself at an end has itself become not only thinkable but trendy. It is not in this sense that I would advocate a retrieval of the seers' freedom from claimed "realism." The seers differ fom this recent trend in that they proclaim the "known world" to be too small not because they have from the inside come to the edge of it, but because God has reached and spoken into it from beyond. In our age "transcendence" is sometimes a code word for the fact that, from within our own system, we know ourselves to be finite, thereby creating by extrapolation the notion of "beyond" even though there be nothing (nothing we can know) "out there."[19] Prophetic transcendence comes from the other end; the "beyond" came first. Divine command, divine agency, divine will are prior to, not derived from, extrapolated from our finitude. An ethic of *torah* and *halakah,* or an ethic of discipleship, is therefore deeper, more rooted in the nature of things, than an ethic which seeks to manipulate the causal nexus for the best.

These are only sample soundings. My hope is that the oddity of the literature of the seers may continue to shake or to shock us into the recognition that the limits our moral systems impose on our moral possibilities need not be the last word.

Toward the end of his paper John J. Collins describes apocalypse as "a way of looking at the world which . . . cannot be verified factually but only authenticated in value by the kind of action it supports . . . . The ethical stance . . . gives rise to the eschatological vision just as much as it draws support from it."[20] This points to a fruitful way of restating the question. To say simply that "apocalypse is validated by the ethics it sustains" would be a wrongly reductionist horizontalism. It would also be self-defeating, since the vision will only support the ethos if the seer considers God and revelation to be real. It would also be petitionary; by what standards from beyond the system would one validate the "kind of action it supports"? But to say that there is a spiral of complementarity, whereby the ethic supports the promise and vice versa, both of them contradicting both the fallen world's defeatism and the fallen Powers' oppression, may enable us to describe both as doxology. The adequacy of the seers' vision is rehearsed and celebrated not so much in the fulfillment of the events they predict as in the divine nature which the predictions clothe and in the liberated life of those who believe.

NOTES

1. There was discussion at the North Park symposium about whether the disciplines of textual analysis or those of "biblical theology" are more apt to accentuate diversity or unity. I am not sure that the literary studies I see all accentuate diversity, or that "theology" necessarily tends prematurely to unify. Yet it is evident that ethics necessarily sets a limit to diversity. One can entertain multiple possibilities or paradoxes within the dialectic of dogmatics or ecclesiology; but when

one must act, one can usually not choose to do "both/and."

2. I am grateful to F. Burton Nelson for suggesting several other directions in which I might have described more directly the ethical payoff of an eschatological orientation; the life of the church as first fruits of the new world on the way, the critique of the idolatries of our age, the contribution of hope to the staying power of a countercultural ethos. . . . .

3. It might well be that particular moral biases in the more ordinary sense—having to do for instance with the value of marriage, of property, of suffering, of delayed gratification—would correlate with specific eschatological views. I would not hesitate to make such a case; but the prior agenda here is the challenge to ethics as a structure for moral discourse.

4. This is a dispassionate statement about the genre, not a reproach. Not all scholarship is supposed to serve "the utility of texts to edify the church." As example of the complexity of the subdiscipline, cf. the pair of essays by David Hellholm and David E. Aune, "The Problem of Apocalyptic Genre and the Apocalypse of John" and "The Apocalypse of John and the Problem of Genre" in *Semeia* 36 13-64 and 65-92.

5. I surveyed some of the themes of this paper in my "Armaments and Eschatology" in *Studies in Christian Ethics* 1, (1988) . 43-61. In that text (pp. 48-49. n. 20) I referred to the problems of definition. If for one party the mark of "apocalyptic" is that its scope is worldwide, whereas "prophets" speak only to Israel, whereas for another party the difference is that "apocalypse" sees God's work as supramundane whereas prophets read real history, and for a third the criterion for apocalyptic is belief in the resurrection, it becomes evident that there needs to be clarification on a higher level of what "definition" means.

6. The most blunt mechanistic models have been modified by Heisenbergian uncertainty on the subatomic scale and "chaos" modeling on a macro scale, but these model changes are still within the deterministic nexus.

7. It may frequently be appropriate to note that the component of the biblical world view that differs from ours is not unique to the eschatological material or to seers. It is not merely apocalyptic that is odd; it is the Bible whose world is strange. Another instance of that strangeness would be the "principalities and powers" cosmology which served the Apostle Paul to interpret history. Should that too be called "apocalyptic" because it strikes us as odd?

8. Cf. my interpretation of the theme "let JHWH do it" as one of the ethical implications of JHWH war; "'To your tents, O Israel': The legacy of Israel's experience with holy war," *Studies in Religion/Sciences Religieuses* 18 (1989) 345-362.

9. Cf. my "The Constantinian Sources of Western Social Ethics" in *The Priestly Kingdom* (Notre Dame: Notre Dame University Press, 1985) 135ff. Constantine is the symbol of this change, and partially its agent; but the conceptual innovation which impacted Christian thought about God and the world is probably more the work of Constantine's biographer Eusebius.

10. The ordinary lay statement is "the end justifies the means:" yet that phrasing is ambivalent. Sometimes "end" means the intended goal, without calculation of the likelihood of its being achieved. Other times "end" means the actual result. Sometimes it means the probable result.

11. At the most the Cuba crisis could be held to "prove" that the threat of a nuclear strike can produce political effects. They included the fall of Krushchev, a new escalation of the arms race, and France's withdrawal from NATO. What the *firing* of a bomb could do, no-one has tested since Nagasaki. None of this short-range consequentialism speaks to the other questions posed by the threat to commit deeds the execution of which would be immoral.

12. I am not arguing that the Christian must avoid being in a position of power, nor that there is nothing to say about how rulers behave. Cf. my *The Christian Witness to the State*, (Newton KS: Faith and Life Press, 1964). What I reject is (a) considering the ruler as the primordial mover of history, and (b) modifying the content of moral obligation in order to approve of the ruler's doing things which would be wrong for others. Cf. *The Priestly Kingdom*, ,138ff.

13. The alternative to truth is not merely falshood but "violence." Gandhi spoke of nonviolent action as "experimenting with truth." Non-violence is not merely a moral rejection of hurting people; it is practical trust in the power of truth.

14. Some of what its advocates call theology of "liberation," when it advocates a radically different end but with traditional violent means, is not as original as it pretends to be. Violence in the service of liberation is an old idea. What Walesa and Havel did, following Gandhi and King, was to change the means to fit the end.

15. The way in which the epistemological privilege of the underdog is operational in liberation theology should not be understood as an innovation; it retrieves a vision that goes all the way back to the Hebrews. The dictum "God favors the underdog" (Elohim m'vakesh et hanirdaf) was current among medieval rabbis. Then there is Dietrich Bonhoeffer: "only the suffering God can help." Bonhoeffer's vision is more profound, but in terms of personal spirituality and as a vision of the divine nature. Yet its setting is prison, not the favela or the campo, and its intellectual challenge is the atheism of a world come of age. Neither the rabbis nor Bonhoeffer was developing a criteriology for discerning the signs of the times amidst the social struggle. Neither made an issue of how the poor become the subjects of their own history. Neither was at home in the idiom of apocalypse.

16. Cf. my "Jesus and Power," *Ecumenical Review*, (1973) 447-454. The paper by Adela Yarbro Collins alluded in passing to Rollo May's differentiating between power which nurtures and that which exploits. Two semantic mistakes regularly cause confusion in this realm. One is to assume that "power" is qualitatively univocal; the only differentiation being between more and less of it. The other is to claim that it is morally "neutral," with its moral value depending on what it is used for.

17. The general shortcomings of quandarism are of two kinds: a) by seeking out for testing the farthest-out specimens where basic values collide, it misrepresents the broad middle of moral discernment, where faithfulness and creativity are able to satisfy most moral mandates; b) by concentrating on decision's needing to be made at one point (I call this "punctualism") it misrepresents most of the texture of moral responsibility, most of which is not punctual. The moral life has length in that the present is predisposed by the past and drawn by the future. It has breadth in that other people and commitments condition our decisions. It has depth in that religious commitments and value insights condition choices.

8. I speculatively took up the challenge of quandarism, around the test case of violent self-defense (which is the one most frequently appealed to) in my "What Would You Do? An Exercise in Situation Ethics" in the *Journal of Religious Ethics* 2 (1974) 81-105, later popularized in *What Would You Do?* (Scottdale, Pa 1983) 13-42. I argue the inadequacy of the dilemmistic paradigm, at the same time that I take up its challenge as an occasion for Gospel communication.

19. Gordon Kauffman's *God the Problem* (Harvard University Press, Cambridge, 1972) 45ff. used this mental maneuver to construct a usable notion of divine transcendence.

20. See in this issue: J. Collins, "Inspiration or Illusion, . . . This statement by Collins represents the general tendency of scholars to telescope the genre and its message; i.e. to characterize at the same time the kind of literature and the seer's witness. This tips us off to the alternative possibility; could the apocalyptic genre serve to communicate an opposite message? One of despair? of self-hatred?

The Apocalypse

Hope, Resistance And The Revelation Of Reality*

CHRISTOPHER ROWLAND

The outburst against Rome in Revelation is one of the many factors which sets this book apart from other New Testament texts. Its apocalyptic form, its symbolism, so difficult to pin down in its precise meaning, its longing for vindication of divine justice and the portraits of God who apparently wreaks havoc on a recalcitrant humanity all have the effect of creating distance between the contemporary Christian reader and the last book of the Bible. No doubt its inclusion in the canon has had a subduing effect when it is surrrounded by more conformist and less subversive texts which manage to buttress social convention. That distance indicates the smugness of the contemporary reader who supposes that the raw emotions articulated in Revelation are products of a primitive religion removed from that of Jesus and Paul. Such a reaction merely reinforces the temptation to deceive ourselves into thinking that we can be cut off from the darker side of ourselves and our world. That Revelation steadfastly refuses to allow. When we read it, we cannot pretend that Christianity is only a religion of light. It helps to remind us that Christians have down the centuries been part and parcel of deeds of unutterable darkness: persecution, genocide, ruthless conquest have all formed part of the sorry story of the Christian Church. Revelation is a potent reminder of collusion with evil and the necessity of the recognition of the demands which are in accord with God's justice. Its apocalyptic form refuses to accept disguises, however sophisticated, behind which bland and empty gestures can cover up the distorted face of an unjust order. Apocalyptic represents Judaeo-Christian tradition's classic form of the unmasking of reality and the refusal to rest content with superficial and cosy appearances.

Revelation and the apocalyptic tradition have frequently been a resource for those who have sought to criticize and distance themselves from existing institutions,

---

* This article adapted from C. Rowland, *Radical Christianity* (Maryknoll, NY: Orbis Books, 1988) 66-81.

whether political or ecclesiastical. What is offered in the following pages is a reading of Revelation which seeks to explore how it might be used as a subversive book. There is no suggestion that it has to be read in this way: apocalyptic offered a realm of discourse which has enabled reactionaries as well as radicals to justify their position. In contemporary theology the politics of conservative fundamentalism are buttressed by an eschatology in which Revelation has its part to play in a sketch of a final scenario where social justice and the option for the poor have little part. Here visions of doom serve only to fortify a well-heeled elect in their convictions that social change is a mask for communism, the hallmark of the Beast. The political quietism of some Christian groups is undergirded by a reading of Revelation which leaves no role for the elect other than a passive spectator of the divine drama in a state of awesome waiting.

An important component of the reading offered in these pages is that Revelation does encourage active engagement. That is not by emulation of the exercise of divine judgment but through patterns of discipleship where protest and witness force a reluctant world to see the divine horizon to human existence which would be otherwise neglected. Seeing things in the light of the messianic redemption (to borrow a phrase from Theodor Adorno) is an essential corrective to a closed view of culture and history which Revelation seeks to combat. This is particularly important for those who maintain allegiance to the Lamb whose victory at present remains unseen but whose reality the Lamb's followers are bound to proclaim. The acceptance of closure, in compromise and tolerance of injustice, is bound to mean a denial of the confession that Jesus, the Lamb that was slain, is Lord. Action of a political kind is involved in maintaining that confession.

Justification of the reading which follows is rooted in the conviction that the divine presence is to be found with the marginalized: the poor, the unremembered, the outcast, the little people of our world. It is that prior hermeneutical assumption which enables Revelation to function as an instrument of social awareness and criticism as well as a resource of hope. It is not a position which is watertight and irrefutable but one that consistently demands the attention of all who claim to be identified with one who lived and died at the margins of his world, outside the city gate.

I. THE APOCALYPSE: VOICE FROM THE MARGINS OF THE CANON?

Throughout the history of the Church the Book of Revelation has posed problems of interpretation and doctrine for Christian thinkers. Its association with fringe movements from Cerinthus and the Montanists to the enthusiastic followers of Joachim of Fiore and the Reformation radicals has added to the suspicion which Christians have felt towards this work. Its peripheral place in the New Testament canon accurately reflects its influence in Christian theology. Eschatology is a matter to which one turns (if at all) only after other doctrinal issues have been fully explored. A glance at the readings prescribed for the Sunday Eucharist in the Church of England shows that the compilers of the readings do not consider the bulk of Revelation an appropriate resource for the edification of contemporary Christians in England. Even when the text does seem to have something challenging and apposite to say (as it surely does on the matter of the State in chapters 13 and 17), the less opaque (and less disturbing) thirteenth chapter of Romans is served up for the edification of believers. That contemporary point is merely an indication of the acute problem posed by the Apocalypse for mainstream conformist Christianity. In the Lutheran tradition the reputation of the Book of Revelation is of being "weakly Christianized Judaism";[1] this is a view shared by many. Its violence stands in stark contrast to the oft-repeated assertions that adherents of the Christian religion should espouse reconciliation and nonviolence, rhetoric which has been subjected to critical scrutiny in recent years. Much of this has been the result of an "internalizing" reading of Revelation in which the struggle represented in its imagery is related not to the historical plane but to the soul of each Christian on its pilgrimage through this vale of tears to the City of God.

But the cataclysmic horizon of late twentieth-century life with the threat of disaster on a cosmic scale has meant that the images of Revelation have had a new appeal, often to those on opposite ends of the political spectrum. Thc members of New Right groups in the USA have resorted to the apocalyptic symbolism of Revelation as a resource to confirm their convictions that disaster is coming to the world order. Revelation can encourage a fatalistic attitude to the nuclear holocaust and an acceptance of the need to use it to keep at bay the hordes of darkness. In such a scenario there is little doubt on the part of the interpreters that the hosts of darkness are to be identified with the forces of world communism, while the elect can easily be seen to be the evangelical Christians and the President of the "free" world whose resoluteness alone can expose the ways of darkness in the face of the insidious activities of thc communist Beast. The fact that Revelation explicitly criticizes the kind of complacent assumption of rectitude and moral decency in the letter to the Laodicaean church[2] seems to make no impact on those who have already assumed that the new age is based on evangelical fundamentalism and a particular version of the American dream. One reason is that concern for the future of the cosmos and God's purposes for it have been deprived of their power by the assurance offered to born-again Christians that before the Great Tribulation comes they will be whisked off to be with the Lord in Paradise. Their only responsibility is to make sure their spiritual state is maintained so that their position with the saints away from a world of sin is not affected.

At the other end of the social spectrum peasants in Latin America find in the stark dualism of the book and the conflict between good and evil a graphic portrayal of their own struggles, as they seek to subsist amidst the violence and destruction of counter-insurgency campaigns in El Salvador, contra-terrorist raids in Nicaragua or the powerful forces of the owners of large estates who seek to drive peasants off their lands[3] in the remote areas of Brazil. What is more, the challenge of imminent disaster to an unrepentant world has begun to find a response in a Western world which has come to despair of the platitudinous certainties of its culture based as it is on exploitation of land and people. The Apocalypse has become a means of unmasking reality and exposing the iniquities which lurk behind the bland utterances of the powerful and the evil structures which undergird a facade of humanity in a sick society.

II. THE CENTRALITY OF ESCHATOLOGY IN THE NEW TESTAMENT

While the book of Revelation may be a product of the Jewish Christian culture of Asia Minor,[4] there is much in it which suggests that it also reflects the beliefs of the mainstream early Christian tradition. The central theme of its presentation of the eschatological drama is the conviction that the death of Christ (who is symbolized by a lamb) and his exaltation to the throne of God is the decisive moment of change in the relationships between heaven and earth and the old age and the new.[5] This was the view of Paul in particular, as is evident in the way in which he talks of the resurrection of Jesus and the indwelling Spirit of God as "the firstfruits" of the new age."[6]

But what of the other features of Revelation? Are the belief in the millennium (a reign of the Messiah on earth), the destruction of the hostile powers and the stark dualism typical of other early Christian texts? The answer to that question is in the affirmative. The presentation of the main features of early Christian hopes for the future is no easy task.[7] For one thing nowhere do we have a systematic presentation of these beliefs. Rather we have various hints in contexts which usually deal with some other subject.

Of the centrality of the belief in Christ's imminent coming in glory there can be no doubt. Most New Testament documents focus on this hope, sometimes without much discussion of the consequences of this belief for the rest of the cosmos. In one of the most extensive passages dealing with the final change from the old order to the new we find material concerning the reign of Christ, but nothing is said about the lot of the saints in the new age, save that at the last trump the dead will be raised and the righteous will be changed into bodies of glory and will share the Messiah's kingdom.[8] In 1 Cor 15:24-28 the subjection of the principalities and powers (and in that Paul includes human as well as angelic potentates) to Christ is a feature of the eschatological process. Nothing is said explicitly here about Rome, but we cannot think that Paul supposes that the status quo will remain permanently. Rather he believes that God has allowed the powers on earth and in heaven free rein for a certain period.[9] Ultimately, however, the powers are called to account, punished and made subject[10] to the authority of God's messiah and in some cases destroyed.[11]

The Gospels indicate that a form of the millenial belief was accepted by the early Church. In the Beatitudes we find that a promise is made to the meek that "they will inherit the earth."[12] It is difficult, however, without excessive spiritualization to suppose that the filling of the hungry and the inheritance of the earth refer to events in a world very different from the present when a new order would bring about a reversal of values.[13] When one adds to these sayings the vow which Jesus is reported to have made at the Last Supper not to taste of the fruit of the vine until he drinks it anew in the kingdom[14] it appears that he was thought to have looked forward to a day when a new order under God would be established on earth: a time when many would come from the east and the west to sit down at table with the patriarchs in the kingdom of God.[15] It is special pleading to attempt to spiritualize all Jesus' hopes. Without resorting to a blind literalism this symbolism should not be evacuated of its evocative force in conjuring up in the minds of hearers and readers the hope for a new and better order in the near future.

Similarly in the Pauline corpus the classic statement of Paul's eschatological belief in Romans 8 includes a statement that the whole creation is moving towards the birth of a new age[16]:

> I consider that the sufferings of this present time are not worth comparing with the glory that is to be revealed to us. For the creation waits with eager longing for the revealing of the sons of God; for the creation was subjected to futility, not of its own will but by the will of him who subjected it in hope; because the creation will be set free from its bondage to decay and obtain the glorious liberty of the children of God. We know that the whole creation has been groaning and travailing until now; and not only the crea-

> tion but we also ourselves, who have the firstrruits of the Spirit, groan inwardly as we wait for our adoption as sons, the redemption of our bodies.

This is a process centered on the present world order, not in some other realm. The majority of early Christians expected a reign of God on earth in the future when the elect would reign with the Messiah Jesus. Thus while there are certainly no signs in either Gospels or Epistles that a specific period of a thousand years was countenanced (such a belief was by no means common in Judaism in any case),[17] belief in the reign of God on earth is an idea which is central to the foundation documents of the Christian Church and is demonstrated by its persistence well into the second century.[18]

III. THE CONQUEST OF THE POWERS

The hostility towards the Roman state and the rejection of its claims and power in Revelation contrast with the blander attitudes expressed elsewhere.[19] Nevertheless the conviction that all that was opposed to God would ultimately be uprooted and destroyed, so graphically portrayed in Revelation 17-20, is at least implicity stated elsewhere in the New Testament.[20] For example, in 2 Thess 2:3-4 we find Paul using the imagery of apocalyptic literature to speak of the ultimate expression of hostility to God which would be overcome by Christ at his coming. Similarly the traditional features of Jewish eschatology, the messianic woes and other cosmic catastrophes, are set out in Mark 13 . Nothing is said in this chapter or its parallels about the overcoming of the forces of darkness and their destruction. Indeed, as it stands Mark 13 seems to be a torso of the traditional eschatological pattern. It mentions the messianic woes and the attendant features which would indicate the coming climax, for example the setting up of the abomination of desolation and the political and social crisis facing those in Judaea, but after the coming of the Son of Man and his angels to save the elect nothing is said about the fate of the rest of creation.[21] As it stands, the chapter leaves the contemporary reader with the impression that the redemption of the elect is from a world fast sinking to destruction (hence the doctrine of rapture which forms part of the stock of current fundamentalist eschatology today). One can only assume that one reason for this truncated eschatological passage has much to do with the preoccupation of the author with the immediate concerns of the elect, their need to persevere in the midst of tribulation and the hope of their ultimate vindication. Possibly Mark 9:1 with its promise of visible signs of God's reign for the followers of Jesus is evidence of Jesus' complete presentation. Also, implicit within the message of Jesus on the reign of God is the belief that the powers of darkness (i.e. everything opposed to God) would be overthrown.[22] In so far as the might of Rome stood in the way of the reign of peace and justice, the coexistence of Roman sovereignty with the dominion of God would have been impossible. Jewish hopes for the future, on which the New Testament ideas are based, made no provision for any such coexistence of the reign of God with the reign of the kings of the earth.

IV. THE PERVASIVENESS OF APOCALYPTIC

Even if parallels can be found to the various items of eschatological belief in Revelation this work at first sight seems to stand out from the rest of the New Testament because of its style of writing. It is the only full-length apocalypse in the New Testament. The absence of the apocalyptic genre from the New Testament does not mean that the apocalyptic religion finds its only example in Revelation. The features which we have categorized as typical of the apocalyptic are in no small part derived from the distinctive experience and claims the work makes.[23] John of Patmos tells his readers that what he saw and heard came while he was in the Spirit,[24] in all probability a reference to a visionary trance. What follows has many of the characteristics of a dream or vision. The beasts and the angels are the product of the visionary imagination taking up scriptural passages which were widely used as a basis for visions, particularly Isa 6:1-3 and Ezekiel 1. In the context of such visions it is only to be expected that their contents may drift towards the bizarre and exotic. Other early Christian writers probably shared this outlook. There is abundant evidence that the claims to visions and revelations were indeed a prominent feature of primitive Christianity. The belief that the spirit of prophecy had returned to the Christian community meant that they thought the voice of God was to be heard directly through the mouth of prophets or by the intuitive apprehensions of the believers themselves.[25] Paul speaks of the importance of glossolalia and prophecy.[26] In the story of the growth of the church in Acts the writer tells of the visions which mark decisive turns in the story: the change in the life of Saul the persecutor of the church;[27] the strange experience of Peter at Joppa which led to the conversion of the Gentile centurion Cornelius.[28] Also, according to the Synoptic Gospels the decisive moment in Jesus' ministry was marked by a vision in which he saw the spirit descending upon him like a dove.[29] Such passages are not common, but they do come at crucial moments in the narratives, so that it would be a mistake to regard their scarcity as evidence of their insignificance. The private nature of such experiences makes it likely that many more remained uncommunicated and, therefore, unrecorded, in the tradition. We can see from 2 Cor 12:2-4 that it was only under severe provocation that Paul resorted to disclosing an experience which he would have preferred to have kept confidential. Such isolated outcrops are an indication of the importance of the claim to knowledge of divine mysteries which Paul refers to occasionally in his Letters.[30]

Early Christianity emerged in a world where contact with the divine by dreams, visions, divination, magic, supernatural enlightenment and other related forms of insight in the quest for knowledge was common.[31] To abstract the early Christian movement from such a quest and from the aspirations to radical change which are frequently embodied in the collections of such knowledge would be to ignore the reasons for its attractiveness within the ancient world. Claims by Christians to be indwelt by the divine Spirit and as a result to know the very mysteries of the divine purposes validated the understanding of the world necessitated by the apparent absence of the fulfillment of the divine will in human affairs. Visions of the divine purposes were an essential component which enabled the continued adherence to religious traditions by those who found little in human affairs to indicate their veracity. Early Christianity offered access to divine power and insight by confession of Jesus' messiahship and acceptance of the rite of baptism. When such convictions about communion with the divine world are linked to the initial assertions about the imminence of a new world order and a pattern of common life where fellowship and mutual support were to the fore it becomes entirely comprehensible why primitive Christianity should offer such an attractive social system for many in the ancient world.

Thus the hints from the rest of the New Testament suggest that the book of Revelation may not be such an idiosyncratic member of the canon. However much its theology may strike a discordant note with the tender spirits of our age we must reckon with the likelihood that both its apocalyptic and its millenarian outlook were vitally important for most early Christian writers. It is a measure of the success of the opponents of millenarianism in Christian theology that suspicion of the book has been endemic in Christian history. To pretend that the centrality of visions and revelations in Revelation is an aberration which perverts the truth of the gospel of Jesus and Paul is to misunderstand the significance which the apocalyptic outlook had for these two figures as well.

V. APOCALYPTIC: UNMASKING REALITY

Since the end of the last century, commentators on early Christian doctrine have had to reckon with the possibility of the pervasive influence on early Christianity of Jewish beliefs concerning the hope for the future derived from the apocalypses.[32] Few today would deny that the hope for a glorious new age in which sorrow and sighing would flee away, loosely referred to as eschatology, has a significant part to play either explicitly or implicitly in the presentation of the early Christian message. While admitting that the word "eschatology" itself has been, and continues to be, a source of confusion, the relationship between apocalyptic and eschatology is frequently left unexplained. Many use the word "apocalyptic" to describe the beliefs concerning the arrival of a new age and see apocalyptic merely as a form of eschatology. This is an area of confusion where some clarification is needed both with regard to the antecedents of the apocalyptic movement and the best way of characterizing it.

In all recent discussions of apocalyptic, a clear distinction is made between apocalyptic (or apocalypticism) and the apocalypse. The latter is a particular literary type found in the literature of ancient Judaism, which is characterized by its claims to offer visions or other disclosures of divine mysteries concerning a variety of subjects. The apocalypse, of which the books of Daniel and Revelation are the two canonical examples, is to be distinguished from apocalyptic, usually viewed as a cluster of mainly eschatological ideas which impinged generally on the theology of Judaism. The distinction between the apocalypse and apocalyptic ideas is an important one. But what is the cluster of ideas, usually labelled apocalyptic? The following summary may help to indicate one pole of the contemporary discussion[33]:

> We may designate apocalyptic as a special expression of the Jewish eschatology which existed alongside the national eschatology represented by the rabbis. It is linked with the latter by many ideas, but is differentiated from it by a quite different understanding of God, the world, and man.

According to such an interpretation characteristic features of apocalyptic include the following:

1) a contrast between the present age, which is perishable and temporary, and a new age, which is still to come, and which is imperishable and eternal;

2) a belief that the new age is of a transcendent kind, which breaks in from beyond through divine intervention and without human activity;

3) a wider concern than merely the destiny of Israel;

4) an interest in the totality of world history;

5) the belief that God has foreordained everything and that the history of the world has been divided into epochs; and finally;

6) an imminent expectation that the present unsatisfactory state of affairs will

only be short-lived.

I would like to draw attention to two features of this treatment of apocalyptic. Firstly, its belief that the future hope is of a particular kind; secondly, its view that there is sufficient cohesion in the ideas contained in the different apocalypses to distil from them an outline of the essential features of apocalyptic; and thirdly, that transcendent eschatology, the hope for a new order *beyond* this world, is the key to our understanding of the thought-world of apocalyptic.

According to this view of apocalyptic there existed in Judaism two types of future hope: a this-worldly, national eschatology found principally in the rabbinic texts (produced by Jewish teachers in the centuries following the fall of Jerusalem in the year 70), and an other-worldly eschatology found principally in the apocalypses. The evidence from the apocalypses themselves, however, indicates that such a dichotomy cannot be easily substantiated. Apart from a handful of passages *the doctrine of the future hope as it is found in the apocalypses seems to be remarkably consistent with the expectation found in other Jewish sources.* If the point of departure for our understanding of the pattern of thought which we call apocalyptic is the apocalypses, and *all* the apocalypses, not just Daniel and Revelation, then we shall have to admit that the description of apocalyptic outlined above is inadequate.

VI. APOCALYPTIC: HIGHER WISDOM THROUGH REVELATION

The belief that eschatology provides the key for understanding the essence of apocalyptic is now seen to be inadequate. We can, however, understand the disparate elements of the book of Revelation if we see the underlying theme to be one which derives from its initial statement "The Revelation of Jesus Christ" (Rev 1:1) rather than from the eschatological message running through much of the rest of the book. Revelation is not merely an eschatological tract satisfying the curiosity of those who wanted to know what would happen in the future. Though it contains much teaching about "what must happen after this," its purpose is to reveal something hidden which will enable the readers to view their present situation from a completely different perspective. When seen in this light, the significance of many of the visions in the Apocalypse falls into place: the Letters to the Churches offer an assessment of their churches' worth from a divine perspective: the vision of the divine throne room in Revelation 4 enables the churches to recognize the dominion of their God; in Revelation 5, the death and exaltation of Christ is shown to mark the inauguration of the new age; and in chapters 13 and 17 the true identity of the Roman emperors and the city of Rome is divulged. Revelation is a text which seeks to summon to repentance and to give reassurance by showing—by means of direct revelation from God—that there is another dimension to material existence, which could be, and was being, ignored by the churches of Asia Minor.

If we think of apocalyptic as "higher wisdom through revelation,"[34] the claim of the apocalypses to reveal mysteries about the future, the movements of the stars, the heavenly dwelling of God, angelology, the course of human history and the mystery of the human plight can *all* be seen to fall within the category of the mysteries which can only be solved by revelation. Such a quest makes sense of the apocalypses, *including* the book of Revelation. Indeed, the impact of the message of the latter depends very much on its claim to be a direct revelation of how things *actually* are, rather than the mere opinion of the wise teacher. Apocalyptic thus offers its readers an answer to that heart-felt plea from the prophet in Isa 64:1: "O that thou wouldst rend the heavens and come down . . . to make thy name known to thy adversaries." Many felt that this echoed the question of oppressed Jews of a previous generation: "where are thy zeal and thy might? The yearning of thy heart and compassion are withheld from me." The apocalypse offered a basis for hope in a world where God seemed to be restrained, by unmasking the reality of what the past, the present and the future of human history were actually about.

There is a kind of historical determinism undergirding this view of human history. The apocalyptic unveiling reveals that the future triumph of the divine righteousness is assured. But the apocalypses do not portray individual human destiny as preordained. That is open; and one of the functions of an apocalypse is to provoke a response of identification with the divine purposes by the individual or community in view of the inevitable outcome of the triumph of God. Several apocalypses do portray the present as the decisive moment in human history when the flowering of the historical development has reached the time for harvest. What stands out in all of the apocalypses is the need for the fulfillment of the totality of God's purposes in history before the new age can finally come. Consequently, it is futile to take any shortcuts to bring that about before the decisive moment in the history of salvation arrives .

Apocalyptic visions offer a hope of a better world which shows up the inadequacy of the present. As such they played an important part in creating a critical outlook on the world order and promoting a distance from the fabric of society as presently constituted. This alternative perspective on the world is the vehicle for reality to be unmasked. The injustice in the world and the temporary nature of the present order is demonstrated as a spur to action in pursuit of the goal of the reign of God.

VII. UNDERSTANDING THE APOCALYPSE

The word apocalypse today is generally synonymous with catastrophe and disaster: *Apocalypse Now* sought to capture in horrific and lurid detail the horror of war. The images of Revelation are what make the book both compelling and frightening; but they seem to be most pertinent to the breakup of society and the world order which comes in war. But if we confine our understanding of the Apocalypse simply to the horrors brought by the Four Horsemen and the torment of the Lake of Fire we shall miss much of significance in this remarkable book.

As we have just noted, apocalypse concerns the unmasking of the reality lying beneath the surface of the society and personal attitudes. The New Testament Apocalypse sets out to reveal things *as they really are* both in the life of the Christian communities and in the world at large. In so doing it gives little comfort to the complacent Church or the powerful world. For the powerful and the complacent it has a message of judgment and doom, whereas for the powerless and oppressed it offers hope and vindication. The characterization of contemporary society in the apocalyptic symbolism of beast and harlot[35] is a vigorous unmasking and denunciation of the ideology of the powerful, by which they seek to legitimize their position by persecution and economic exploitation; it is an ancient Christian form of the critique of ideology.

The critique of the present is effected by the use of a contrast between the glories of the future and the inadequacies of the present. The process of unmasking involves an attempt to delineate the true character of contemporary society and the superhuman forces at work in the opposition to God's righteousness in the world. The enormous power of those forces which undergird the oppression and lack of righteousness of the world order are shown to be unstable and destined to defeat. In contrast the apparent fragility of the witness of those who follow the way of Jesus is promised ultimate vindication.

VIII. THE STRUCTURE OF THE APOCALYPSE

To assist with the exposition of themes from the Apocalypse, a survey of the book and its imagery is here outlined:

1:1-8 Introduction

1:9-20 Call Vision

2 - 3 Letters to the Seven Churches

4 The vision of heaven: a door is opened for the seer to witness the contrast between the acknowledgement of God's sovereignty in the world above and an unresponsive humanity below.

5 The Lamb is shown to be worthy to open the seals and thus to initiate the process of divine judgment and the reconciliation of God and humanity which reaches its climax in 21-2.

6, 8-9, *and* 16 The sequence of seals, trumpets and bowls which periodize the eschatological process which must precede the establishment of the divine reign on earth.

7 First interruption in the sequence of seals, trumpets and bowls. The opening of the seals in Revelation 6 is here interrupted with a description of the sealing of the elect and the promise of ultimate vindication for those who are faithful in the period of divine judgment.

10-15 Second interruption in the sequence: the eschatological witness of the Church.

- 10-11 the prophetic task of the Church
- 12 Divine protection for the people of God and the acknowledgement of ultimate victory but with the imminent threat from the Devil.
- 13 the earthly embodiment of the Devil in the state revealed and the consequences for those who refuse to compromise (i.e. having the mark of the Beast).
- 14 the Elect are those who are marked with the mark of the Lamb; they will be the ones to achieve ultimate vindication: the contrast with the fate of those who have the mark of the Beast.
- 15 Song of victory over the enemies of God.

17-19:10 Babylon's identity and character revealed and her judgment described.

19:11-15 the victory of the Son of Man over the enemies of God.

20:1-10 the messianic reign on Earth with the restraining of evil.

20:11-20 The Last Judgment.

21-22:5 New Creation, New Jerusalem.

22:6-21 Final admonitions.

The first three chapters of the book describe the call of John the seer who is imprisoned on the isle of Patmos,[36] followed by a series of letters to the angels of the seven churches in Asia Minor in which the Heavenly Christ offers reproof and encouragement in varying degrees, fostering a steadfast witness and the arousal of the complacent from attitudes of compromise. The apocalypse proper begins in chapter 4 where John sees God enthroned in heaven surrounded by the heavenly host who laud him as creator and redeemer. That scene is transformed in the very next chapter which describes the coming of a Lamb to God to receive a scaled scroll which symbolizes the historical process leading up to the establishment of divine justice on earth. The Lamb has earned the right to open the scroll and start this process leading to the climax of human history.

The book of Revelation is interested in human history as the arena where the divine promises will be fulfilled. There is an unequivocal link between God and the historical process; in continuity with the Jewish tradition there is no suggestion that the world is out of God's control. Rather, unseen to human eye, but laid bare by the apocalyptic seer, the action of God is shown to be behind the dissolution of the stability of the cosmos and society. The dramatic picture of the coming of the Lamb (a symbol of the executed and martyred Jesus) to the throne of God in chapter 5 expresses the conviction that already God's purposes for humanity are in the process of being fulfilled.

IX. LIFE IN THE LAST DAYS

The sequences of seals, trumpets and bowls outlines the predetermined evolution of the divine purposes in history as the structures of the world give way to the messianic age (the millennium). That process which is symbolized by the repeated sequence of sevens is long and drawn out; there is no rapid transfer of the world to the sovereignty of God. The millennium comes only at the end of the predetermined process of divine judgment. There can be no shortcuts to the millennium; the period of tribulation and suffering must be accepted with fortitude and patience, the latter being a favorite word in the book of Revelation. Judgment is necessary because there is no sign of repentance. Human reaction to the horrors of the surrounding world is not to repent but to curse God.[37] God's righteouness reveals itself in judgment against humanity because of the alienation of human society from the way of God. The maintenance of that structural injustice which is unresponsive to the need for change in line with God's will results in ultimate destruction.

The reasons for the shortcomings of the state are laid bare also. The Beast is the incarnation of the powers of the Devil and attracts universal admiration for acts which *appear* to be beneficial.[38] The pressure is to conform and be marked with the mark of the Beast.[39] Those who refuse to do so are offered reassurance that being marked with the Lamb is a sign of righteousness even if it means social ostracism.[40] In the present age those marked with the Beast apparently have freedom to go about their business, whereas those who refuse to be so marked and side with God and the Lamb are persecuted and their deaths are greeted with glee by the inhabitants of the earth.[41] In reality it is those who maintain their integrity, even at the price of their lives, who will be vindicated, whereas those who have the mark of the Beast "drink the wine of God's wrath."[42] Those who persevere are shown that the might of state power is itself extraordinarily fragile, and its affluence, so attractive and alluring, is destined for destruction at the hands of that power which has maintained it.[43]

X. THE PROPHETIC WITNESS OF PROTEST

The apocalypse contrasts with the utopian tract offering its readers a blueprint of some future, ideal society. As an evocation of a future age of glory it challenges the present order and enables those who accept its message to have their own consciousness infused with its critical spirit and an optimistic attitude towards the future. But Revelation is not a detailed blueprint of an ideal society to be contemplated at leisure or one which engages the reader only temporarily. Hope inspires action, readiness to suffer, and an awareness of the urgent need of repentance in the face of catastrophe. It seeks to persuade its readers that the present moment is a time of critical importance. The outline of future history is offered as the basis for a change of heart to engage the whole of life in its drama which will have drastic consequences for the one who reads it. Acceptance or rejection of its message is nothing less than the difference between alignment with the reign of God which is to come and sharing the fate of the Beast in the Lake of Fire.

That demand is evident in the letters to the churches which introduce the vision of hope and in the concluding admonitions which stress the authority of the text and the imminence of the fulfillment of its message.[44] The readers of the Apocalypse are not allowed to dream about millenial bliss without being brought face to face with the obstacles which stand in the way of its fulfillment and the costly part to be played by them in that process: they have to wash their robes and make them white in the blood of the Lamb, and avoid being marked with the mark of the Beast.[45] The strictures against those who recommend eating food sacrificed to idols indicate the need to create some distance between the conduct of Christians and the typical behaviour of society.[46] The references to idolatry and immorality in these passages are to be understood as in the tradition of the Jewish concern for holiness, that distinctive pattern of life over against the nations: "it shall not be so with you."[47] There is a challenge to the assumption that the disciple will be able to take part without too much comfort in the social intercourse of the contemporary world. As Klaus Wengst has put it:

> According to John the decisive question with which he sees the Christians of his time confronted is not How can I survive this situation with the least possible harm? . . . Rather, the question of the possibility of his own survival is completely put in the shade by the one question which is important to him: In this situation, how can I bear witness to the rule of Christ, his claim to the whole world? . . . . He calls for an exodus . . . as joining in, life along the usual lines, necessarily means complicity with Rome. The consequence is social separation. . . . By refusing to "join in", by contradicting and resisting, they dispute that the world belongs to those who claim to rule over it . . . "Here is a call for endurance of the saints, those who keep the commandments of God and the faith of Jesus" (14.12). This sentence can be regarded as a summary of all that John wants to say. This endurance puts Christian life into the role of the outsider.[48]

The role of the follower of the Messiah is not quiet resignation. Rev 6: 9-11 suggests that martyrdom actually contributes to the coming of the kingdom. There has to be a quota of martyrs who must share the testimony of Jesus and take their stand against a rebellious world before the vindication can finally come. According to chapters 10-11 the seer is involved in the unfolding eschatological drama of the Apocalypse when he is instructed to eat the scroll and commanded to prophesy. This is a direct call to participate actively as a prophet rather than to be merely a passive spectator. Revelation is insistent that the role of the martyr or witness is of central importance. Jesus of Nazareth is the faithful prophetic witness, and his followers have to continue his testimony.[49] That will involve suffering in the great tribulation, but those who join the messianic throng are those "who have washed their robes and made them white in the blood of the Lamb." In chapter 11 the Church is offered a paradigm of the true prophetic witness as it sets out to fulfill its vocation to prophesy before the world, utilizing thc figures of Moses and Elijah. That prophetic witness takes place in a setting opposed to God and ends in martyrdom and death: "the martyr defends not his life but his cause."[50]

This is similar to the main thrust of the message of the eschatological discourse in the Synoptic Gospels[51] which must not be separated from the narrative of Jesus' proclamation and inauguration of the reign of God. It is that context which is necessary to prevent the discourse about the future becoming the focus of the narrative. Discipleship involves sharing the way of the cross of the Son of Man as he goes up to Jerusalem. What is offered the disciple is the sharing of the cup of suffering of the Son of Man rather than the promise of sitting at his right hand or his left when he reigns on earth.[52] This request is not repudiated but, as the eschatological discourse makes plain, there can be no escape from the painful reality of the present witness with its need to endure the tribulations which precede the vindication. That is the challenge which faces those who wish to live out the messianic narrative in their own lives; no short cuts to the messianic reign are to be found here. Similarly, in Revelation the promise of a part in the New Jerusalem is linked with present behaviour.[53]

XI. OVERCOMING THE CONTRADICTIONS OF THE PRESENT IN THE NEW CREATION

In reading the unfolding eschatological panorama of Revelation it is not often realized what a significant piece of theology is to be found in this work.[54] First and foremost, Revelation offers canonical justification for the cosmic and historical context of divine activity. That view, so deeply imbedded in the Jewish scriptures, was subordinated in mainstream Christian doctrine to the concern for the individual soul, a process already evident in the New Testament. The struggle between darkness and light in human affairs was neglected in favour of that conflict in the human heart. The book of Revelation has provided encouragement for all those who look for the fulfillment of God's righteousness in human history.

There is similarity of language between the description of the new age in Revelation 21 and the prologue of the Fourth Gospel.[55] In Rev 21:3 the tabernacling of God with humankind is fulfilled in the new creation. It is an eschatological hope which awaits the completion of that process of judgment on the unrighteous institutions which barred the way to God's reign. In contrast John 1:14 speaks of the tabernacling of the Divine Word in history as an event not in the future but in the past, in the person of Jesus of Nazareth: "the Word became flesh and tabernacled among us and we beheld his glory, the glory as of an only son from his father."[56] While in Revelation 21 the dwelling of God with humanity takes place in a world made holy and acceptable for this, in John the Incarnation takes place in an environment where the "world knew him not."[57]

The contrast between the vision of the new Jerusalem in Revelation 21 and the initial vision of the heavenly court in chapter 4 also should be noted. In Revelation 4 the seer is granted a glimpse into the environs of God. Here God the Creator and Liberator is acknowledged, and, as we notice from the following chapter, it is from the God of the universe that the historical process begins which leads to the establishment of a new aeon. In the chapters following 4 and 5 we find the picture of a world afflicted but unrepentant; indeed, manifesting precisely the kind of misguided devotion to evil which has to be rooted out before God's kingdom can finally come. In Revelation 4-5 God is still in heaven, and it is there that the heavenly host sing his praise and magnify his name.

HEAVEN: God surrounded by those who do God's will

EARTH: Humankind unwilling to do God's will

Heaven on earth in new creation (Revelation 21-22)

This contrast between heaven and earth disappears in the new creation. Now the tabernacle of God is with men and women, and they shall be his people. God's dwelling is not to be found above the cherubim in heaven; for his throne is set right in the midst of the New Jerusalem where the living waters stream from the throne of God and his servants marked with the mark of God will see God face to face.[58] Here we have an example of theological immanentism which is predicted for the new age. It is only then that there will be the conditions for God and humanity to dwell in that harmony which was impossible while there was rejection of the divine righteousness in human affairs. Heaven on earth is what the new age is all about. God is no longer transcendent but immediate—part and parcel of that world of perfection and evident in it. Indeed, those who are his will be his children and carry his name on their heads: they will be identified with the character of God and enjoy his presence unmediated.[59]

As we have seen, early Christian writers were convinced that this divine immanence was not reserved solely for the new age. The glory which the apocalyptic seer enjoyed in his revelation was a matter of living experience here and now for those who confessed Jesus as Messiah and participated in the eschatological Spirit. Already those who possessed the Spirit of God were sons of God;[60] already those in Christ were a new creation[61] and a Temple of divine spirit.[62] That hope for the final resolution of the contrast between heaven and earth was already perceived by those who had eyes to see and know it. Already the people of the Messiah were being "taught by the Spirit . . . what God has prepared for those who love him, God has revealed to us through the Spirit."[63]

The Apocalypse can remind readers of early Christian literature of the hope for a reign of God on earth, when injustice and oppression will be swept away and the structures of an evil society replaced. This is an important component of the Christian gospel. One can imagine how easy it would have been for the early Christians to have capitulated to their feelings of political powerlessness by concentrating on individual holiness only. But even Paul finds it necessary to speak of a process of salvation which is firmly rooted in the process of liberation for the whole of creation.[64] The Apocalypse does not easily allow a retreat into the conventicle as the main arena of divine activity, for it persuades the saints to prophesy before the world about the righteousness of God and the dreadful consequences of ignoring its implementation. In the midst of the old order the presence of God is to be found in the prophetic witness of protest, the unmasking of injustice and the pointing forward to the messianic age. The visions of a world above where perfection reigns are symptomatic of the fractured existence of injustice and an expression of longing for resolution and an end to alienation.

NOTES

1. Bultmann, R.,*Theology of the New Testament,* vol. 2, trans. K. Grobel (New York: Scribners, 1955) 175.

2. Rev. 3:14-22. For an example of contemporary North American usage of Revelation see A. Mojtabai, *Blessed Assurance.*

3. An example of an exegetical approach which takes these points into consideration is that of Carlos Mester *Esperança de um povo que luta. O Apocalipse de São João: uma chava de leitura.*

4. On this see the literature cited in C. Rowland, *Open Heaven* (New York:Crossroads, 1982) 403ff.

5. Revelation 4-5.

6. 1 Corinthians 4-5.

7. O. Cullmann, *Salvation in History,* trans. S. G. Sowers (New York: Harper and Row, 1967) and *Christ and Time.,* trans. F. V. Filson (Philadelphia: Westminster, 1964) 64.

8. The crucial passage is 1 Cor 15:23-28 which Schweitzer, *The Mysticism of Paul The Apostle* (New York: H. Holt, 1931), interpreted as a reference to the millennium. Cf. W. D. Davies, *Paul and Rabbinic Judaism* (London: S.P.C.K., 1948) 286-90.

9. Rom 13:1-4, cf. Rev 12:12 and 13:5.

10. 1 Cor 15:28.

11. 1 Cor 15:24.

12. Matt 5:5.

13. Luke 6:22-24.

14. Mark 14:25.

15. Matt 8:11. For an attempt to spiritualize Jesus' hopes see , J. Jeremias, *New Testament Theology,* vol. 1 (New York: Scribner's, 1971) 248.

16. Rom 8:18-23. See J. P. Miranda, *Marx and the Bible,* tr. J. Eagleson (Maryknoll:N. Y. Orbis, 1974) 27-76.

17. See article *chilioi* by E. Lohse in *TDNT* 9 (1971) 466-71.

18. See Irenaeus, *Against the Heresies* v. 33.3 and J. Daniélou, *The Theology of Jewish Christianity* 377-85, trans. J. A. Baker (Chicago: Regnery, 1964).

19. Romans 13; 1 Pet 2:14 and Titus 3:1.

20. See O. Cullmann, *The State in the New Testament* (New York: Scribners, 1956).

21. Mk 13:14-27.

22. E.g., Mk 3:22-25 and W. Wink, *Naming the Powers* (Philadelphia: Fortress, 1984).

23. See Rowland, *Open Heaven* .

24. Rev 1:10 and 4:2.

25. Acts 2:17-18; 11:27-28; 1 Cor 2:6-13.

26. 1 Cor 14:12 and 26.

27. Acts 9:1ff. cf. 22:6ff and 26:12ff.

28. Acts 10:11.

29. Mk 1:10.

30. Rom 11:25; 16:25; 1 Cor 2:1; 2:7; 4:1; 13:2; 15:51.

31. See E. R. Dodds, *The Greeks and the Irrational* (Berkeley: University of California Press, 1951), and *Pagan and Christian in an Age of Anxiety* (Cambridge: University Press. 1965); also Rowland, *Open Heaven,* 9ff.

32. On this subject see Rowland, *Open Heaven.*

33. P. Vielhauer in Hennecke, Schneemelcher, *New Testament Apocrypha,* vol. 2 (London: Lutterworth, 1965) 608ff,

34. As Martin Hengel has described it in *Judaism and Hellenism*, vol. 1, (London: SPCK, 1974) 210.

35. Revelation 13 and 17.

36. On the major themes of Revelation see further Rowland, *Open Heaven*, 423ff; E. Schuessler-Fiorenza, *The Book of Revelation* (Philadelphia: Fortress Press, 1985); *Justice and Judgement*, (Philadelphia: Fortress Press, 1985), and K. Wengst, *Pax Romana: and the Peace of Jesus Christ* (Philadelphia: Fortress Press, 1987).

37. Rev 9:20 and 16:21.

38. Revelation 13. Cf. Revelation 12 which speaks of the descent of the devil from heaven; the juxtaposition of Revelation 13 with ch. 12 suggests that the consequence of the fall of the devil from heaven is the demonic inspiration of the power of the state.

39. Rev 13:8.

40. Rev 13:16-17.

41. Rev 11:10.

42. Rev 14:10.

43. Rev 17:16 and note the graphic description of the fall of Babylon the Great in chs. 18-19 (on which see now A. Boesak, *Comfort and Protest. Reflections on the Apocalypse of John of Patmos* (Philadelphia: Westminster Press, 1987).

44. Rev 22:10 and 18-20.

45. Rev 7:14 and 14:9.

46. In 2:14 and 2:20 and see Wengst, *Pax Romana*, 120 and 132-33.

47. Mark 10:43.

48. Wengst, *Pax Romana*, 133-34.

49. Rev 1:5 and Rev 19:10.

50. L. Boff, "Martyrdom: An Attempt in Systematic Reflection", in *Martyrdom Today*, eds. J. B. Metz and E. Schillebeeckx (Concilium, 163) 13, trans. P. Burns (Edinburgh, T. & T. Clark, 1983).

51. Matt 24-5; Mark 13 and Luke 21.

52. Mark 10:35-45.

53. E.g. 2:7.

54. There are helpful comments on the climax of the book in M. Rissi, *The Future of the World*((SBT 2,3; Naperville, IL: Allenson, 1972)

55. John 1:1-18. On the relationship see Rowland, *Christian Origins*, 252ff.

56. John 1:14.

57. John 1:10.

58. Rev 22:4.

59. Note similar themes elsewhere: 1 John 3:2 and 1 Cor 13:12.

60. Rom 8:9.

61. 2 Cor 5:17.

62. 1 Cor 3:16; 1 Cor 6:19. Further on this theme see Rowland, *Christian Origins*, 255.

63. 1 Cor 2:10-13.

64. Rom 8:19-25.

THE CONTRIBUTORS

LESLIE ALLEN
Fuller Theological Seminary - Pasadena, CA

GEORGE BEASLEY-MURRAY
Southern Baptist Theological Seminary - Louisville, KY

ADELA YARBRO COLLINS
University of Notre Dame - Notre Dame, IN

JOHN J. COLLINS
University of Notre Dame - Notre Dame, IN

AGNES CUNNINGHAM
University of St. Mary of the Lake - Mundelein, IL

GABRIEL FACKRE
Andover Newton Theological Seminary - Newton Centre, MA

JACK DEAN KINGSBURY
Union Theological Seminary in Virginia - Richmond, VA

KLAUS KOCH
Hamburg University - Hamburg, Germany

CHRISTOPHER ROWLAND
Mansfield College - Oxford, England

DAVID M. SCHOLER
North Park Theological Seminary - Chicago, IL

TIMOTHY WEBER
Denver Conservative Baptist Seminary - Denver, CO

JOHN HOWARD YODER
University of Notre Dame - Notre Dame, IN

PICKWICK PUBLICATIONS

4137 Timberlane Drive
Allison Park, PA 15101-2932

Critical Realism and the New Testament
By Ben F. Meyer
ISBN 0-915138-97-2 $19.95

The Epigones: A Study of the Theology of the Genevan Academy at the Time of the Synod of Dort
By William A. McComish
ISBN 0-915138-62-X $36.00

Social Concern in Calvin's Geneva
By William C. Innes
ISBN 0-915138-33-6 $19.95

Freedom and Civilization Among The Greeks
By A. J. Festugière
Tr. by P. T. Brannan
ISBN 0-915138-98-0 $15.00

A Gentleman in Every Slum: Church of England Missions in East London, 1837-1914
By David Brown McIlhiney
ISBN 0-915138-95-6 $15.00

The Kitchen Saint and the Heritage of Islam: Conversations, Spiritual Maxims and Letters of Brother Lawrence
Tr. by Elmer H. Douglas
ISBN 1-55635-003-1 $10.00

Luke the Theologian. Thirty-three years of Research (1950-1983)
By François Bovon
ISBN 0-915138-93-X $35.00

The Present and the Past
A Study of Anamnesis
By Richard J. Ginn
ISBN 1-55635-004-X $12.00

Searching for Lost Coins
Explorations in Christianity and Feminism
By Ann Loades
ISBN 1-55635-000-7 $12.00

Theology Beyond Christendom. Essays on the Centenary of the Birth of Karl Barth
Ed. by John Thompson
ISBN 915138-85-9 $29.95

A Theology of Electricity
By Ernst Benz
Tr. by Dennis Stillings
ISBN 0-915138-92-1 $19.95

The Triune God. An Ecumenical Study
By E. L. Mascall
(Co-published with Churchman Publishing)
ISBN 0-915138-96-4 $12.90

The Quest for Church Unity
From John Calvin to Isaac d'Huisseau
By Richard Stauffer
ISBN 0-915138-63-8 $15.00

The Will of God and the Cross
An Historical and Theological Study of John Calvin's Doctrine of Limited Redemption
By Jonathan H. Rainbow
ISBN 1-55635-005-8 $24.00

Anselm: Fides Quaerens Intellectum
Anselm's proof of the existence of God in the context of his theological scheme
By Karl Barth
ISBN 0-915138-75-1 $15.00

The Holy Spirit in the Theology of Karl Barth
By John Thompson
ISBN 0-915138-94-8 $24.00

God With Us
By Joseph Haroutunian
A Theology of Transpersonal Life
ISBN 1-55635-008-2

Jeshua: Nazareth to Jerusalem
By Moelwyn Merchant
ISBN 1-55635-010-4